Ordinary People, Extraordinary Lives

Recipients of the
Order of British Columbia

Ordinary People, Extraordinary Lives

Recipients of the Order of British Columbia

Goody Niosi

Goody Niosi

Heritage House

Copyright © 2002 Goody Niosi

National Library of Canada Cataloguing in Publication Data

Niosi, Goody, 1946-
    Ordinary people, extraordinary lives

    Includes bibliographical references and index.
    ISBN 1-894384-52-0

    1. Order of British Columbia. 2. British Columbia—Biography.
I. Title.

CR6257.O68N56 2002   929.8'1711   C2002-910906-X

First edition 2002

Heritage House acknowledges the financial support for our publishing program from the Government of Canada through the Book Publishing Industry Development Program (BPIDP), Canada Council for the Arts, and the British Columbia Arts Council.

Cover and book design by Darlene Nickull
Edited by Terri Elderton

HERITAGE HOUSE PUBLISHING COMPANY LTD.
#108 - 17665 66 A Ave., Surrey, B.C. Canada V3S 2A7

Printed in Canada

BRITISH
COLUMBIA
ARTS COUNCIL
We acknowledge the support of the Province of British Columbia
through the British Columbia Arts Council

The Canada Council | Le Conseil des Arts
for the Arts | du Canada

Dedication

For my father, Willi Sobottka, who led an extraordinary life. He was and still is my hero and role model. Thank you, Pom, for your love and inspiration.

Acknowledgements

I want to thank the wonderful crew at the Heritage Group: Rodger Touchie, my publisher, who continues to believe in me and encourage me so much; Terri Elderton, the most thoughtful editor on earth; and Darlene Nickull, whose artistic input is so valuable.

I also want to thank every person I interviewed. I know how difficult it was for them to make time for me in their more-than-busy schedules.

Contents

Foreword

It was my very good fortune to be Chief Justice of British Columbia when the Order of British Columbia was created by an Act of the Legislature of British Columbia in 1989, and my further good fortune to become, by virtue of that office, the chair of the Advisory Committee that recommends the appointment of new members to the Order each year, subject to the approval of the Executive Council. In my years as chair, the Executive Council never once interfered with the recommendations of the Advisory Committee.

Another benefit I enjoyed as chair was the opportunity to meet and work with the wonderful, public-spirited citizens who served on the committee with me. They were the Speaker of the Legislature, a deputy minister, a representative of the Union of B.C. Municipalities, a president of one of B.C.'s universities, and two members of the Order appointed the previous year. Of these, I was the only one with tenure, until retirement. The others rotated on and off the committee as their positions changed. They were a most enjoyable, conscientious group, and it was a credit to them, with some persuasion on my part, that permitted the committees to agree on the identity of those selected for recommendation.

The selection of such a small number of wonderful candidates was, of course, a most difficult assignment because each nominee, in his or her own way, was often as richly deserving as those selected. Because of the need to reduce the list to the manageable number required, it was necessary to establish unofficial categories and to apply some other criteria to ensure, as best we could, that the election fairly reflected the profile of our great province. If I have one regret about the Order it is that we could not recommend a greater number of the excellent British Columbians for appointment every year.

The investiture ceremony at Government House and the following reception and dinner hosted in honour of the new members of the Order was always a highlight of the social part of my responsibilities. I often thought how pleasant it was to be at a function where everyone wanted to be, quite unlike many of the other functions over which I had to preside where some would have much preferred to be elsewhere.

The lieutenants-governor who presided at the investitures, and the premiers who attended these important events always spoke warmly and accurately about the quality of the new members of the Order. Many of them commented that these deserving candidates were truly representative of the people of British Columbia—talented, dedicated, and caring—but most important of all, British Columbians who made us all proud.

Being involved with the Order of British Columbia has been one of the most rewarding parts of my official life. I congratulate the author, Goody Niosi, for making this remarkable organization and its members better known by her handsome book.

—Allan McEachern
Former Chief Justice of the British Columbia Supreme Court
and former Chief Justice of British Columbia

Introduction

When my friends ask me what it was like to write this book, what comes to mind is a feeling of honour to have met the extraordinary people in these pages and also one of privilege to be entrusted to write their stories.

The idea for the book came to me in 2001 when I attended the investiture ceremony for that year's recipients of the Order of British Columbia at Government House in Victoria. Among the recipients that year were well-known people like Sarah McLachlan, Robert Bateman, and Judith Forst. There were also people I had never known about: Dr. R. Hayward Rogers, who has done such outstanding work treating cancer patients, and Dr. Leonel Perra, a champion for accessible education. And there was Merve Wilkinson, Canada's icon of sustainable forestry, who had invited me as his guest and whose biography I was just completing.

In the weeks following the ceremony I found myself wanting to share the feeling of inspiration that imbued me that day. When I talked to people about my experience, I was surprised to hear that many had never heard of the Order of B.C. or about the outstanding people who have received it since 1990; that's when I became determined to write this book. Surely these recipients of the Order of B.C. deserved to be better known, I thought, not because they wanted fame—in fact, most had no desire for the spotlight—but because I believe that in today's world we need all the inspiring role models we can find.

British Columbia is a glorious province, bursting with natural wonders and resources. I believe the most precious of these resources is its people. The Order of British Columbia was established by statute on April 21, 1989, to recognize and honour citizens who have demonstrated exceptional determination to work towards a better world for all citizens. Each year about fifteen people receive the award.

I'd hate to be on the selection committee. How do they choose from among the outstanding candidates? Ric Careless, whom I interviewed, told me that what makes the Order of B.C. so special is that it is not a political award. It is a citizen's award. Anyone can nominate someone to receive the Order of B.C. The selection committee is made up of citizens led by the Chief Justice of British Columbia.

I wish I could have profiled every single person who has ever received the award. But I somehow don't think my publisher, Rodger Touchie, was prepared to print a 3,000-page tome. So, how did I choose the recipients to include? Heck, it was a bit like throwing darts at a board.

I started with Grace Elliott-Nielsen because she lives in my town. I'd met her on several occasions before and was awed by her accomplishments and her quiet sense of self. When I'd finished writing her story, I knew I'd have to work hard to top it or even equal it. Here was a woman who had been born into a family that had very little, that struggled to get by; but, more importantly, it was a family where love made up for a shortage of money, and the children were treasured and encouraged to make the most of their paths in life. Grace Elliott-Nielsen did find her path. It may have been littered with obstacles and challenges, but she removed every one that came at her, and where there was no path to follow, she built her own road.

I soon discovered that there were many other inspiring stories to learn. My second interview was with Dr. Roger Tonkin on Gabriola Island, who chose to become a doctor at the age of eleven and never stopped working towards making that vocation richer and more rewarding, not just for him but for others as well. I talked to Mel Cooper, the man who owns Victoria's CFAX radio station and who sits on so many boards and contributes so much to the community that I still wonder how he finds time to sleep. I talked to Geraldine Braak, who became blind but carried on with her life as though nothing had changed and who then set out to make a difference for blind people—and others with disabilities—all over the country.

I sat in Robert Bateman's studio on Salt Spring Island, watching him paint his glorious birds, listening to him talk about his boyhood in Toronto, his travels around the world, and his love of nature. I spent time in Richard Hunt's garage-turned-studio in Victoria, listening to him talk about his passion for his Native culture and its art and then being awed by the bright and life-affirming pieces he showed me. I sat in Dr. Roger Hayward Rogers' tiny office in Sidney, trying hard not to drip tears on my notes, not because his story was sad but because it was full of hope, and I always cry at happy endings.

I was privileged to talk to Rick Hansen, a true Canadian hero and an inspiration for thousands of people all over the world, and to Tim Frick, the man who coached him. Tim told me that when he received the Order of B.C. he was amazed and delighted that it was possible for "a little man in the trenches" to receive such an honour and not just the big names. Funny, I don't think of Tim Frick as a "little man." His quiet manner, his confidence, and his pure dedication to helping disabled athletes achieve their full potential make him a giant in my eyes.

There isn't a person in this book who is not a hero: Dr. Leonel Perra, who brought education to people in impossible places and often hilarious circumstances; Dr. Michael O'Shaughnessy, who has dedicated his career to AIDS research and who has never lost touch with the human face of this awful disease; Hilda Gregory, who trusted her faith and did such landmark work with deaf children; Joan Acosta and her revolutionary *Westcoast Reader* newspaper and books for newcomers to B.C.; Ric Careless, to whom we—and future generations—no doubt owe for much of the preservation of our precious wilderness areas such as the Nitinat Triangle, Tatshenshini, the Height of the Rockies, South Moresby Island, and more; and Ross Purse, who emerged from a horrendous wartime experience to dedicate his life to his fellow man and his country. I had an amazing interview with Takao Tanabe. During our time together I heard his anger over his wartime experience, and once or twice I feared he might just walk out of the coffee shop and cut our interview short. But I also saw his serene smile, and then, he offered a transparency of one of his glorious works of art for the cover of the book. I am deeply grateful for his gift and also for his allowing me to gain some insights into the events of his life. And what do I say about Merve Wilkinson, the man I saw every week for a year while I wrote his biography, a man who has proved that sustainable forestry is not only possible but necessary?

Not one of these Order of B.C. recipients was born with a headstart; not one of them was coddled or given great advantages while growing up. Most overcame great odds to find their chosen vocations or avocations. Some chose their paths by what might seem like serendipity, and some had caring family or mentors to guide them. But once on their paths, they did not give up or turn back; they blazed the way for others to follow. They are special because their actions have defined them so.

I hope these stories inspire you as much as they did me. These seventeen citizens of B.C. have made an enormous difference in the lives of others. I'm glad the Order of British Columbia was created so that we—as citizens of the province—can give them the acknowledgement they so richly deserve.

Merve Wilkinson:
Magnificently Unrepentant

M erve Wilkinson was the inspiration behind this book. I had almost finished writing his biography, *Magnificently Unrepentant*, in January 2001, when he telephoned me and told me he had been awarded the Order of British Columbia. He asked me to come to Government House in Victoria to be a guest at his investiture.

Among the fifteen recipients of the Order of B.C. that year were Robert Bateman, Dr. Leonel Perra, and Dr. Roger Hayward Rogers, all of whom I would later meet and interview. The pomp and ceremony were impressive. The sound of bagpipes filled the reception hall as the recipients of the award were marched in to take their places in the front row of seats. One by one they were called to the podium, where the Master of Ceremonies read a list of their accomplishments. Each recipient received tremendous applause, but when Merve took the stage he "brought down the house," as they say in show business. As the Master of Ceremonies read, "Merve Wilkinson began harvesting trees off Wildwood, his 138-acre property in 1945. Now, over 50 years later, he still has the same amount of timber he started with," Merve, leaning heavily on his cane, slowly raised one hand in a "thumbs-up" gesture. Even Premier Gordon Campbell and Lieutenant-Governor Garde B. Gardom applauded and joined in the laughter.

Merve later told me that when he shook hands with the premier he told him, "You know, you boys ought to give this sustainable forestry a try."

That's Merve—always outspoken and never intimidated by rank or titles.

Merve Wilkinson, 2001

So, I tell Merve's story because it deserves to be in this book that he inspired. It took me almost a year to write his biography. Every Friday I would drive down his impossibly long, tree-shaded drive to the rambling log house on the edge of Quennell Lake, where we would sit at his kitchen table while he told me about his life. Merve has a prodigious memory. At age 86 he could remember the names of his childhood friends, his grade school teacher, and men he had worked with and had not seen in 50 years.

Sometimes I would arrive and Merve and his wife, Anne, would be sitting at the kitchen table eating their lunch, so they would ask me to join them. Many times I would leave their house loaded with pears and apples from their fruit trees or eggs from the hens. Sometimes visitors would be gathered around the table, all of them wanting to know more about the legendary Wildwood, many of them asking, "When is the book coming out?" because they wanted to know about Merve's life as well as his forest.

Merve was born in Nanaimo in 1913 and grew up on the shores of Quennell Lake just south of town. "I grew up in this environment," he says, "and at that time all the original settlers were here. They were marvelous people. They were as different from each other as day is from night, but when it came to the community, they were not individuals—they worked together. From them, I learned the value of working *with* things, not against them. It was a community where people meant something to each other and where nobody ever suffered; the neighbors came to help when it was needed. That's the way community should be."

Merve attended the East Cedar School until the end of his third year when two families moved from the area, leaving only six school age children to attend class—not enough to warrant hiring a teacher. So the school shut down, and Merve enrolled in the provincial correspondence course.

"It was a very good course," he recalls, "because it put you on your own. If you had a question for a teacher, you'd either have to wait a week or you got out and researched it yourself and found the answer. The head teacher of the correspondence course, Mr. Hargreaves, very quickly realized that because my parents had lots of books available— and knew where to get books—that I was a prime candidate for coaching on how to find my own information. He always encouraged me to go out there and find the answer, even if it was a different answer from what he had. He acknowledged that different people had different answers for different things."

In 1934, with his mother's help, Merve bought the 147 acres of land in Yellow Point that he would later call Wildwood. He and his wife, Mary, planned to raise vegetables and chickens and turn the land into a small farm that would sustain them. But in 1937 when their son, Denis, was one year old, they had the opportunity to study agriculture and homemaking skills at an eight-week farmer's institute course offered at the University of British Columbia. It was there that Merve met a Swedish professor, Dr. Paul A. Boving.

During class Dr. Boving would quiz his students with the intention of steering them into the area that would best work with their terrain, climate, and location. "What sort of farm do you have?" he would ask. "What's the land like?" "What about the climate?" When he questioned Merve and discovered that the young man had 147 acres of old-growth timber, Dr. Boving said, "Good Lord! You should be studying forestry!"

Unfortunately, there was no curriculum offered in North America that the professor cared to recommend, so he arranged for the latest forestry course to be sent from Sweden. The Swedish method of sustainable forestry made sense to Merve, and he determined to put it into practice on his land. When he graduated, Dr. Boving said to him, "Don't think this has made a forester out of you; it's only given you the tools to learn to become one. Take it from there." Merve calls his words the best advice he was ever given.

Back home at Wildwood, Merve began to assess his land. Wildwood was a beautiful piece of forest land, typical of coastal Vancouver Island, with trees of all sizes, ages, and species, including fir, cedar, hemlock, balsam, arbutus, alder, maple, crab apple, aspen, juniper, and yew. The land supported every kind of wildlife and every sort of bug and insect. Worms crawled over the ground when it rained and burrowed under the soil when the sun shone.

Before Merve cut down his first tree, he walked his land many times, carefully deciding what to take and what to leave. He looked for trees that were past their prime, and he noted trees that were home to eagles and woodpeckers and was careful not to fall those. He selected single trees and sometimes three or four trees in a group where density or disease warranted their removal.

When Merve finished his first cut in 1945 the forest was still intact, but it had returned to him all the money he had invested in the property, paid for the cost of building the roads, and covered his wages. He removed no more trees from his land for five years, and during that time he marvelled at how quickly the forest filled back in. If a person had visited Wildwood a year after the first cut the only evidence of logging they would have found was the odd stump here and there.

Merve and Mary became involved in all the local neighbourhood activities such as the social club, the dance group, and the club that went out paddling in their canoes or camping overnight. Merve was one of the moving forces behind the creation of the local Credit Union, the Co-Op store, and the Nanaimo District Museum.

In 1948 Mary was working in the garden when a late summer shower passed overhead. The soft warmth of the rain felt good on her bare head and she remained outdoors, tending the vegetables while the cloud passed by. Several weeks later she began to complain of terrible headaches. Her health deteriorated quickly, and when she was certain she was suffering from a brain tumour that would either kill her or leave her helpless, she walked into the woods with Merve's shotgun, held it to her head, and pulled the trigger. Years later, after much research, Merve concluded that the shower that had fallen on Western Canada contained atomic residue from the bombings at Hiroshima and Nagasaki, but by the time the Canadian government admitted it was aware that the radioactive rain had reached B.C. and Alberta, it was too late for Mary.

After Mary's tragic death, Merve's friends helped him through his grief. One of them, Ron Riley, convinced him to help him in his bid to win a seat for the CCF (Co-operative Commonwealth Federation) in the provincial elections of 1952. The campaign in the B.C. Interior not only helped Merve heal, but also gave him a first-hand view of politics.

In 1954 Merve married Grace. Denis, Merve's son, had graduated and moved to Saskatchewan, but Merve wasn't done with parenting. He and Grace adopted two Native girls, Marquita and Tisha, and later fostered a family of four children. While Merve involved himself in his children's activities and education, he continued to log his land. Word of what he was doing at Wildwood gradually began to spread, and visitors came to ask questions about his system of forestry. Merve welcomed them. After his second cut in 1951, his enthusiasm for sustainable forestry had grown and with it his desire to teach others and tell them that there was a better way of doing things. "The more serious visitor wanted to know what my systems were," Merve says. "How did I arrive at my growth rate? How did I decide which trees I was going to cut? Why? Why did I put the roads where I put them? Why not put them straight through the middle? Some answers were simple but very effective. You don't put a road through the best piece of timber you have on your property. Sure, it'll help you take the wood out fast, but you're taking land out of growing potential by putting that road where it doesn't need to be. It can be 200 feet farther away and not destroy good forest land."

Some people looked at what Merve was doing and said, "This system has potential."

When Merve finished his third cut in 1955, he couldn't keep his success a secret any longer. He had gathered enough statistics to know he had the answer to sustainable forestry in B.C., so he wrote to the provincial minister of forests, inviting him to come to Wildwood and have a look.

The minister declined, but sent his chief forester, Dick Spillsbury, who looked over Merve's land and said, "This is a wonderful system." But he also added, "The way Canadians are and the way they love the dollar, it will be difficult to make it fly."

Dick Spillsbury's visit didn't change the way trees were logged in B.C., but Merve was undeterred and kept writing letters. He didn't care just about himself; he cared about the future of his children and his grandchildren and the grandchildren of his friends and neighbours. Merve had grown up with the understanding that he was a member of a community, and he was responsible for how that community functioned. So when he realized that clear-cutting forest land was not necessary, and when he knew he had an alternative system that would work, he said to anyone who would listen—and to some who would not, "Enough already, those bums are destroying the earth!"

One spring evening in 1986 Merve was watching the CBC's *Pacific Report*, hosted and directed by Cam Cathcart. The host was interviewing the mayor of Fort St. John, B.C., who was complaining that his region's forest industry was dying. "I listened to this guy's wails. He was a good enough mayor probably, but when it came to forestry he was as far off the track as a locomotive is when it's being built," Merve says.

When the program ended he wrote to Cam Cathcart: "This man should learn something about forestry before he gets on the air with this kind of uninformed talk. It's not necessary for B.C. to run out of timber. We are going to if we persist in doing what the Fort St. John mayor thinks we should do." Then he outlined his own practice of sustainable forestry at Wildwood. Days later Cathcart phoned.

"I'm glad he was paying the phone bill," Merve says. "He called me at ten-thirty in the morning and we talked until about noon."

Cathcart asked many questions: What had Merve been doing in his forest? Was it working? Could it work on a broader scale? And lastly, he asked, "Can I come and film your operation?"

"Sure," Merve said. "I'd be delighted."

A week later, a camera crew arrived from Vancouver, and two weeks after that the program aired. When the show ended at 7:30 p.m. Merve's telephone started ringing and didn't stop until long after midnight. People called from the states of Oregon, Washington, and Wisconsin, and from all over Canada. Was this kind of forestry real? Was it possible? Merve said, "Yes it's possible. And if we are to save our forests for future generations, it is the only sort of forestry that is viable on our planet today."

Almost overnight Wildwood became a classroom for girl guides, boy scouts, elementary schools, high school and university classes, and a wide variety of environmental groups. Professional foresters from all over the world came to study at Wildwood. Since then foresters have come from Germany, Holland, Finland, Norway, Sweden, Luxembourg, Switzerland, Spain, Jordan, France, Japan, China, Borneo, Java, Australia, Chile, Bolivia, Brazil, Coast Rica, Mexico, Cuba, Nigeria, Libya, and from all parts of the U.S.

Merve greets them all with unabashed joy. Whether it's a group of Grade Six students or an official government delegation, he welcomes them with the same sincerity and the same eagerness to share his knowledge. He tells them that he has acquired some knowledge in his years of working in the forest and that he will answer their questions to the best of his ability. "I don't know everything," he tells them. "But don't hesitate to ask the question, and please keep it in plain language."

He tells them he won't invent fancy phrases to cover his ignorance and that he is not ashamed to say he doesn't know, although if he knows where a person might get the answer to his question he will refer them to that source.

"Phrases like 'silvicultural prescription' mean nothing," Merve says. "Only people who want to sound important make up such gobbledygook. And what about 'site specific'? If site specific means that some trees will grow in one area and not in another, then say that! Don't say site specific. Pompous phrases accomplish only one thing: they shut out people who want to know."

He never talks down to anyone, not even the tiniest child, and he never talks up to anyone either, no matter how impressive their name or title. He treats questions with honesty and care and talks about the most important things he has learned about forestry. "The principle of sustainable forestry means keeping trees of every age, size, and variety growing in the forest. When you choose the trees for a cut, you are selecting a volume that is less than the annual growth rate. You start by selecting trees that are windfalls—every forest produces the odd windfall. Then you select trees that may have died, weighing its value as a wildlife tree against its value as lumber; keeping birds in the forest is a prime consideration. The third category is trees that are beginning to fail—that are dying back and producing yellow needles. These trees are producing wood slowly. They may take another 50 years to die, and you are simply speeding up the process by taking them out. Always keep in mind that you want to leave enough dead trees for your wildlife habitat. After that you are just taking out trees to thin the remaining forest, keeping in mind that you want to help the remaining trees grow tall and strong. Above all, you must not cut all one size of tree. It is imperative to keep diversity in the forest."

"Use the smallest equipment in the forest that will do the job. Large equipment damages the soil and the systems in the soil on which the tree depends." Merve recalls an experiment where he used a 30-horsepower cat one year and a 50-horsepower cat five years later. Using the larger cat was more expensive and gave a lower return.

"When falling be careful not to damage other trees. Learn to put your tree down where it will have minimum impact. Don't fall from early May until mid-June because that is when the birds are nesting. You can't see the nests from the ground but they are certainly there. Another factor at that time of year is bugs. In May and June the wood-boring beetles fly and lay their eggs. If you have timber on the ground, you'll have pinworms in your logs. You'll do damage to the site if you take out long logs. Cut them down; the mill will anyway. Take out logs no longer than sixteen to 26 feet. Be careful to maintain a network of seed trees spread over your property in such a way that the local winds will distribute the seeds. You will never have to plant trees. Seed trees should be clearly marked out."

In 1979, after 25 years of marriage, Merve and Grace divorced. Ten years later, the Raging Grannies visited Wildwood. They were a group of women who were rapidly becoming notorious throughout the province for their political activism spiced with flamboyant dress and musical parodies on the issues of the day. Among them was Anne Pask, a woman with a bright wit and a deep commitment to the environment. After a two-year courtship, Anne and Merve married, and she joined him in his work at Wildwood.

The next chapter in Merve's life is perhaps my favourite: the Clayoquot Sound protests. I've often thought that the story of Clayoquot Sound has all the makings of a great Hollywood movie. The elements are certainly there: corruption, conflict, drama on a grand scale, humour, and—best of all—the hero winning in the end.

Clayoquot Sound encompasses one of the largest tracts of temperate rain forest remaining in North America, extending from Estevan Point on the west coast of Vancouver Island down to Pacific Rim National Park, and encompassing nine major watersheds and several large islands. Its 2,440 square kilometres of lush rain forest are considered to be one of the most spectacular wilderness areas on the continent. When Mike Harcourt's NDP government and B.C.'s largest forest company, MacMillan Bloedel, announced in 1991 that Clayoquot Sound would be clear-cut, it was no surprise to anyone when the environmentalists raised a clamour.

By 1992 the protests over Clayoquot Sound had reached a near-global level, but while many voices were shouting in anger, others were

pleading for the government to re-consider its options. Merve's was one
of the voices that called for compromise. He invited the premier and his
cabinet to come and look at his operation to show them that clear-cutting
was unnecessary, but the government refused to come.

The logging at Clayoquot Sound triggered the biggest incidence
of civil disobedience Canada has ever known. Beginning in June 1992,
thousands of people travelled to Tofino to blockade the logging road
and defy a court injunction prohibiting them from doing so. They
camped in the woods and on the beaches. They brought banners and
placards, and each day they assembled on the Kennedy River bridge,
which was the beginning of the logging road and the only access to
Clayoquot Sound.

The first time Merve visited Clayoquot Sound, he came as a speaker
invited by The Friends of Clayoquot Sound. He talked eloquently and
passionately, but his speech was liberally laced with good common
sense. He suggested that "no logging" was an unattainable goal and
that "no clear-cutting" was a viable alternative. The protesters agreed
and changed their placards to "No Clearcutting."

Each day they packed the bridge leading to the logging road, and
each day the RCMP arrested them and carried them off. On July 10,
Merve and Anne took their turn on the bridge at 5:00 a.m., near the
back of the crowd of 680 protestors. The police arrested them, put
them on a bus, and sent them to the recreation hall in Ucluelet that
served as a temporary detention centre.

The mass trials took place later that year. Everyone was found guilty,
despite irregularities and what Merve terms "much skulduggery," but
when it came Merve's turn to speak and defend himself, he told the
judge that one of his purposes in being there had been to swing the
group away from a "no logging" mindset to a "no clear-cutting" paradigm.
"I made my case for having been arrested. I told the judge why I considered
that important. It was necessary in the overall picture of trying to make
progress in forestry. I stated my case quite clearly and told him that I had
no regrets whatsoever. I told him that I went up there to attract more
attention to the fact. I knew people were watching to see what I was
going to do. I wanted to let people see in no uncertain terms that I was
quite willing to put my feet where my mouth is. I was willing to get out
there and do something about it—not just talk about it."

In his written judgement that was entered into the court records, Judge Skipp ended his assessment of Merve Wilkinson by calling him "magnificently unrepentant." He sentenced Merve to serve 100 hours of community work, which he carried out by helping to create nature programs at the Morrell Sanctuary. But the court case and Merve's "unrepentant" stand made his name even more well-known than it had been previously. Publicly owned television networks from the U.S. and from South America, the BBC from Britain, and television crews from Germany filmed at Wildwood. Here was a man who knew a better way to take lumber from the forest, and he had stood up for his beliefs.

In 2001 Merve was awarded the Order of British Columbia. Later that year he was informed that he had been chosen to receive the Order of Canada in recognition of his 60 years of sustainable forestry at Wildwood and the work he has done educating people all over the world in his methods.

Because Anne was not well enough to travel to Ottawa for the investiture, her Honour Lieutenant-Governor of B.C. Iona Campagnolo made the presentation at the Yellow Point Lodge on February 25, 2002. Upon presenting the award, Campagnolo said to Merve, "You are a treasure. You are respected in every community I have visited."

Campagnolo, a past recipient of the Order of Canada and the Order of B.C., said she had visited Wildwood 30 years ago and was proud to know that today Wildwood contains more timber despite having been logged continuously every five years. "It is a record that deserves repetition as well as honour," she said. "Mervyn Wilkinson is a British Columbia treasure. His integrity shines through as an example of the kind of dedication for which the Order of Canada was created." Leaning towards him, she added quietly, "You're really doing God's work, you know."

After receiving the medal, Merve said, "I feel very honoured because when I look at the list of people receiving the Order this year, there's a tremendous amount of people in education, social workers—people who have done something for the country—and there's a dearth of politicians and industrialists, and that's good."

Today, thousands of young people make the pilgrimage to Wildwood, and Merve speaks to them about his philosophy and the need to preserve the earth. I attended a ceremony at Wildwood on March 27, 1999, when a tree was felled that was to become the central mast of the *Lifeship 2000*, an ecologically built tall ship that would serve as the expedition vessel for LIFE (Leadership Initiative For Earth). The ship was to travel the world with young people and elders as mentors, carrying a message of peace and sustainable living. These words of blessing were spoken at the tree's felling:

> I have listened to the voice of time and have heard the elements sing—and now I know that my spirit will pass on. It will glide through the waters and fly with the wind and follow the path of the stars. The end of my life will lead to the beginnings of others. My spirit will travel on: the cycle complete and within the future again, we all will meet.

And I thought how fitting these words would be for Merve, when his time comes.

Geraldine Braak:
The "Little Lawyer"

Although Geraldine Braak has lost most of her sight, I am convinced that she is a woman with profound vision. She overcame the hardship of blindness by helping others like her and by educating those others who do not have to cope with a disability.

Even before my meeting with her, I had decided that Geraldine is a woman who knows what matters most to her. When I request an interview, she says in a distinct Dutch lilt, "Yes, but not on the telephone. I prefer to be face to face." Although she sounds rather forthright, she also chuckles at something I say. Even when she stops, I can detect the bubble of laughter close to the surface, about to erupt.

I study her photograph before meeting her: pale grey-blue eyes unfocussed and out of alignment, looking in the general direction of the camera, a shock of thick grey hair, and a wide toothy grin.

It's a warm spring morning when we meet in her office in Powell River, B.C.. It's a sparse, uncluttered space washed in sunlight, the windows framing an attractive view of the harbour and the ferry docks. Although Geraldine can't enjoy the view she is happy to point out the sights beyond her windows. There are few clues to her visual impairment—only the lack of furniture, perhaps, and the reading equipment attached to her computer. Many awards hang on the walls; the Order of British Columbia and the Order of Canada are most prominent.

Geraldine Braak, 1997

She is busy and running late—a last-minute lunch meeting at the Chamber of Commerce has come up. She invites me to join her, but I decline.

"Fine," Geraldine says, then she instructs her assistant to call an associate to come and pick her up in 30 minutes to drive her to the luncheon. Her decisive orders are tempered by "Please" and "Thank you" and a chuckle that she uses like a period at the end of her sentences. Still, her efficiency belies her grandmotherly appearance. I get the distinct feeling that Geraldine's gentle demeanor hides an iron resolve.

Even before we begin talking about her early years growing up in the Netherlands, she lists some of her personal achievements, such as creating affordable housing for people with disabilities in Powell River and promoting increased accessibility and independence for the disabled right across the country. Geraldine admits easily that she is an achiever. Even as a young child she aimed to be the best at whatever she did, but she also points out that she never tried to attain her goals at the price of fairness.

Geraldine was born on December 2, 1936, in the small town of Brunssum in Holland, near the German border. Her father, Herman, was a bookbinder. Geraldine was baptized in the Catholic Church, and she was one of five children, growing up in a comfortable middle class family. She spent her days playing with her brothers and sisters, or trailing after her mother, generally leading an ideal and carefree childhood. Then, when she was three years old, Germany invaded her country, and everything changed. Army trucks loaded with German soldiers, cradling rifles and submachine guns, rumbled into town. As they passed through, the soldiers depleted the stores and stripped the shelves of any food and goods they could find. Herman began to spend all his spare time scrounging and bartering for food. Elizabeth, Geraldine's mother, altered and re-altered her growing children's clothing, sometimes ripping apart her own dresses to make new ones for them.

Brunssum escaped the shelling and bombing but not the effects of the war. Since the town was only minutes from the German border, Hitler Youth often crossed the line to march through the streets and sing their rousing songs. Geraldine and the other children of Brunssum thought their songs very exciting and their uniforms flashy and handsome, so they would march along with them and join in the singing. The adults of the town wisely said nothing against the Hitler Youth. They believed the surest way to keep their children safe was to not provoke fights.

When the German army invaded his village, Herman got a job working in the coal mines, which the Nazis had declared a protected industry because they needed coal for their factories. Herman and the other men working in the mines escaped incarceration in prisoner-of-war camps. For four years Herman and Elizabeth just managed to maintain some security for their family, and in October 1944 the Germans retreated back to the border on the road through Brunssum. It was a different army than the one that had marched through the town in 1940. This time the German soldiers patrolled every street and square in a bid to make their flight an orderly retreat.

The next day dawned eerily quiet. Elizabeth rose early, picked the ripe pears from the tree in the garden, and sent Geraldine and her sister to an aunt's house in the country with a basket of fruit to trade for eggs. The girls had left town and were trudging through the deserted countryside when they heard a distant rumble and felt the ground begin to tremble. They stopped. More German jeeps and tanks? They didn't have to wait long before an enormous convoy of army trucks appeared on the horizon. But they weren't German trucks. The trucks were loaded with Canadian and American soldiers who, when they spotted the two little girls at the side of the road, leaned out of the trucks and called, "Does your daddy smoke?"

The girls were too astonished to reply. They nodded, and the soldiers showered them with cigarette packets, chocolate bars, chewing gum, and packets of cookies. Geraldine stared at the riches in open-mouthed amazement. Her sister, with quick presence of mind, dumped the pears out of the basket and scooped up the treats lying on the road. When the basket was full, they covered their treasure with the pears and lugged it all home.

When they showed their mother the contents of the basket, Elizabeth started to cry. It was not the sight of candy that filled her eyes with tears but what the treats and cigarettes meant: The Allies had come to liberate her country.

Elizabeth divided up the spoils and sent her daughters back out with the basket to share the sweets and cigarettes with their relatives. The aunts and uncles were so delighted they filled the basket right back up again with eggs, butter, vegetables, and anything else they could spare.

The Allied soldiers set up a headquarters in Brunssum and took inventory of the local accommodation for billeting soldiers and officers. Because Herman and Elizabeth lived across the street from the headquarters, they had six officers assigned to their house. Nothing could have excited the children more than having these handsome foreign soldiers sleeping in their front room.

But the initial euphoria of freedom quickly wore off. The front lines were so close that the officers could march into battle in the morning and come home to fall into bed at night, exhausted. Sometimes an officer did not return.

On New Year's Day 1945, Geraldine's family took part as usual in the traditional Dutch custom of visiting friends and family to wish them a Happy New Year. Their route took them past the cemetery, where a convoy of army trucks was parked. The open trucks were stacked high with bodies wrapped in shrouds. Geraldine and her family watched as the soldiers, with tears frozen on their cheeks, tenderly cradled one body after another in their arms and placed them in one of several enormous pits in the ground. Each grave held about eight hundred bodies. "That is a picture I shall never forget," Geraldine says, and for once the smile is gone from her face, the chuckle missing from her voice. "Even though I was very young ... It was the sadness of it—the realization that all these poor young people were killed, and they were in a strange country. They were being put into great big graves, and they did not have anybody there to give a funeral for them. I remember the total sadness of the soldiers that were carrying them. I can still see the frozen tears on their cheeks."

After the war, people gathered up the threads of their lives. They went back to their jobs or to the fields, and the children went back to school. Geraldine excelled in her studies. She wanted to be a lawyer because she believed lawyers helped people and always tried to do what was right and fair. Her friends gave her the nickname

"Little Lawyer" because of her uncanny knack for seeing all sides of an argument and for her dedication to fairness. If there was an argument or a dispute in the playground, Geraldine was the one who would know how to sort it out. In retrospect, she laughs, "I think I would have been one of those poor lawyers who helps every underdog." She was certainly bright enough for law school. She skipped three years in her studies and graduated from high school at age fifteen.

Right after she graduated, and before she could apply to a university, Herman and Elizabeth decided to immigrate to Canada. Their decision was largely based on their hopes for the future of their three sons. They knew that unless they moved to another country the boys would eventually go down into the coal mines. Herman and Elizabeth decided that such work wasn't a good future for them.

When the Canadian immigration department registered the family, they put Geraldine down as a high school student because she was only fifteen. When she said she had already graduated and produced her diploma to prove it, the department—with some surprise—admitted that her diploma was equal to a Grade Thirteen certificate in Canada.

Immigration assigned the family to Saskatoon. They arrived in October, completely unprepared for a Canadian prairie winter, with no inkling of how low the temperature could dip, how raw the northeast wind could be as it whipped across the open plains, or how long the freeze would last. When they first arrived, they rented rooms in a family hotel for six weeks until they found more permanent accommodation—a house across the street from the Catholic Church. It was not until May that they realized there was a paved street underneath the layers of snow and ice.

Geraldine knew she would have to forget her dreams of studying law, yet she felt no resentment. She accepted the fact that her life had changed: she was in a new country, and it was her duty to contribute to the family. During the day she worked as a dishwasher in a Chinese restaurant and at night she went to secretarial school to study shorthand and typing. When she graduated she got a job in an office. Shortly afterwards she met John Braak.

John had also come to Canada from Holland and he was also Catholic. When he arrived in Saskatoon, he visited the Catholic parish to introduce himself to the priest.

"Are you Dutch or German?" the priest asked John.

"I'm Dutch."

"Well, you should go across the street. A Dutch family lives there, and you could have some contact with people from your own country."

John thought that was a good idea, so he thanked the priest and walked across the street to knock on the door. Geraldine opened it and fell in love. So did John. It was really that simple. There may or may not have been bells ringing inside their heads—Geraldine recalls only a deep certainty that this was the man for her for the rest of her life. A year later, in 1956, they were married and moved to Kitimat in northwestern B.C., where a local construction company had hired John, a skilled carpenter.

While John went to the job site each day, Geraldine looked after the house and began to do volunteer work in the community. She was beginning to feel that Kitimat was home when the giant Alcan plant shut down and 1,700 people lost their jobs. The workers and their families left town; house construction ground to a halt.

John and Geraldine moved to Vancouver, where Geraldine got a job working as a window decorator for the Woolworth department store. She was responsible for the displays in thirteen windows that fronted Granville Street, and she discovered she had a genuine artistic flair.

John was also working with Woolworth on store renovations. The company was so pleased with his work that they hired him to work on their other stores, including a Woolworth in Powell River. John took one look at the small community on the Sunshine Coast and knew he wanted to stay. It's easy to see why. Although from a distance—on the ferry, crossing Georgia Strait from Comox—the town is overshadowed by the giant pulp and paper mill, up close it looks more pleasant. Its main street meanders gently along the waterfront, and the hillside it is situated on rises steeply up from the water, lined with streets of well-kept houses, boasting tidy little front gardens. The pace is slow. On a warm spring afternoon people stroll along the sidewalks or skip stones in the water down by the beach.

In 1960, John and Geraldine moved to Powell River. Soon they had two children: Diana and Steven. Geraldine drove them to hockey, dancing, baseball, and all their other activities. She volunteered for various committees, made cookies for bake sales, helped her children with their homework, and always managed a well-kept house. Her home, family, and community were her priority. Geraldine was content with her life when her eyesight began to fail. She had always been nearsighted, but she had simply worn glasses or contact lenses and had never given it a second thought.

She was diagnosed with glaucoma in 1968. She used stronger contact lenses to compensate for her weakened vision, but then her retinas shattered. Although she still had some vision, she was now diagnosed as legally blind. Her immediate reaction was the utter disbelief that follows a shock. How could this have happened? She didn't dwell on the question and would not give in to fear, anxiety, or sorrow. She concerned herself with carrying on her day-to-day duties without upsetting John and the children.

"I know that I never cried," Geraldine recalls. "I was not going to give in."

Like Geraldine, John did not let the news discourage them. When they went to the doctor, he took her hand and said, "We'll fight this one. You know you are not alone. You know that it's okay."

Diana and Steven took longer to assimilate the changes that their mother's visual impairment brought to their lives, but they did adapt. When she realized nothing could be done, Geraldine decided to act as though nothing was different. She loved her life. Why change it? She could still clean her house—it just took longer. When she cleaned a window, she did it twice just to make sure she was not missing any spots. Just because she couldn't see the dirt didn't mean she was going to tolerate it.

She registered with the Canadian National Institute for the Blind (CNIB) and travelled to Vancouver for mobility training and orientation (white-cane travel training). She learned how to use the white cane to detect curbs and other obstacles on the sidewalk; however, when she arrived back in Powell River, she realized that her training was going to do her no good whatsoever. Vancouver had proper sidewalks, often with wide strips of grass on either side; Powell River had few sidewalks, and those it did have were often old and crumbling.

Geraldine didn't get around as much as she could with her full vision, but she got rides with friends and trusted that with time she would gain more independence. Then one day in 1974 a woman named Isabelle, who was an official with the CNIB, visited Powell River. After meeting Geraldine, she called Frank Hodge, the president of the BC/Yukon Division of the Canadian Council of the Blind (CCB) and asked him to go to Powell River to meet this woman with the big smile and unusual attitude. The CNIB representative confessed later that she had said to Frank, "I have a real live one here. She does not feel sorry for herself. She worries about other people and carries on as if nothing is wrong."

Isabelle told Geraldine she wanted her to start a chapter of the CCB in Powell River. She explained that the CNIB was the agency that delivered services to the blind, and the CCB is the national organization of blind people.

"Well, are there many blind people in Powell River?" Geraldine asked. "I've never seen any."

"There are more than fifty people who are legally blind in Powell River," Isabelle said.

"Well, okay," Geraldine said. "I will listen to what it is about."

The CCB and CNIB organized a joint meeting, giving written invitations to their registered clients in Powell River, and about twenty people showed up. Frank Hodge explained the mandate of the Canadian Council of the Blind and what services it provides. He said it would be a good idea to form a chapter in Powell River because a united voice is stronger than individual voices. Those at the meeting agreed that a Powell River chapter of the CCB was a good idea, and when they were asked to elect a president they turned as if on cue towards Geraldine. Before she had a chance to think about it or to protest she was acclaimed president, and she has held that post ever since.

As soon as the Powell River chapter of the CCB was officially founded, it was like a snowball had been pushed off the side of a mountain with Geraldine caught up in the momentum. As president, Geraldine was the delegate to the BC/Yukon Division conference of the council, where she was elected to the division's board of directors. She became a director of legislation, and then she was elected as the delegate from BC/Yukon Division to the national board of directors. At the national level, she was elected second vice-president of the board, then vice-president, and eventually president.

Geraldine devoted as much passion, energy, and enthusiasm to her new work as she had to her housework, her children, and her various volunteer activities. But others recognized this work, and she enjoyed how much of it involved looking for ways to change legislation to better accommodate people who were visually impaired. She could use all her natural abilities as a helper, a peacemaker, and a person who was determined to be fair.

In the early 1980s, Geraldine took part in the Spicer Commission. She served with the committee representing the CCB, which submitted a brief to Spicer. The committee stated its position on national unity: it was good that Canada is made up of many nationalities and peoples and that it should remain a unified country. Geraldine participated in another royal commission hearing on the transfer of federal funds to the provinces. Speaking as the president of the CCB, she questioned the ramifications of decentralizing medical services for disabled people. The issue, she argued, was that transfer payments to provinces might not be used equally for disabled people, and disabled persons had to have equal access to medical services nationwide. "I wanted to make sure that all the provinces were sending people to these royal commissions to make their voices heard so that all the health care funding wouldn't go into one lump of money for health care. There still had to be a separation of the health care dollars, with money set aside for rehabilitation for disabled persons. We had to know that every province had the responsibility of doing some rehabilitation work."

In 1986, when the CCB nominated her for the position of national president, she flew back home from Ottawa and called a powwow at the kitchen table with John, Diana, who was now seventeen, and fifteen-year-old Steven.

"They want to nominate me for president," she told them. "I don't think I should take it because it means going away from home quite a bit."

"What's wrong with that, Mom?" her children asked.

"There would be some pretty big disorder around the house," Geraldine said.

"You know, Mom," Diana said, "you're not the kind of mom that will be happy sitting around at home not doing anything. Next year I will be graduating, and Steven a couple of years later. You've taught us how to clean, how to cook, and how to look after things. We can look after the house when you're away. Mom, you have to think of yourself and what you can do for others. You should do it."

Geraldine was surprised at Diana's sensible attitude, and wondered if she had not been paying attention while her beautiful daughter was growing up and becoming an adult.

"We're proud of you, that you are out there doing things instead of sitting back and complaining," Diana said.

When John supported Diana's viewpoint, Geraldine realized that she really did want to be president. Her family's support gave her the renewed energy to pursue her ambition. She called the nominating committee, agreed to run for president, and was duly elected.

As it turned out, the domestic arrangement worked better than Geraldine could possibly have anticipated. She says that Diana and Steven were better cooks than her, and mealtimes became a real treat. "I never ever came home from anywhere to find dirty dishes around or the beds unmade or the house untidy," Geraldine says. "And I think they felt they wanted to do the work because they had been part of the decision making."

The job of president required Geraldine to work 40 to 60 hours a week, none of it paid labour. "I did it because I saw the need," Geraldine says. "I realized that I was able to do this, and I was capable of speaking up and bringing an issue to the forefront. I knew it would make a difference in the long run."

Every committee she joined—and there were countless committees—was volunteer work. She was a member of the Premier's Advisory Committee on Disabilities, which travelled all over B.C. in order to talk to people and take a new look at the services being provided. The committee published a paper, which was accepted by the government as a guideline for legislation. The *Vancouver Sun* lauded the paper as one of the best it had ever seen. It stated that many people with disabilities, including those who were brain damaged and those with mental disabilities, had never been recognized. The change in legislation made it possible for many marginalized groups to stop requesting welfare and start collecting disability payments.

Geraldine was also a member of many advisory committees to various federal ministers. When she began to list some of these committees—with impossibly long names—I said, "Hold it!" "How many of these committees have you been on?"

Geraldine grinned. "I have no idea. I'd say at least between 30 or 40."

In the early 1990s, she was part of the Advisory Committee on Accessible Transportation (ACAT) to the Minister of Transportation. Geraldine's objective was to make sure that all disabled persons were well served—not just those who were blind and not just those in wheelchairs, but everyone. She was on committees that studied the accessibility of washrooms, airplanes, buses, and elevators, and pondered every detail of that accessibility.

When the Canadian Paraplegic Association (CPA) argued that it needed elevator buttons within easy reach, Geraldine pointed out that this change would not serve blind people or older people who would have trouble bending down. Her solution? Split the difference. She laughs when she tells me about it. "And so I got called 'the 50/50 Lady.' They still tease me about that because I always said, 'Yes, it should be there for you, but it should be there for us as well. You can accommodate both.'"

Years earlier, lobby groups for persons in wheelchairs had been successful in having sidewalk edges removed at street corners. Geraldine pointed out the danger to blind people who counted on their white canes to tell them where the sidewalk ended. Her solution was to introduce a one-quarter-inch edge at street corners.

Given a problem to tackle, Geraldine did not stop until an equitable solution was found. It was never a question of ego. Not once did she hold to her opinion as being the "right" one. Through the process of negotiation, the various associations for disabled persons began to understand and care about one another's needs. But Geraldine did not stop with government in making the needs of disabled persons known: she also talked to business and industry leaders. A deaf person might want signs on a display board, but that wouldn't work for someone who is blind. Her attitude of realism and her willingness to compromise helped ensure that she was heard. She knew she would never get everything she wanted, but she kept herself focussed on key goals—one of which was eliminating the marginalization of blind people. Blind people are the most underemployed in the country—74 percent of working-age blind people are unemployed.

"This is absolutely, very unacceptable," Geraldine says. "Society looks at blindness as one of the worst possible things that can happen. They view blind people as people who cannot do anything. Even today, that is still true in many cases. It is a lot easier to make a desk a little bit higher so that a wheelchair can fit it than it is to make the equipment adaptable for blind people."

Most people who are blind are old, and many of that generation view blindness as demeaning, she says. For them, the image of blindness is still epitomized by a man sitting on the street, selling pencils from a little cup. Geraldine realized that blindness could tear up a person's self-esteem. "When I saw that [they still have this idea], it really touched me," she says. "It made me want to make sure that this is something that must slowly disappear. If you see a person in their early '60s and they feel they are no longer the same, that is very sad because it really does not make any difference. You are still who you are."

Creating jobs and building self-esteem for blind people became Geraldine's biggest personal ambition in 1981, during the International Year of Disabled Persons. The focus was on people's abilities, not their disabilities. Geraldine was determined to keep the momentum of 1981 going. With the urging of many disabled persons groups, the government created a National Access Awareness Week (NAAW) Committee, in which she participated and advertised to raise awareness in the five areas that particularly concerned persons with disabilities: transportation, housing, education, recreation, and employment (THERE).

"Awareness is important," she says. "If people see you manning mall displays and they see that you know what you are doing, they see you in a different light."

All the committees and all the campaigns have made a difference, she says, some of them good and some of them still lacking. For example, Geraldine believes that when specialized schools for people with disabilities closed, not enough was done to take their place. The closures benefited those children who were taken out of boarding schools and brought home to their families and communities, but the public school system into which they have been integrated are still not capable of handling children with special needs. There are not enough special needs teachers, but more importantly, integration has not translated into inclusion, and children with disabilities are still chosen last for games and teams. "They're always the ones that are on the sideline," Geraldine says. "They're always the ones who feel they are not good enough. We have done a very poor job in that area."

She doesn't believe a teacher can successfully teach a classroom of 30 children that may include students who are blind, or deaf, or with comprehension problems. She talks about the case of a little girl in a public school who had a comprehension problem. While she was getting ready for gym class, the alarm rang for a fire drill, and the girl ran outside into the schoolyard, dressed only in her underpants. There she stood, shivering in the rain, while the other children laughed at her. "Why did a teacher not immediately throw her own coat over the child to cover her?" Geraldine demands. "There are still so many things that are wrong with our education system," she says. "Yes, you can say you'll integrate kids, but you also have to know what is involved. You can't just put them into the classroom and let the chips fall where they may."

While she knows there is still a lot of work to do, she also acknowledges that much has been accomplished, particularly in the raised awareness around people with disabilities. But when asked about her proudest achievement, she says with no hesitation, it is that she found the middle ground, the compromise that would work for the greatest good of the majority. Not once did she say, "It has to be my way."

In 1987, Susan Jersak, Maggie Hanson, and Carol Hamilton, three local people who wanted to do something to help people with disabilities, founded the Powell River Model Community Project for Persons with Disabilities (MCP). No sooner had they got the MCP established than they approached Geraldine and said, "We want you to come and work for us."

"I don't have time," Geraldine said. "I've committed to another term as national president of the CCB."

By then she was also a Canadian delegate to the World Blind Union (WBU), a non-governmental United Nations organization representing over 160 countries. She later became a member of the world executive.

"When I finish being national president I might consider your offer," she said.

In 1994, when she finished the maximum number of terms a board member can sit as national president, Susan, Carol, and Maggie approached her again.

"Remember, you said you were going to come and work for us."

"Oh yes," Geraldine said. "Well I'll be interested in doing something, but not too much."

"Not too much" for Geraldine meant that she became the Executive Director of the MCP and worked a minimum of 40 hours a week. It was her first paid job as an advocate for persons with disabilities; however, working a full-time job did not mean she stopped doing her volunteer work with the WBU and the CCB.

Today the MCP focuses on THERE: transportation, housing, education, recreation, and employment. Geraldine's achievements in her community include establishing a HandyDart system and a Para-Transit system that operates outside the municipal borders. When the MCP became aware of a government initiative to sponsor affordable housing units, it had only seven weeks to meet the application deadline. Unfazed, Geraldine set to work. She was well aware that one criterion for the housing grant was community backing, so she talked to every community organization and business in Powell River, asking for letters of support.

The community backed her, and shortly before the deadline, she received a phone call from the minister's office. "Please, will you stop sending us these letters?"

"If you look," Geraldine said, not even bothering to suppress the chuckle in her voice, "you'll notice they are all signed by different organizations."

"Yes we know. We've got the message."

The MCP got the grant and built a 31-unit housing complex, some units completely wheelchair accessible and 60 percent of them income supported. In 2000, the Sunset Home Society turned over the management of another housing complex, Brew Bay, to the MCP. In the area of recreation, the MCP built a wheelchair-accessible recreational area along a local lake. It includes a 13-kilometre trail that is completely wheelchair accessible and four cabins near the trail that are set-aside for persons with disabilities. The MCP also sponsored two telethons and received foundation funding for the playground equipment that is accessible to all at the nearby Willingdon Beach play area.

Geraldine then turned her attention to education. Working with the local school board and Malaspina University College, she ensured that all courses were accessible to people with disabilities, whether that meant computers with screen readers or sign language interpreters. Because she knows the importance of literacy, one of Geraldine's pet projects is supporting Braille as the most valuable teaching tool for the blind. She notes that although technology has made many advances for blind persons, it will never replace the importance of knowing how to spell, read, and write. After several meetings with representatives of a variety of organizations of and for the blind, Geraldine convinced the various groups to establish the Canadian Braille Authority, working with the American Braille Authority and the International Braille committee to create a unified code for Braille throughout the world. Geraldine became an interim committee member and worked on establishing the organization's constitution and bylaws in order to get the Canadian Braille Authority accepted by the government for Revenue Canada status as a not-for-profit organization. Geraldine was also a member of the first executive committee in the Canadian Braille Authority and was awarded a certificate of outstanding service and a life membership.

Employment for the blind is Geraldine's biggest challenge. She has instituted training and counselling programs to help persons with disabilities enter the workforce. Often, when she felt that people needed a boost in their self-esteem, she would hire them. Although the MCP had no budget for staff, she paid them from her own wages. What was important was not the money, but what it represented.

Geraldine is anxious to list her accomplishments and is meticulous about accuracy, but when I mention that all she has achieved must excite her, she shakes her head.

"No, all of these things should have been done without all the work involved. Maybe one of my achievements is that the recognition of that is there now."

In 1997, Geraldine received a phone call from Government House in Victoria. "Congratulations Mrs. Braak. You have been chosen to be the recipient of the Order of British Columbia."

"Oh sure," Geraldine said, letting her chuckle bloom into outright laughter. "Who are you?"

"My name is Heidi. I am with the honours and awards office for the Government of British Columbia. We will be mailing this to you within the next couple of days."

It wasn't a joke—it was real! Geraldine was so excited she could barely contain herself, and she certainly couldn't wait to rush home and tell John. "It's something you don't even think about," she says. "You're not even really aware that it's there. I had never known anybody who had received it. It was a very big surprise."

At the investiture, Geraldine remembers listening in awe to the citations of her fellow recipients. "Why am I here?" she asked herself.

Afterwards, one of the recipients said to Geraldine, "You know, when I listened to everything you had done, I wondered, 'Why am I here?'"

Geraldine says, "I think perhaps we all feel like that—how people would consider us worthy of being nominated—as it's such an honour."

In 2000, Malaspina University College awarded Geraldine Braak an honorary Doctor of Laws degree. The "Little Lawyer" had become a lawyer at last.

When Dr. Richard Johnston, the president of the college, informed her of her award, she thought, "How is this possible?"

It was possible because of how Geraldine views things and how she has always argued for fairness and justice and has worked for the benefit of all.

In 2001 Geraldine received another telephone call—this time to inform her that she was to be awarded the Order of Canada; and because of her international work, she was to be invested as an officer of the order—a very high honour indeed. Once again she stood on the podium, wondering, "Why am I here?"

Geraldine now answers this question. "The biggest gift you have is your life," she says. "You can waste it, or you can live it with all you've got."

As I leave her office to head back to the ferry that will take me across Georgia Strait to Comox, I think about her words. It seems to me that Geraldine Braak has taken her gift of life and created a larger gift for all those she has found needing her energy and vision.

Dr. Michael O'Shaughnessy: Champion for AIDS Research

*D*r. Michael O'Shaughnessy describes himself as an achiever. Given his accomplishments, particularly in the field of HIV research, it's a fitting description, but there's more to him than a lifetime of achievement. After I talk to him in his office at St. Paul's Hospital in Vancouver, I form a picture of a man who is smart, funny, irreverent, and tenacious. His office, tucked away on the sixth floor in a wing that looks old and almost deserted, is large but cluttered with chairs, a round table, a large desk, lots of bookshelves, with family photos, various awards, and certificates scattered among the desk and walls. We meet on a Friday, casual Friday, as Michael explains, because he is wearing casual pants and a sweatshirt. I like his lack of self-consciousness, his open manner, his big, booming voice and his rich Bronx accent, and his disarming willingness to talk about his life and philosophy.

We have arranged for a two-hour interview. "I have one hour," Michael says as soon as I sit down.

"But we said two hours," I remind him.

"Well something's come up," he says. "It's a very busy time. Let's just start and maybe I can go a bit longer than one hour."

We start at his beginning. Michael was born on February 11, 1944, in the south Bronx, as the second oldest of five children. His parents were Irish immigrants. His mother, Bridget Hart, had been sent to America in 1918 as a six-year-old orphan to live with her cousins. Her name is engraved on a special plaque on Ellis Island with other child immigrants that needed special approval from the U.S. government to enter the country.

Dr. Michael O'Shaughnessy, 1998

Dr. Michael O'Shaughnessy

Michael grew up poor, but he grew up in a neighbourhood rich in culture. The Bronx was populated by Italians, Irish, Germans, Jews, Hispanics, African Americans—almost every language on earth filled the streets with a sweet cacophony of sound. But no matter how different the families were in language and customs, they all shared the same poverty.

"You know what's funny," Michael says. "We didn't know we didn't have. It's only later that you realize you didn't have anything. We were happy."

Bridget's brother, Thomas, had come to New York a year after his sister. He was a priest and an academic with a PhD in Sociology and became one of Michael's earliest role models. "He was so smart and so well read," Michael recalls. "I think he helped push me that way—the curiosity and the reading. That's what I remember most—him telling me there wasn't much that was more important in life than reading and understanding."

Michael's parents were another strong influence. His father, Michael senior, was a quiet, thoughtful, and gentle man, who worked as a policeman. It was his mother, Bridget, who was determined that her children would be successful. "My mother took no prisoners," Michael laughs. "She was ambitious for all of us, and we all did well."

Michael attended Catholic schools that gave him a good grounding in the classics. He muses, "I had an education that I suppose is anachronistic in today's world, but it was good. I'm sure glad I had it."

He left high school with a scholarship that paid part of his tuition for university. To pay for the balance he took on any job he could find during summer holidays and after school. At just over six feet tall and 220 pounds, and very muscular, athletic, and tough, he could do almost anything. He worked in cement construction, laid hardwood floors, did office work—if someone was willing to pay him to do it, he would.

He was working towards a Bachelor of Science degree at Manhattan College. Despite studying hard and trying to apply himself to school, he didn't really take his first two years seriously. In his third year he took part in a project headed by a team of professors at the University Research Institute, studying a virus that makes plant

45

cells turn into a tumor. Michael's attitude abruptly shifted; he became serious about his work because he realized that his research wasn't involved with just an isolated virus on an isolated plant—it related to all life. "What changed my attitude was the professors," he says. "It's who they were and how they thought. I had had some very memorable professors, but not until then had I looked at something that I thought I wanted to do."

Michael graduated from Manhattan College with a Bachelor of Science degree and enrolled at Adelphi University in New York to work on his master's thesis. There his research centred on interferon, a substance the body cells produce that inhibits the replication of viruses. He was fascinated with the compound, so when he finished his Master of Science degree, he went to Dalhousie University in Halifax, Nova Scotia, to do his doctorate studies with a group of scientists working on interferon. He could have attended any number of outstanding U.S. universities that offered him National Science Foundation Scholarships, but he turned them down to work with the scientists at Dalhousie, who—in his opinion—were the best group he could find.

The head of the department at Dalhousie was the world-renowned scientist, Carl van Rooyen, who wrote the first textbook on clinical virology. Van Rooyen retired the year Michael arrived, but his academic team was still in place, and as far as Michael was concerned, it was the team that counted. "I loved being a student," he recalls. "You know, it's amazing; there's so much stress because you have no money, but it's fun because it's your whole life."

Michael enjoyed probing and questioning and making discoveries. It was his whole world—almost. During this time he also met, fell in love with, and married his wife Susan in New York City.

In 1972 he achieved his PhD degree and went to Queens University in Kingston to work with a senior scientist, who was also doing research on interferon. Research was still his passion, but to earn a living, he took on two jobs: managing the Public Health Laboratory for eastern Ontario, and teaching virology and microbiology at Queens University. "A lot of the students you teach are just there to pass the course," he says. "And I didn't enjoy that. But every once in a while you see one that is exceptional and that makes your day."

Dr. Michael O'Shaughnessy

Michael found the job at the Public Health Laboratory was more challenging than the teaching job, but also generally more fun. When he took over the lab it was an isolated unit separate from the university scientists, who were doing research on diseases like tuberculosis. It made no sense to him that they should not have access to the Public Health Laboratory, which did an enormous amount of work with tuberculosis, so he restructured the organization and integrated it into the academic community. He was convinced that the researchers would learn more from seeing the people that would benefit from the work they were doing.

He worked at the Public Health Laboratory for ten years. When he noticed that he was no longer excited by the work, he decided it was time to quit. One day, while he was mulling over what to do when he left his job, Susan pointed out an advertisement for a position in Ottawa at the Laboratory Centre for Disease Control. "Michael," she said. "You ought to apply for this. You would like to do this job."

The federal government was looking for someone to manage the national virus surveillance unit. Michael applied and was hired for the position. In 1982 he and Susan moved to Ottawa. His new work was very interesting: Michael and his team kept track of the viral diseases in Canada, ran a quality assurance program, did testing, and issued findings and publications on the various diseases they studied. But the program was so meagrely financed that he and the department struggled to do their job properly. It wasn't until 1984, when he picked up a scientific journal and read two papers written by Dr. Robert Gallo, the director of the National Cancer Center in Washington D.C., that Michael discovered the direction to take in his work on viruses. Dr. Gallo's articles described the idiologic agent that causes AIDS (acquired immunodeficiency syndrome, which is the last phase of human immunodeficiency virus disease, or HIV). When Michael read about Gallo's work, he thought, "My God! Here is the guy who has actually found the cause of HIV disease!"

He was overwhelmed by this discovery. The data was compelling; here was a major breakthrough! "Everyone, including ourselves, had just been barking up the wrong tree. Even if you weren't working on it, if you were in the public heath arena, you had to say, 'Oh my God! It *is* a virus. It *is* transmissible!' But it's a different type of virus.

And the excitement was that it's a virus that integrates into the host genome and it becomes part of us, so that's why you can get infected and not get the disease for two decades. The virus gets in there and just hides."

Journal in hand, Michael went to his superior and said, "Look at these papers. This is it. This is the cause. This is the stuff. We should learn this technology. We should go and visit Gallo's laboratory. Somebody from this place has to go!"

Michael was the most junior man in the department and, consequently, the least likely to be selected to go, but no one else volunteered when his boss asked every scientist in the laboratory, "Who want's to go to Gallo's lab and learn how to do this testing, get a handle on this material, and grow this virus?" Michael concedes the other scientists were all busy men and may not have had time to go, but that in the 1980s the fear of contracting AIDS was also enormous. He, too, was apprehensive, but he believed that his job with viruses and public health necessitated going to Gallo's laboratory and learning everything he could about HIV. After all, he reasoned, people with HIV were part of the public he served. "We'll protect ourselves the best way we can and get on with the job," he said.

Michael flew to Washington, D.C., to work with the charming and notorious Bob Gallo, who had a reputation for rarely spending time in his own lab. Those who knew him liked to tell a Bob Gallo joke: "The difference between God and Gallo is God is everywhere and Gallo is everywhere but here." When the government of Canada called Gallo to request permission to send someone to his laboratory, he said, "Sure, you can send someone down here, but when he gets here, I'm going to be away."

When Michael arrived in Washington, Gallo's staff didn't care why he was there, refusing to let him enter the laboratory. He spent two days sitting, reading, and pacing in the library. At the end of the second day he talked to his brother, John, who was the assistant secretary of health of the U.S. "What is this?" Michael complained to John. "What's going on here?"

"You need to tell them who I am," John said. "And you need to say that you are an official visitor from the government of Canada, and that I will expect a report on how this official visitor is accommodated."

The next morning Michael talked to Gallo's chief assistant, who checked the organizational chart of the U.S. government. "He came back to me just about shitting himself that he was so rude to me," Michael recalls gleefully.

The staff opened the laboratory to him and he went to work. His research partner, Marjorie Robert-Guroff, was committed, gracious, and helpful. "And that's how I got started working on HIV," Michael says. "It's amazing. They put me in the library for two days, and if circumstances weren't that my brother happened to be the assistant secretary of health, I'd probably still be there, waiting for these turkeys."

Gallo was nothing like his senior staff that had so rudely ignored Michael. He came back to the lab, gave him all the help he needed, and sent him back to Canada with enough HIV virus to run tests for two years. Gallo was keen to see his discovery make a difference in the world.

Michael spent two months in Washington, and he continued to make trips back to Gallo's laboratory to continue his research. The medical community knew that HIV was a problem in Canada, but it did not know the full extent of that problem until Michael and the scientists in Gallo's lab worked together on refining and applying a test for the disease. Although the work Michael was doing gave him the excitement of discovery, the thrill was tempered by the realization that there were people whose health had already been affected by the virus. It wasn't a cold virus that was going to disappear in a week or two; it was different from anything he or any other scientist had ever seen.

At that time some people believed that not everyone who contracted the HIV infection would get AIDS. Michael was one of the scientists who said, "You're dreaming. If they have the virus, they will get the disease."

He and the others who agreed with him were later proven right: 99 percent of people infected with HIV get AIDS.

HIV became Michael's life work. Peter Gill, the head of microbiology at the Laboratory Centre for Disease Control, believed the work Michael was doing was important and exciting, and encouraged him to continue his work with HIV. "I got so much support from him and so much enthusiasm from him. We had a great relationship," Michael says.

The battle to find a cure—or at least a vaccine—for AIDS became more personal for Michael when he met an actor named James St. James, whom he came to know and care about. Michael listened to James speak eloquently on the subject of AIDS. His words painted a poignant picture of the pain of living with the disease. When James died, Michael felt the world had lost a good man. Then he discovered that his friend, Dr. Randy Coates, a scientist and epidemiologist, was HIV positive. "When you start to get to know people like James and my friend Randy, you need to get involved. You can't sit by," he says.

Then he met another man: a young scientist who had AIDS and who died within a year of diagnosis. Michael stopped viewing the disease impersonally. For him, HIV disease had become more than a challenging problem to solve; it was a disease that was cutting short the life expectancy of good people that he knew.

In the late 1980s the federal government created the Federal Centre for AIDS to look after HIV research; Michael transferred to the new department. The other people who applied to work there were people who, like him, were genuinely interested in working on the HIV problem. But in 1992 the minister for health closed the centre simply because in the grab for funding by various health departments, the centre for AIDS was the lowest priority.

As director general of the centre, Michael had to give the news to his staff, help them transfer to a new job, and shut the centre down. When he began his own job search, he noticed that St. Paul's Hospital in Vancouver was advertising for a director to establish the B.C. Centre for Excellence in HIV/AIDS. Michael applied and won the competition.

He arrived in Vancouver in April 1992. The centre started with four people: administrator Brian Harrigan, Irene Goldstone—who had been head nurse in an institution that cared for HIV patients, Michael, and a secretary. Today the B.C. Centre for Excellence in HIV/AIDS is one of the leading treatment and research centres in the world, blending the clinical and research facets of HIV, and serving as the model for other centres worldwide.

When Michael arrived at St. Paul's Hospital, it was the only hospital that had made a decision ten years previously to treat HIV positive patients while other hospitals were turning them away. One large hospital in Vancouver would send HIV patients to St. Paul's by taxi because they wanted nothing to do with them.

The core people for the centre were already in place when Michael arrived: Dr. Julio Montaner, Dr. Martin Shechter, Dr. Richard Harrigan, and Dr. Bob Hogg, all of whom Michael calls "stars." "All I did was come in here and recognize the incredible strengths that were here and incorporate them into the centre," Michael says. "Some days the toughest job is managing the egos. We're all 'Type A' and we have our own visions, but it's great because we've done some incredible things."

The "stars" are media savvy. Michael handles reporters like an old pro. He knows about picking up cues on radio and television and how just the right turn of phrase will grab an audience's attention. He likes to show off his collection of *Canada AM* mugs from his numerous appearances on the popular television show. He laughs about the attention he receives from the media, but he notes that publicity isn't just fun. It's serious business because it keeps the government and the public focussed on the importance of finding a cure and treatment for the disease.

Michael's team has two questions that guide everything they do: "How do you treat people with HIV disease?" and "What's the most effective way?" In the quest to answer those questions, the centre was the first in Canada to use combination therapy, that is, using two or more drugs. It was the first to adopt the viral load assay as a treatment tool. It was the first to adopt triple drug therapy in a publicly funded plan. It was the first to develop and implement resistance testing not only for residents of B.C. but also for people nationwide. It developed a method to measure drug levels in people who are failing treatment, to determine whether the drugs are being processed badly, or whether the patient is not taking the drugs. "We challenge ourselves every day," Michael says. "How do we know? What if we do this? What if we do that? What if we take people off treatment and wait a while?"

Michael's team published a paper on delayed treatment in the *Journal of the American Medical Association* in 2001, and the international press picked up the story. It was exciting news: money could be saved and side effects could be avoided if treatment could be delayed without putting the patient in jeopardy! Michael and his team have published papers in the *New England Journal of Medicine* and every other reputable medical journal in the world. "It's been a blast," he says. "We built a model. We built this team, and how we looked at it is that we have a relationship between the clinicians and the scientists and there's always this interaction."

Every day they ask themselves, "Is what we are doing the best we can do for the patients?"

"I wouldn't do this job if I didn't care about the patient," Michael says. "I need to be an advocate for them. It's my job." He believes he has two responsibilities. The first is to look at each new drug that comes along and ask, "Is it effective?" If it is, his second responsibility is to convince the doctors and the people who pay the bills that these drugs are worth using. Treatment for HIV/AIDS is expensive. The centre's drug budget is $35 million per year to treat about three thousand people. The centre has taken another 1,000 people off treatment, operating on the hypothesis that they can wait to be treated more aggressively without compromising their health. Those who are not receiving drugs are not suffering side effects, and the medical system benefits by saving money.

"But we didn't do that to save money," Michael says quickly. "When you determine that a drug is effective and plays a role, you need to negotiate hard. HIV is a disease where, because there is such a downward drift in health, a lot of people who have it don't have access to money, and so the population that is affected is quite poor."

Michael established a committee at the centre that created a comprehensive set of guidelines for the treatment of HIV/AIDS, and the centre ensures that physicians conform to the guidelines. Before the guide was published there were no set procedures. The centre also has a close partnership with the Centre for Persons With AIDS Society, and together they developed a program called "The Treatment ABC's," where the centre sends teams out into communities all over B.C. to teach doctors about treatment and to help them overcome their reluctance to treat HIV disease. The centre has also given doctors in small towns and rural communities a 1-800 line that allows them to speak to an expert and not feel isolated with a problem they feel ill-equipped to handle.

Twenty years ago the life expectancy of people infected with HIV was eight years. Today it's twenty years, but that's still not good enough, according to Michael. "We can't accept that as the status quo, but that's where we are. We're pushing to make it longer. We don't have a cure. People will die early with HIV disease, and they will die young. We don't have a cure yet."

His dream is to find a cure. "The best day of my life will be when I can close this door and turn the key because they don't need us any more. I've met a lot of people, who I like a lot and who have this virus, and if you told me there was a cure for them and for the people I don't know, I would say that's the greatest news I've ever had. But I won't see that in my working life." But a cure isn't the only thing Michael's team is searching for; they are also trying to develop a preventative HIV vaccine. Michael believes they are still years away from achieving that goal. Ten thousand people in British Columbia live with what he calls "this damn virus." We can't ever forget them, he says. We can have all the preventative vaccines in the world, but they won't help those already infected. Science has to find both a preventative and a cure, or at the very least, better and better treatments.

In the ten years he has been at the B.C. Centre for Excellence in HIV/AIDS, Michael has helped set up the Centre for Health, Outcomes, and Evaluation Sciences that Dr. Martin Schechter gleefully dubbed "Cheos." Michael is co-director of the Canadian HIV Trials Network. He helped raise the money that put a health van in Vancouver's downtown east side with a physician and a nurse on board to dispense care to the people on the street. He and Dr. Julio Montaner found the funds to establish an AIDS ward at St. Paul's Hospital. He and his team set up a Maximally Assisted Therapy Program for addicted people on the streets, which serves as a centre for people to get the anti-HIV drugs they need. It also serves as a drop-in, where they can get a sandwich or help from the staff with finding housing or even just getting access to a telephone. The Maximally Assisted Therapy Program may not seem to have a lot to do with HIV, but Michael's argument is that it reaches people who need treatment and who otherwise might be reluctant to access it. He loves Vancouver's downtown east side because in many ways it reminds him of his old neighbourhood in New York. "Where else can you walk on the street and have such a mix?" he asks. "The colours and languages—that's what I grew up with."

In 1996 Michael co-chaired the International Conference for AIDS that brought 15,000 people to Vancouver and helped raise $25 million for HIV treatment and research. Dr. Martin Schechter and Michael set up the Vancouver Injection Drug Users Study that took a look at the activity on downtown Vancouver's east side streets. Their latest project is a clinical trial for medically prescribed heroin instead of methadone. "I may be stoned for that one," he laughs. Heroin for clinical use may be controversial in society, he says, but not among scientists. Besides, Dr. Michael O'Shaughnessy would never let a bit—or even a lot—of controversy stop him. "You have to look at what's the right thing to do," he says. "And this is the right thing to do. So just suck it up and do it."

Michael received the Order of British Columbia in 1998 because all his life he has been doing what he believed was the right thing. It isn't the only recognition or award he has received, but it's the one that makes him most proud because the Vancouver Native Health Society and the Persons With AIDS Society—two community organizations—recommended him for it. He was so excited when he got the phone call, he can't even remember who he spoke to.

"And then, when I went to the ceremony, with the people who received the award at the same time—I was so impressed with them. I thought, 'My God, these people are really something!' I was so impressed that I was there with them." Michael was recognized for his scientific work and for being an advocate for people with HIV. He believed his job was to make the government understand why expensive drugs are worth funding and why the funding must continue to be made available in order to supply those drugs to people with HIV.

"I've had a superb career," he says. "I've done just about everything I wanted to do. I have had great recognition and very good productivity as a scientist. I was president of this and the chair of that … The Order of British Columbia meant more to me than all of that. It really did."

Michael's business card is double-sided. On one side it reads: Michael V. O'Shaughnessy OBC, PhD, Centre Director, Centre for Excellence in HIV/AIDS. On the flip side it says: Michael V. O'Shaughnessy OBC PhD, VP Provincial/Tertiary Programs and Research Providence Health Care. Beneath that title is another one: Assistant Dean of Research, Faculty of Medicine, University of British Columbia. Providence Health Care runs St. Paul's Hospital, and when the position of vice-president came up, Michael applied for it. I say that it seems he was already overworked, but he says he doesn't mind working 60 hours a week. I remind myself that he's already confessed to being a "Type A" personality.

So when he says, "Look at this," shows me a framed photograph, and explains, "That's my place in the Chilcotin, and that's where I'm going to retire to," I am a bit taken aback. The photo is of him and Susan on horseback on a hillside overlooking a green valley. I say, "I can't imagine you retired."

When he leaves St. Paul's Hospital, Michael plans to let go of the job completely; however, he doesn't expect to spend all his days riding up and down the hills of his ranch. He hopes to use his experience in dealing with government to help the community of which he will become a part. "I've worked with the government," he says. "I understand the system, and I don't take any shit."

I don't believe that Michael has ever taken any baloney from anybody. His pugnacious streak may be a family trait; but he also grew up poor and in the Bronx. From his mother, he got the desire to achieve; his uncle Thomas gave him a love of learning and an insatiable curiosity. The way they combined to create a man who cares enough to advocate for one of the most disenfranchised groups in our society is pure Michael O'Shaughnessy.

I think it's probably typical of Michael that during our one-hour talk, which turned into 90 minutes, he never once glanced at his watch, never once rushed me, and never once mentioned his next appointment. He gave me his full attention, and I'm guessing that's what he does with every person and every project in his life.

Richard Hunt, 1991

Richard Hunt:
A Man That Travels
Around the World Giving

$H$is Native name is Gwel-la-yo-gwe-la-gya-les, meaning, "a man that travels around the world giving." It suits Richard Hunt well. It is because he has given so much of himself that he has been awarded the Order of British Columbia and the Order of Canada. Richard Hunt has many accomplishments to be proud of; perhaps the most important of those is how he helped to revive and raise awareness of Northwest Native art, elevating it from the ranks of anthropological curiosity to its rightful place as an integral part of the Aboriginal culture. However, when I ask him what his proudest achievement was, he says it was graduating from high school.

In a family of fourteen children, Richard was the only one to complete his secondary education. When he attended school, it wasn't easy to be a Native in a largely non-Native educational system. Richard says it still isn't easy. He lives in Victoria with his second wife and daughter in a modest suburban house, where he has converted the garage into a studio. It is there—in that slightly chilly space—that we talk. To begin with he is somewhat cautious, as though he doubts my motives. "Have you looked at my website?" he asks when I inquire where he was born.

"Yes," I say, "But I want to hear about your life in your own words."

He tells me he was born on April 25, 1951, in Alert Bay, a small town on Cormorant Island near Port MacNeil on northern Vancouver Island. His family lived in nearby Fort Rupert, but because there was no hospital there, his mother had travelled to Alert Bay to give birth to him, her seventh child.

Richard's family belonged to the Kwa-giulth Nation, which shares its language and culture with other First Nations known collectively as the Kwakwaka'wakw. In the traditions of the Kwakwaka'wakw, family and kinship are paramount. Their most treasured heritage includes the owned rights to the performance of songs, dances, and the display of historic crests. Although the Kwa-giulth suffered tremendous setbacks when white people arrived—through infectious diseases and the establishment of reserves and residential schools— they kept their traditions alive.

Anthropologists collected the Native art of the Northwest Coast for storage in museums. They treasured the pieces as examples of primitive art that was dying and would never be revived; but the traditions didn't die, and the rebirth of Native art can be attributed in large part to the Hunt family. George Hunt, Richard's great-grandfather was an early ethnographer, who detailed the culture of the Kwakwaka'wakw people.

In 1951, the year of Richard's birth, the British Columbia Provincial Museum invited the 70-year-old Chief Nekapenkim (Mungo Martin), one of the only talented Native carvers still alive on Vancouver Island, to replicate the totem poles in Victoria's Thunderbird Park because the originals were deteriorating, and the museum wanted to move them indoors for preservation. Mungo was Richard's adopted grandfather. He had rescued his mother, Helen, from the Alert Bay residential school years before and had adopted her in a traditional potlatch ceremony. When Mungo arrived in Victoria he asked Richard's father, Henry, to come and work with him. Henry was a logger, fisherman, and trapper, but he had also learned to be a carver. When Henry joined Mungo at Thunderbird Park, he promised that a member of the Hunt family would always work there.

Richard started carving when he was thirteen years old. That summer he had gone berry picking to contribute to the family income.

Everyone had to help out, Richard explains, because Helen was a generous woman. When a relative or a friend needed something, she gave it to them without ever worrying whether or not she could afford to. After that first day of berry picking, with his back bent over and aching under the blistering sun, Richard was exhausted. He recalls, "I dreamt about berries all night and said, 'I don't want to do that for a living.' I knew I wanted to be a carver like my dad, and the next thing I knew I was going to Thunderbird Park."

Richard began his apprenticeship after school, watching his father carve, and listening to him explain what he was doing. He learned that carving was part of his culture and that according to tradition he would own every carving he created. He also learned that he did not have to invent anything new, all he had to do was follow in his ancestors' footsteps and do what they had always done.

Richard believes he was fortunate in many ways. His mother, Helen, never talked about her years at the residential school, but she had made a promise to herself and her family that none of her children would ever go to one of those institutions. So Helen and Henry's children were among the few Natives who attended public schools. "I fought my way through school," Richard recalls. "I was a patrol captain in Grade Three, when one of my brothers was getting dragged around by his hair and the guy was laughing at him, so I threw my patrol gear off and had a big fight with him and got kicked out and got the strap … I put up with racism all through school."

"How did you feel about that?" I ask.

"For the longest time I couldn't figure out why people didn't like me. Then I realized I was Native." Richard laughs, and although it's not a happy laugh, it transforms his round, handsome face to look twenty years younger. He adds, "It was when I started dating girls that I started realizing it. You're my friend until I want to date your daughter."

Richard was a strong athletic youth who was a champion football and soccer player. He also excelled at art. Mr. Hemming, his art teacher at Victoria High School, recognized his talent, so whenever Richard had a full day of art classes, Hemming allowed him spend the day working with his father at Thunderbird Park instead. He knew that no instruction he could give the aspiring carver could equal that which he was learning from his father.

Although Richard shone in art and sports, he did not do well academically, and he failed two grades. But he did graduate. "It took me fourteen years to get through school," he says. "I wasn't the greatest student, but in the summer of 2001, I gave a talk to a graduating class and I said, 'I wasn't the sharpest pencil in the pencil case. It took me a few more years to graduate. I thought an "E" meant excellent and "P" meant perfect.' I was only doing it because my mom made me, and I would be the first in the family to graduate. But when I gave my talk at the school I told them it wasn't that my brothers and sisters were dumb—it's just that they were trying to make a living to help and support the family. I graduated, and I told them how important that was."

Richard went to work with his older brother Tony, who had also apprenticed at Thunderbird Park with their father and who had opened Arts of the Raven Gallery in Bastion Square in downtown Victoria. Richard quit after a year because he believed carving was solo work and he thought of himself as an artist in the cultural tradition of his people. Whatever he started, he wanted to finish. He still works alone in his studio. He has not had an apprentice or an assistant since leaving the museum. Richard Hunt always creates a Richard Hunt carving, down to the last painstaking detail.

When Richard left Arts of the Raven, the Royal British Columbia Museum hired him to work with his father in Thunderbird Park. Shortly after Richard became his father's assistant, Henry quit, saying that his job at the museum was done. He had made a promise to Mungo that one of the family would always be there, and now Richard was that person.

Richard had his grandfather's and his father's talent, both as a carver and an educator. Thousands of people visited Thunderbird Park each year, and Richard answered their questions with care and respect. He also taught them about his culture, traditions, and art. He carved totem poles, ceremonial masks, and other valuable pieces of art. A 30-foot totem would take three months to complete. Richard's net salary was about $1,600 a month, and it began to rankle him that he wasn't being paid more for his work. "I pointed out to the government that my job wasn't to carve, it was actually to inform the public and teach them about our people," he says.

In response, the museum administration rewrote his job description and specified in his contract that everything he carved at Thunderbird Park belonged to the museum. "So I signed it," he says. "Because I thought if I didn't I'd probably lose my job." He still believes that everything he carved before signing the contract probably legally belongs to him, and everything his father and grandfather carved while they were at the museum belongs to the family as well. He dreams of one day retrieving his family's art and taking it to Fort Rupert, his ancestral home, where it could become a tourist attraction and help the local economy.

Although Richard believes his working conditions were not fair or just, he remembers his time at Thunderbird Park as good years, where he learned from more experienced carvers and developed his own creativity. He was not the oldest or most experienced person there, but he was the head carver because the title was passed to him from his father, who had in turn inherited it from Mungo.

Richard took pride in his work because he believed Thunderbird Park belonged to the Natives. It had been created as a centre for the Kwakwaka'wakw people, but it was built on Salish territory, which became a source of conflict. The Kwakwaka'wakw chiefs said that no other tribes could use the Big House without receiving permission, which they had no intention of granting. Richard's view was that any Native—whether from Vancouver Island, the United Sates, Mexico, or South America—should be allowed to use the Big House. When he told his mother what he believed and said, "We're all brothers," Helen told her son, "This is a game we play. You shouldn't take the game too seriously or you're going to get confused and angry." But he did get angry, so he concentrated on his work instead of getting involved in the political game. Years later he learned that Thunderbird Park belonged to the government, not his people or any other Native people, and the sense of ownership and freedom he had experienced there was an illusion.

While he worked for the museum, Richard created major sculptural works. In 1976 he carved a fifteen-foot totem pole for the Museum of Ethnology in Osaka, Japan. In 1978 he and his friend,

Nuu-cha-nulth artist Tim Paul, carved a fifteen-foot totem pole for the Captain Cook Birthplace Museum in Middlesbrough, England, and in 1979 Richard carved a 26-foot totem pole that was erected at the main entrance to the Royal British Columbia Museum.

In 1980 he was beginning to feel frustrated and tied down. Although he didn't feel bound by his father's promise to Mungo that a member of the family would always be at Thunderbird Park, he did feel obligated to honour it while his father was alive. So he decided that travelling would be one way to change the pace of his work and to meet new challenges.

He went to Los Angeles with Tim Paul to carve a totem pole and then to Edinburgh Scotland, where he carved and erected a twelve-foot totem pole at the City Art Centre in conjunction with the Edinburgh Festival in which "Canada" was that year's theme. He also carved a totem pole for the International Garden Festival in Liverpool, England.

In 1985 Richard and Tim Paul travelled to England again, at the request of Queen Elizabeth II, to repair and repaint the totem pole carved by Mungo and Henry and presented to her by the Province of British Columbia in 1958 to honour her centennial visit. Richard was excited about the opportunity to meet the Queen. "I always thought I wanted to be like my dad," he says. "I wanted to be a carver like my dad and do what my dad did. I know he met the Queen a few times, and so I kind of wanted to do the things he did. My parents were very poor, but they had a lot of things happen to them. They knew a lot of important people in Victoria."

In England, as in other places that he travelled, Richard encountered the familiar problem of racism. His proposed accommodation in a tiny room in a Windsor hotel reminded him of the time he had repainted a totem his father had carved for Expo 67 in Montreal, where he had been housed in an old hotel next to the bus station. It seemed to him that he was always being treated as less than his fellow citizens. But as time went on, he spoke up more and more. He wasn't angry, he says, he just wanted to be treated the way he was by his Native brothers.

Richard then describes being treated with respect when he was invited to a powwow in Fort Collins, Colorado. "I got up and spoke after three hours of dancing. It was the first time I had been at a powwow and after the dancing I had to get up and make a speech. I told them, 'I'm not embarrassed to talk to you because I feel like I've just come from my house on the Coast to talk to my brothers in the Interior.' One guy got up and gave me his chest plate because he liked what I had said. 'Take this,' he said. 'I don't want it,' I told him. 'It's beautiful but it's part of your regalia. You should keep it.' He said, 'No I've got another one,' so I said, 'Okay I'll take it.' That was kind of neat." The breastplate is one of Richard's treasured possessions. Another is a paddle he received from the Chemainus Nation for his contribution to the 1994 Commonwealth Games, for which he carved the designs for the bronze medal and was one of the artists who created the carving of the "Queen's Baton."

"I carry that paddle as my medal," Richard says. "I should use the paddle because it's beautiful, but I just leave it and look at it and think."

In Windsor, when Richard saw the room he was supposed to live in while working on the totem pole at Windsor Park, he demanded something better for both him and Tim.

"It's tourist season," said Roland, the assistant park ranger and the man assigned to look after the carvers. "All the rooms are taken. I can't get anything for less than a hundred pounds. So why don't you come and stay with me in Windsor Park?"

Richard and Tim moved into a stately 500-year-old mansion on the grounds where there was a swimming pool in the garden and their spacious rooms had baths and televisions.

One day while Tim and Richard were working on the Queen's totem, they heard a sound that Richard describes as "a herd of stampeding coconuts." They put down their tools and turned to see a carriage pulled by a team of six horses.

"I thought this was a hoot," Richard recalls. "So I started jumping up and down and waving both my arms and yelling at the footmen perched on top of the carriage. 'Hey, you guys! How are you doing?'"

No one waved back.

Roland tapped Richard on the shoulder. "Excuse me, Mr. Hunt. That might be Philip."

"Philip who?"

"Prince Philip, the head park ranger."

"What makes you think that?"

"Well, he's the only one who's allowed to ride a six-horse carriage in Windsor Park."

Richard and Tim didn't meet Prince Philip, but when the totem pole was almost finished, Roland said to them, "Tonight we're going to have a few beers together to celebrate the completion of the totem pole. Tomorrow at one o'clock you're going to meet the Queen."

Tim and Richard drank with their host until 5:30 in the morning. The next day, feeling tired and headachy and also nervous and excited, they stood in front of the totem pole as the Queen drove up in her Jaguar. A bodyguard opened the door for her. She stepped out and exchanged words with the other guests as she moved towards the pole. When she stopped in front of Richard and Tim, she took off her glasses and slowly looked up and down the totem pole. "It's quite bright," she said.

"Yes," Richard said. "It's brand new paint." He groaned inside. *You idiot,* he thought.

"I remember when this pole was put up," the Queen continued. "I had the flu and my mother had to stand in for me."

"I was only about ten years old then," Richard said.

"Oh you're a young lad. Don't talk about age." And—too late— Richard remembered that age was a taboo topic with the Queen. *You idiot,* he told himself again. But he thinks there must have been something about him she liked because Queen Elizabeth spoke with him for twenty minutes about his art and the hedgehogs that were creating havoc by digging holes in the park grounds.

Richard continued to travel. His carvings were admired in New York, Philadelphia, Washington, D.C., Los Angeles, and wherever they were exhibited. But Richard refused to take personal credit for his art. "It's my history," he says. "My father and grandfather—I'm just carrying on what they did. I'm not trying to invent anything new. All I'm creating is a different interpretation of the same thing."

He also liked to go to the local pubs, meet new people, and make friends. He wanted to be an ambassador for his people and he ignored the well-meaning advice of his friends at home, "Be careful. Don't talk to strangers. Take cabs."

In 1984 Richard married his second wife, Sandra. His first marriage had lasted only five years. "I was young and dumb," he says. "I was still wild and crazy." He hadn't wanted to get married again, but when he met Sandra, he fell in love. That same year he also took time to study his people's history, and the more he learned the more he felt drawn to his culture and more strongly felt the injustice of how his people had been treated.

After his father died in 1986, Richard left the museum. He had never believed he was bound by the pact his father had made with Mungo, and now there was nothing to hold him. When he made the internal commitment to leave, Richard was worried about how he would survive without a dependable income. "I thought, 'Does anybody want my work? Do they know I'm out there now?'" But even before his final day, people heard that Richard Hunt would soon be carving independently, and by the time he collected his severance pay he had commissions for the next year.

Richard started exhibiting his work, and the Derek Simpkins Gallery of Tribal Arts in Vancouver began to represent him. When he had shows, his work sold instantly. He branched out and began to design jewellery, clothing, street banners, and logos for events, conferences, and organizations.

The demand for his work is still high. If he tried to take on all the orders that come his way, he would be carving seven days a week. "I don't think I'm any better than anybody else," he says. "I think this is a job. It's how I interpret what my dad and my grandfather did. I don't have to invent anything because it's already there. I just have to do it the way I want it done." It is how he interprets the old tradition that sets Richard's work apart. He employs a modern clarity of line and form, and while his work retains all the primitive simplicity of the old ways, there is a refinement that is subtle yet strongly personal.

Many of his designs are for charity because Richard rarely says no if he is asked to contribute to his community. Each year he donates prints to organizations such as the B.C. Children's Hospital, the B.C. Paraplegic Association, Project Literacy, and many others. "I have a lot of relatives that don't read," Richard says. "I can read, but I'm not the greatest reader. People like that need help."

Each year Richard also designs a special print for the Boys and Girls Club because when he was young he and his siblings "hung out" there. He donates a shirt design to the Victoria Diabetes Run/Walk in honour of his mother who had diabetes. In 1987 Richard's donated design first appeared on the Royal Victoria Marathon sweatshirts. Since then the event has grown from 600 to a record 7,500 runners in 2001. The Royal Victoria Marathon supports the Greater Victoria Hospital Foundation as its charity and has helped purchase valuable equipment for the hospital. Explaining his involvement with the marathon Richard says, "I know people with heart trouble, and I also figure some day I might need it."

When his daughter's school needed to raise money for a breakfast program, he donated a print for them to raffle. The kids raised so much money they had enough left over to buy socks for the soccer team.

"How many charities do you support?" I ask.

"At least twenty."

"Why?"

"Because it's in me to give. It's hard to say no when someone comes up to you in dire straits and needs money. The only way I can help is with my art."

He continues to live up to his name, travelling around the world and giving. He has carved the world's largest diameter totem pole in Duncan, B.C. He has designed and carved a dance screen for the Canadian Museum of Civilization in Ottawa and a bear transformation mask for the Science Museum in Minnesota. He has given carving demonstrations in Los Angeles and New York City. He carved the *Thunderbird* and *Killer Whale* showpieces for the Vancouver International Airport, and wherever he goes he teaches about his people and his art.

In 1991 he was the first Native artist to be awarded the Order of B.C. His citation reads in part:

> Richard Hunt has played a leading role in the renaissance of Northwest Indian art. It is a rebirth that has spread throughout North America and influenced indigenous art around the world. A master carver, ritualist, and dancer, Richard Hunt has created

a diverse body of art that contributes much to the preservation and perpetuation of Kwa-giulth culture and traditions. His totems, prints, drums, masks, and bowls are the pride of museums and private collections around the world.

In 1993 Richard received the Canada 125 Medal that was created in honour of Canada's 125th birthday, for contributions to the City of Victoria and to the country. In 1994 he was awarded the Order of Canada. The highlight of his trip to Ottawa was meeting Frank Mahovlich and Serge Savard, who were also awarded the Order of Canada that year. Richard recalls riding on the elevator with Frank. "I know who you are," Richard said.

"I know who you are too!"

They had their picture taken together, and Richard says he will always remember the thrill of standing between two of his childhood hockey heroes.

In 1995 Richard was appointed to the board of the B.C. Arts Council. When the newly elected NDP government cut the grant it had promised them, Richard protested loudly that this was not right. He did not choose his words carefully and ended up saying, "You guys just used us in a big press release. I thought I could do something good for us, and now I find out we're just little scapegoats for you." A government representative at the meeting responded with, "I take exception to that," and Richard said, "I don't care if you do." He added that he had no issues with individuals but with the policies of the government.

After his outburst Richard did not expect to be elected again to the board of the B.C. Arts Council, but it was because he was willing to speak with honesty that he was re-elected and continued with it for five years.

He continues to speak honestly. He says, "We're turning into a tourism economy, and now we have all these non-Natives becoming hooked on Native art. It's taught in the prisons because it keeps the prisoners calm. When they get out they think they own it. We are the ones who own it. My whole thing is to try to save our culture. If the government is not going to do that they have to help us get into the market of mass production. The only way we're going to get China and Japan and Taiwan out is by going into competition with them. The thing is not to ship our product over to China and Japan and get them to make it and bring it back here. The thing is to put our people to work."

Richard's other social passion is the question of land claims and treaty negotiations. These issues have been debated for generations, he says, and nothing happens. "The research has already been done. Why go over the same ground again and again?"

But now, he admits, he is becoming tired of speaking out. He just wants to be a carver. He spends his days in his garage, where he carves. When young people come to him, he gives them the adzes that have been used by his people for generations. "An electric tool works, but this is the traditional way, and this is what I want them to learn."

Although he prefers to work alone and doesn't want to mentor youths, whenever young carvers come to him, he examines their tools, sharpens them, or gives them an adze along with advice on how to use it. He gives them books and tells them to finish school and make carving their hobby until they have completed their education.

He says that although he wants the young people to graduate from high school and perhaps go on to college, he also wants them to carve because the culture is important. "A lot of our people are coming back to our culture. They are not going to the church any more; they're going to the Big House. They don't want to know what's happening in the white world; they want to know what's going on with their culture, and they want to become a part of it. That's a great thing. If you can call a Big House a church because it will save our culture, maybe that's what we should call it. Our totem pole is our cross."

In 1996 Richard was asked by the Governor General of Canada to sit on the selection committee of the Caring Canadian Award and to be a member of its board for the next four years. In 2001 he was made an Honourary Citizen of Victoria in recognition of his many contributions to his community. Even with all the honours he has received, he is most proud of graduating from high school. "And I made people look at the Northwest Coast and made them realize that we're not dead yet. When I was in school I thought Geronimo was my relative. They never taught us about us."

Richard is pleased that his two daughters take pride in their Native heritage, but he also tells them, "Be proud of who you are on the other side—not just on my side."

He has many more exhibitions scheduled and private commissions to fulfil, but he also wants to dance again. "I'm not a real dancer any more. I used to dance all the time. I have all my regalia. It doesn't hang on the wall of my house. No one sees it. It's all in boxes. For me, it's my culture, and I put it away."

He also wants to investigate the possibility of mass production of Native art because he believes tourism is the economic future of B.C. and that Native art has a large role to play in the new economy.

As I begin to put my tape recorder away, Richard tells me that September 11, 2001, changed the way he thinks and the way he creates his art. He showed me the most dramatic change: his colour palette. All his art since that day is brighter and more vivid. He says, "I thought, man, I gotta make things bright because I'm tired of things being dark. That event made me think, 'So many things aren't really important if these are the things that are going on in the world.' I was in the World Trade Center, so I couldn't believe how those towers could come down like that. I told my daughter, 'If you had ever seen the size of those things, you just wouldn't believe that had happened.' I watched every day. I still watch today what's happening because of that attack … Maybe I am just trying to brighten the world up for me. If you look at my work nothing really looks grouchy. I've always tried to create a happy look instead of a sad look."

When I examine his work closely, I can detect a subtle joy in everything he has ever done. Even his sea monsters and eagles look happy. It is as if Richard's carved creatures carry a secret message—of a hope that humans are so seldom aware of. Despite the anger he has felt due to discrimination, despite the reasons for him to feel hatred, Richard Hunt has transcended it all through his art, which embodies universal love.

Mel Cooper, 1992

Mel Cooper:
Mr. Enthusiasm

*I*n Victoria, he is known as "Mr. Radio." In Vancouver, he is still known as the man who helped make Expo '86 one of the most successful world's fairs ever held. To everyone who has ever talked to him, ever worked with him, or ever heard him speak, Mel Cooper is "Mr. Enthusiasm."

Within minutes of meeting him on a Saturday afternoon in the boardroom at CFAX, his radio station in Victoria, I have to concur that "Mr. Enthusiasm" is absolutely the right moniker. He wants to show me everything: the plaques and awards on the walls, family photographs, and a file folder full of adages to live by that he has collected over the years. These are some of them:

- How fast you do something is never as important as how well you do something.
- Anticipate problems—don't wait until they bite you in the butt.
- There's nothing wrong with being wrong unless you won't admit it.
- Never get too big to do small things.
- Share your ideas—they often come to bloom in another brain.
- Enthusiasm is contagious—spread it around.

Mel Cooper doesn't just talk about his adages—he lives them. He learned his winning philosophy early in life, growing up in St. John's, Newfoundland. Mel was born George Neldon Cooper but became "Mel" in 1951, when he got a job as a radio announcer at

CKMO in Vancouver. The program director said, "What's this thing about George Neldon? As of today when you go on the air your name is Mel."

Mel was born on December 10, 1932, and grew up in the shadow of Cabot Tower, where Marconi received the first radio signal. "That's what did it," he laughs. "What's really interesting is that I used to play on Signal Hill in the old fort, which is now a heritage building, and that's where I think I got a signal. Not only Marconi got a signal, I did too." Mel used to play "radio" with his friends because radio was glamorous, mysterious, and wonderful. "It's amazing how things happen," he says.

He describes his childhood as "wonderful." He had no idea that the economy was bad or that almost everyone was struggling, or that many people were on the dole. Mel's father, Ron, completed Grade Nine and left school because he wanted to earn a living. Ron's mother, a teacher, had wanted her children to go to college and become doctors, lawyers, or professionals. Although his siblings lived up to her expectations, Ron disappointed her. He started up a number of small businesses with very little money and by working hard built up some capital with which he eventually built a series of grocery stores. Mel recalls that Ron was determined to rise above the poverty he saw all around him. Mel's mother and father worked hard, but they also managed to have a good time. Everyone who knew Ron Cooper liked him.

Mel was the oldest of five children and grew up helping out in the stores. During the war, Mel's parents brought soldiers and sailors into their dining room to feed them a home-cooked meal, and Ron would listen to the stories the men told of their own homes far away. One evening Ron listened attentively to a young soldier talking about B.C., a place the Coopers would not have been able to find on a map.

Compared to Newfoundland, where things were so bad, B.C. sounded like a land of unlimited opportunity. Ron Cooper always managed to make enough money for the necessities, but he gave credit to most of the people who shopped at his store, and sometimes they couldn't pay their bills. When they didn't, Ron tightened his own budget; he never said no because they were his neighbours and friends, and he knew they would pay him when they could. The dream of a better life in the west filled his head for a few months until one day, when Mel was fourteen years old, Ron said to his family, "We're going to British Columbia."

"It was quite a surprise to us," Mel recalls. "We were true blue Newfoundlanders. We loved everything about the place we lived— the wind, the snow, the rain—we loved it all. But my dad said, 'No, I've got four kids,' and he sold his business and packed us into a plane."

"I remember coming into Vancouver," Mel says. "I couldn't believe it. I had never seen such greenery. I had never seen trees and flowers like that in my life. It was unbelievable compared to the starkness of Newfoundland."

The family checked into the Hotel Vancouver, and Ron talked to the hotel manager. He told him he had just sold everything he owned and that he had no idea what he was going to do in B.C. Could he give him some advice? The manager must have liked Ron's attitude because he introduced him to the "right" real estate person and the "right" bank. Through a combination of shrewdness and serendipity, Ron bought a small house in the "right" area of Kerrisdale off Marine Drive, and a 50 percent partnership in a grocery business nearby. Shortly afterward, he bought out his partner's share of the business and went on to own a chain of supermarkets throughout the Okanagan. He was able to send Mel to Vancouver College, which was run by the Christian brothers of Ireland.

Mel had always done well at his studies; he liked his new school, and as far as he was concerned life just didn't get any better. He recalls writing a letter to his grandmother in which he professed: "You've always been truthful with me. You always talked about the importance of truthfulness, but you lied because you told me you had to die in order to go to heaven. Well, I'm in heaven right now."

The "truth" was as important to Ron as it was to his mother. Ron told his children, "No matter what, tell the truth to me." Stealing was the worst thing a child could do—no matter how minor or trivial the theft. Ron wanted his children to go into the grocery business with him, and although the four younger children did, Mel wanted a university education instead. Ron didn't argue with his son; however, he told him he would have to pay his own way.

Mel enrolled at the University of British Columbia (UBC) in the liberal arts program. On his first day, standing in line to get his class schedule, the student behind him introduced himself and asked, "So what are you going to do?"

"What do you mean?"

"I mean what do you like to do? What are your hobbies?"

"Well, I like jazz. I like baseball. I like to write. In high school they told me I knew how to write an interesting story—I guess that's something I like to do."

"Well then, why don't we join something where you can do some writing?"

"It's my first day at university, and I really want to get settled in. I'll get involved in clubs later."

"No, let's get involved now. Come on, let's go. Let's see what clubs there are where you can do some writing."

"Quite frankly I'm not a follower," Mel says. "But he pushed and said, 'Come on, let's go.' So we went to Brock Hall, where they produced the student newspaper, and it looked a little too far out for me. I was a conservative kind of individual. I was never a trendy kind of guy."

When Mel's new friend noticed that he seemed less than enthusiastic about the paper, he said, "Let's try the radio society next door." The radio group's welcome was overwhelmingly friendly. "Come and join the club!" they said. So they did. Mel wrote scripts and did some on-air announcing. He also enrolled in some off-campus broadcasting courses at CKWX, a local radio station that liked to mentor the students.

"I liked school," he says, "But what I liked even better was radio—and I was a very poor young announcer—but I loved it to the point where I thought, 'Hey, I'm not going to do justice to my courses here.' If I had the choice of doing a one-hour radio show or going to a chemistry class, I'd take radio. The radio bug had me."

When Gae Eaton, another member of the radio society, got a summer job with CJAV in Port Alberni, she recommended they hire Mel as well. He applied with an enclosed a letter of recommendation from CKWX that read in part: "Mel is not as accomplished as some other announcers, but he works very diligently and you'll get his full effort. Mel has potential."

Mel was hired. "It was work, work, work, and it was not work," he recalls. "It was really enjoyable. I did everything." He wrote news stories, reported on sports, and handled request shows while Gae wrote the commercials. At the end of the summer CJAV offered him a full-time job. He said no and went back to university in Vancouver, where he got a part-time job at CKMO. Within weeks, the program director offered to hire him.

"Today I may not have made the same decision because an education is so important," Mel says. "But I truly thought, 'I'm never going to be offered a full-time job at a radio station in Vancouver again. I'd better grab it while I can.'"

A couple of years later, in 1952, CKWX offered Mel a job in Trail in the Interior of B.C., running the news department at the local station. He accepted the offer, but first he married Gae—who had become his sweetheart—so that they could move to Trail together. Right after the wedding, Mel began a three-week training course at the Vancouver station. After two weeks, the CKWX news director said to him, "How happy are you with the idea of going to Trail?"

"I'm all for it," Mel said.

"Would you be unhappy if you didn't go there?"

"Why? What's going on?"

"Would you stay here? We'll send somebody else up there."

Mel was happy to stay and work in the news department at CKWX—the highest rated radio news station in Western Canada. He remembers Bert Cannings, the news director, as one of the most supportive people he ever worked for. Bert took the time to go over every piece of copy Mel wrote and made suggestions that would help him become a better news writer and editor. "He really helped me so much," Mel says. "He was a great, great supporter."

There were others who helped him as well. "I was very fortunate," he says. "I had people who were so helpful. I didn't seek them out as mentors, but it worked out that way."

"Why do you think they were eager to help you?" I ask Mel.

"I think it was my desire and my passion and my commitment to getting it done and doing it right," he says. "There's a plaque on the wall in my office calling me 'Mr. Enthusiasm.' I guess it was my enthusiasm for it. It is contagious, and I guess they will look at your lack of abilities or lack of experience and say, 'He's got a good attitude about learning and a good attitude about working.' And my natural Newfie Irish friendliness didn't hurt either."

One night in 1954 Mel received a telephone call in the newsroom from Bill Rea, who had the reputation of being the most dynamic and creative station owner in Western Canada. His latest enterprise was station CKNW in New Westminster. "I've heard a lot of things about you," Rea said. "I would like to offer you a position with our company, but I would like to meet you first."

Mel said, "Mr. Rea, I am flattered beyond belief. I know you have a reputation for being a forward thinking individual. But I'm married, and I have two young children and frankly, I can't afford to consider your offer. And I like what I'm doing. I love being in the news department of CKWX."

"Why don't we just meet anyway?" Rea said. "I'd like to meet you. I notice you're on the night shift. When do you go to work?"

"I head downtown at about three o'clock."

"Where do you live?"

"Near McDonald." Mel gave him the address.

"Do you have a car?"

"Oh no, I take the bus. One of the perks I get as a news editor is a bus pass."

"I'd like to pick you up and take you to work."

"Well, Mr. Rea—"

"Let me just pick you up. I'd like to meet you in any event."

The next day Mel waited in the front room of the small house that he'd bought for $500 down and a $4,500 mortgage. With his salary of $165 a month he managed to keep the mortgage paid.

When a big pink Cadillac convertible pulled up at the curb, Mel picked up his lunch bag, and walked down the drive to meet Bill Rea while Gae stood on the porch with the babies, waving good-bye.

"Is that your wife?" Rea asked.

"Yes."

"Do you rent the house?"

"No, I bought it."

"How old are you?" Rea asked.

"Twenty-two."

"And you bought a house."

"Well, I don't own much of it—the mortgage company does. But I'm working on owning it."

When Bill parked the pink Cadillac in front of CKWX, he turned to Mel and said, "I want you to work for me, but not in my news department."

"What have you got in mind?" Mel asked.

"I want you to run a promotion, merchandising, and marketing department. I think that's where you'll shine."

Mel thought that Bill Rea was probably right. When he was in university, he and a friend had run a small advertising company called B.C. Creative Promotions that worked with local businesses to get their ad messages out to the students, and they had done well.

"How much do you make?" Bill asked.

"Well Mr. Rea, I'm not that proud of it, but I make $165 a month with a bonus plan. Every once in a while I get $25 or $29 a month as a bonus."

"I'll pay you double that," Bill said.

"What?"

"I'll pay you $330 a month."

"Whoa!" Mel thought, but he didn't say anything. The money was exciting. He needed it, but he didn't want it to be the most important reason to take the job.

"You don't have a car," Bill said. "I'll give you a company car to drive. You'll need it anyway for your promotion work."

Mel promised to think about it. When he got into the newsroom, the staff asked him, "What happened? Did he make you an offer?"

"I don't want to talk about it," Mel said.

But Bill Stevenson, one of the senior sportscasters, said to him, "Mel, Bill Rea is good. If you can work for him in the promotional and advertising side, you'll be working for the best there is. He must see something in you to offer it to you. Take it. Don't hesitate—just take it."

Mel said, "Bill, I think you're right." He didn't want to leave CKWX because he liked the station, his job, and the people he worked with, but he also thought it would be foolish not to take such a generous offer.

Four weeks after Mel joined CKNW the station burned down, and Bill Rea suffered a heart attack. People said it was a direct result of the tragedy. The company scrambled to reorganize. People in management moved into more senior positions or took on new titles, and in the shuffle Mel was made national sales manager. Eighteen months later he was promoted to general sales manager and took over sales for the entire company. "I loved promotion, marketing, and merchandising," he says. "I really loved it, and I've been known to have a creative mind for ideas. But when I went off the air as an announcer I missed it immensely. I fell in love with everything I did."

When the new owner, Frank Griffiths, interviewed Mel for the number two position at the station, he said, "Do you mind my asking you how old you are?"

Mel looked younger than his 24 years and could easily have been mistaken for a teenager. Even today he looks at least a decade younger than his age with his round, unlined, cherubic face and red-blonde hair with almost no touch of grey.

Despite the loss of Bill Rae and the fire, CKNW grew to become the biggest radio station in Vancouver. Mel's reputation grew along with it. The word in radio circles was, "If you want a good marketing idea, talk to Mel."

When Frank Griffiths bought CJOB in Winnipeg he gave Mel the opportunity to buy 8 percent of the station. "I'll do my best," Mel said. "But I don't have much money to bring to the table."

"You don't have to worry about that," Frank said. "Here's a piece of paper. Go down to the Toronto Dominion Bank. They'll expect you and the money will be there for you to borrow."

"But I don't have any collateral," Mel said.

"It's okay," Frank said. "I've signed for it."

A couple of years later, when Frank Griffiths' radio station went public, he offered Mel cash for his 8 percent or shares in the new company. "I'm making the same offer to the other people, and if they don't pick up the shares, I'll be happy to offer those to you as well."

"I got as many as I could," Mel says. He went to the manager of the Toronto Dominion Bank with the shares he owned and asked, "How much will you let me borrow on these?" When the answer didn't meet his expectations, he went to the Royal Bank, where the manager gave him a much larger loan; Mel's lifelong relationship with the Royal Bank began then.

"Griffiths was great to me—as everybody had been," Mel says. "It was a great moment because it gave me my first ownership and it gave me the opportunity because the company stock was very successful. It doubled and it split and it doubled and it split …"

A few years later Griffiths made Mel vice-president of the company, overseeing all seven radio stations across the country, including CKNW and CFMI—a new Vancouver FM station. "Frank was a very bright and smart financial man, who let his management run things," Mel says. "He did not micro-manage. He never came in except to sit down for reports and even then those meetings were short."

Frank Griffiths' style fostered creativity, so whenever Mel saw an opportunity in the radio representation business he talked to Frank about it. Advertising agencies were booking their radio air time with advertising representatives in Toronto, which made little sense to Mel. He suggested the station form a company that would allow advertisers to book local time with representatives throughout B.C. "I think we should get into the business," he told Frank. "We have our own stations. The 15 percent commissions that are being paid would be coming to us instead of going to another rep company. And we could attract all kinds of stations. Would you like me to put together a plan?"

"Why don't you own it?" Frank asked.

"Well, I thought it would make sense for the company to do it."

"No. Why don't you do it?"

Well, and why not? Mel thought. If it was fine with Frank, why not? "Here he was, allowing me some ownership. You've got to thank people with that kind of attitude."

Mel called his company Western Broadcast Sales, and it did as well as he had predicted it would. One of the company's clients was Clare Copeland, who owned CFAX in Victoria, a station that was doing reasonably well but not as well as the owner would have liked. One day in 1973 Clare asked Mel if he would come to Victoria to give him some ideas on improving the station.

Mel went to Victoria, and as they were talking, Clare said, "If you could wave a magic wand, what would you like to do?"

"Clare, don't ask those kind of questions," Mel said. "If I was to dream wild dreams, they wouldn't be practical dreams. Do you want something practical, or do you want something that's way out there in left field?"

"What would be out in left field?"

"Oh, I don't know. Maybe I'd like to be a producer of movies some day, or maybe I'd like to be a producer of Broadway plays. On a practical basis, if I had a magic wand, I'd own your radio station."

"You would?" Clare said.

"Yes, I would."

"You know what's funny," Clare said. "I surely don't want to sell my radio station to anyone, but I have a desire to work hard to get the new New Democratic Party (NDP) government out of power, and I can't do it as the owner of a radio station in Victoria that is the news station. So I'd be prepared to talk to you about selling this station."

Mel entered negotiations with Clare, thinking he wanted to sell CFAX to Frank Griffiths' company, Western Broadcasting. Its proximity to the legislature made it a natural acquisition. At the end of the day he said, "I'll bring an offer to you, but I want to talk it over with Frank."

"Why would you talk it over with Frank?" Clare asked.

"Well, for Western Broadcasting to buy it."

"No, no, no," Clare said. "I don't want to sell it to Western Broadcasting. I want to sell it to you. I want you personally."

At first Mel was stunned and then he felt the familiar mixed emotions he experienced every time a new opportunity came his way. "I'm happy as a clam with what I'm doing," he told Clare. "But I'd be happy to talk to you about it. What kind of money do you have in mind?"

Clare wanted $1.5 million.

"I can do that," Mel thought. Within days he brought Gae to Victoria, and while he sat down with Clare and the lawyers, he said to her, "Why don't you go out and scout the city for some property just in case I make a deal."

"What do you want me to look for?"

"Don't look at anything unless it's on the water."

Mel purchased CFAX early in the afternoon and minutes later Gae telephoned, "I've found a house that I think you'll love." Mel did love the waterfront home on Beach Drive and made an offer to purchase it.

When Frank Griffiths heard that Mel had been negotiating to purchase a radio station, he called Mel into his office. "What's this I hear about you buying a radio station?"

"Yes, Frank, I already have a meeting set up with you to talk about it."

"How much did you pay for it?"

Mel told him.

"That's a good price. You did well. Why don't I buy it from you? I'll give you a quarter of a million more than you paid for it."

"Frank, I couldn't do that to Clare," Mel said. "He sold it to me. He didn't sell it to me to flip it."

"Okay then, own it, but don't run it. Stay with me and stay with the company and put someone else in to run it." Frank offered him more money, a new contract, and a bonus, but Mel turned it all down.

"No," he said. "I've committed myself to this."

He sold his Western Broadcast Sales company to Frank and went to Victoria. CFAX was known as an "elevator music" station, and although Mel had no objection to soft instrumental music, he knew it wouldn't attract a large audience. He also recognized that there was no station in Victoria that was the news leader. At CKNW, he had seen how successful radio news could be. What's more, CFAX was located in the province's capital; it seemed no better time and place to concentrate on issues, commentary, and politics.

He made changes gradually, and within a few years he transformed CFAX from a virtually all-music station to talk radio. Today, CFAX is the only station in the community with talk radio personalities, public affairs programs, and programs that involve the audience.

At the same time, Mel and CFAX began to serve the community. He recalls, "I used to talk about the station at home and my youngest son would hear me talking about it, and then I'd be talking about service, and years later I found out he thought I ran a service station."

Mel joined the Chamber of Commerce, and in 1975 was elected president. In 1977, Marilyn Cann, a local woman who had been running a small charity called Santas Anonymous, asked Mel to take it over because it was getting too big and she felt she could no longer manage it. CFAX Santas Anonymous is now in its 25th year, taking Christmas requests from children in need and—with the help of its listeners—making those wishes come true. In 2001, CFAX distributed 6,500 gifts to needy children, and volunteers delivered an additional 1,000 food hampers to families. "The best part of it is that the kids get what they want," Mel says. "I like that. I feel really good about that."

When an organization asked him to help he couldn't say no and didn't much want to. He got involved in the Belfry Theatre, the Victoria Symphony, and countless charitable groups. He sat on their boards, chaired special projects, and used his spare time to contribute to the community simply because, as he says, "It was the right thing to do." He has been president of the Boy Scouts, and when he became involved with the Nature Conservancy, he campaigned to save wilderness areas as far away as Ontario.

The awards and certificates he has received for his work hang on the walls of his office and boardroom. I can't count them. Mel says there are more in drawers and at his home. I don't even want to guess at their number. "My biggest problem is that I have to turn down so many board requests," Mel says. "I have a difficult time saying no." Because he rarely says no, he still works long hours. "I had been accused for a long time of being a workaholic. And I think they were correct. When I was working long hours, long days, and long weeks, I never felt I was a workaholic. I was doing 70 hours a week. I worked hard because I had to pay the bills, but later on, I replaced that with community. I was doing an average of 20 hours a week minimum of actual time working with organizations—raising money and so on."

He was also becoming a well-known motivational speaker. In 1981, when B.C. fell into a deep recession and the media broadcast stories of doom and despair, Mel was one of a group of business leaders called Team B.C. that decided to do something to change the intensely negative attitudes in the province. They acknowledged that times were tough, but they pointed out that there were businesses that were doing well despite the terrible economic climate.

Mel was one of the speakers who travelled around the province with the message: "Yes, you can succeed in a down economy." One of the men on Team B.C., Perry Goldsmith, had just started a speaker's bureau, and when he heard Mel he said to him, "You should be doing more of this."

"I haven't got time," Mel said.

"How many requests a year do you get to speak right now?"

"Oh, I don't know … about a hundred."

"How many do you do?"

"About 40."

"How do feel about saying no to those other 60?"

"I hate saying no to them. I'm flattered that they want me to do it, but …"

"I'll be the one to say no. You're going to get 150 requests and you may get more than that."

Mel has been a member of the Speaker's Bureau since 1982. For many years he gave almost 100 talks annually. In 2000 he decided to reduce his speaking engagements to 40 a year, but when he was made honorary chairman in Victoria for the Year of the Volunteer in 2001, that number dramatically rose.

While he was working in the community, Mel met Carmela, a woman who also liked to volunteer. Mel fell in love, and so did she. "It was a difficult situation," he says. "I was thinking, 'This has got to stop. I can't afford to feel this way. I can't afford to be interested,' but the feelings …" His emotions won: he divorced Gae and married Carmela. Mel admits he was not proud of breaking his marital commitment to Gae, but he also says that he and Carmela are still in love today and intensely happy together.

In 1985, Mel embarked on his most ambitious project. He had met Jim Pattison in the early 1950s and had been a member of Pattison's board when Air BC was formed, becoming chairman in 1980 at Jim's request. One day Jim Pattison telephoned and asked Mel to meet him on board his yacht that he'd berthed in Victoria's inner harbour. "I want to have a chat," he said. Pattison was chairman of the board of 'Expo '86, a project that was reported to be in trouble. "Mel," he said. "We've got big problems. I'm going to take over as president of Expo, and I'm going to go on the line.

I want some good people around me, and I want you to come with me."

"Jim, I can't do that," Mel said. "Leave Victoria and leave my family and move to Vancouver …"

"Just do it three days a week," Pattison said.

"How can I do justice in three days a week to what you've just told me? You want me to run all the marketing and raise all the corporate money!"

Pattison agreed it was going to be tough and riddled with near-impossible obstacles.

"Jimmy," Mel said. "You just spent ten minutes telling me that it's a difficult job, so why should I do it?"

"Because you're a giver, and this is the ultimate gift to your province."

Jim Pattison had hit him in his soft spot. Mel asked no more questions and just did it. He raised a record $174 million in corporate funds, and Expo '86 became the model for future world's fairs. "I felt good about that," Mel says. "Because it was a success, and I was involved in the management team."

I ask him, "What motivates you to do all of this? To keep saying yes?"

"Accomplishment is one thing—getting it done," Mel says. "You put yourself on the line, but I don't mind putting myself on the line. I think more than anything, I like to give back if I can." Then he tells me about his grandson, who is a student in university, winning national awards for humanitarianism and for his volunteer activities. "I love that part of him," he says. "He's in university and he's doing now what I didn't get around to doing until 1974, and I've been doing it ever since. Maybe I've helped influence him a bit too."

In 1988 Mel was on the bid committee that brought the Commonwealth Games to Victoria. He served on the board of BC Tel and later on the board of Telus. Being on the board of the Royal Bank of Canada was one of his proudest achievements. When it was announced nationally in 1992 that Mel Cooper had joined the board of the Royal Bank, Jim Pattison called him. "Mel, I had no idea you were going on that board and I have to tell you, I think it's the best board in Canada."

Mel remembers walking into the boardroom for his first meeting, thinking, "What am I doing here?"

When he had arrived at the upper age limit for board members and had to retire in 2002, he gave a retirement farewell speech, saying, "You know at my first board meeting, I looked around the room and these were the best-known names in Canadian business. My name was the only one I didn't recognize."

In 1989, Mel received the Order of Canada and in 1992, the Order of British Columbia award. He believes the work he did for Expo '86 was pivotal in giving him both awards, but in fact, he was cited for his numerous contributions to the community and for his unflagging enthusiasm.

"I was the most surprised person," he says, recalling the Order of Canada. "If you had asked me, 'Do you think you'll ever receive the Order of Canada?' I would have said, 'Of course not! Why would I ever receive the Order of Canada?' When I went into Rideau Hall and sat there in the row with all the others, I looked around and thought, 'I'm not in this company. This is a mistake. They shouldn't have me here.' These people were so wonderful. They were the cream of the crop. And I wondered, 'What am I doing here?' I was sure pleased, but I was totally surprised."

When he received the Order of B.C., he was pleased because it represented acknowledgement from the community that he thinks of as his home.

While we talk about his awards, Mel takes me on a tour of his office and boardroom, pointing them out to me one by one. But the ones he lingers over and explains in greatest detail are the ones his staff and radio station have received. "I believe in ultimate contribution," he says. "I believe in contributing more than you're expected to as a radio station. I believe in excellence, and I talk a lot about it. I figure if I'm going to talk about it it's because I believe in it. I haven't won these—the staff have. We have won more awards of excellence for news, for community, for creativity than any radio station in Canada. I feel good about that."

He still goes to the office each day. What he calls "slowing down" is what other people would call a full day's work. He is chairman and CEO of CFAX and his new FM station CFEX. "I like to sit in on meetings," he says. "We get together and come up with ideas and get involved in community things, and this is still fun. I like to be actively involved. People ask me when I'm going to retire, and there are lots of rumours about that. My answer to them is, 'I will definitely retire the day I no longer feel I can contribute. If I can't run at the speed I want to and I can't do it good enough, I will definitely go on to other things.' And I certainly don't feel that way today."

He says it has never been important to him to be the biggest or the richest. "What really is important is not what you own, it's what you are and the role you play in the place you live in and the people you deal with."

Before leaving our interview, I ask Mel for copies of some of his adages so that I might include them in his "story" and read them quietly in my own time. Reading them later, I find them almost trite. But then, maybe not, I decide. After all, they have come from a man who really believes that "Enthusiasm is contagious—spread it around," and here I am, having proven his belief, by taking his adage with me.

Grace Elliott-Nielsen:
All Things are Connected

G race Elliott-Nielsen has talked with visionaries, world leaders, drug addicts, movie stars, displaced people, and kings. She is at home in a longhouse or a palace. When she received the Order of British Columbia, the province's highest honour, Grace was called a visionary and cited, among other things, for developing programs to meet the needs of the Aboriginal community and for starting the first Aboriginal Health Centre in B.C. She was also one of the founding members of the Aboriginal components to the Building Better Babies program in Nanaimo, a program that has now spread to 32 urban centres in B.C. and 623 across Canada.

Grace Elliott-Nielsen never expected fame or recognition. She has devoted her life to others because she believes the earth can be a better place, that all things are connected, and that all things are important. Each person can only do a small piece to effect change, she says—her life has been about working on her small section of a giant patchwork quilt.

Grace is a large woman with a round face and deep brown eyes. Her soft voice rises and falls in a rhythm I find mesmerizing and appealing. I imagine her telling stories to her grandchildren and holding them spellbound for hours. She learned about storytelling from her father, Norman Elliott. He passed on to his children the old legends of his people and he taught them about the past. "Some things that happened were good, some were not," he told her. "But if people work hard enough, they can bring back the spirit of the good things and learn from the bad experiences."

Grace Elliott-Nielsen, 2000

Norman owned 360 acres of land on Coffin Point, a spit of land that thrusts out from Yellow Point, south of Nanaimo, and which forms the Ladysmith Harbour. Grace's mother, Matilda, was a member of the Chemainus Nation, whose reserve backed onto the Elliotts' land. Norman's grandfather was English while his grandmother, a member of the Cowichan Nation, traced her family back to Seattle. The famous Chief Seattle was her grandfather.

Grace Elliott was born on July 8, 1944, the youngest of six children. Norman Elliott taught his young daughter that you could pray anywhere—on the water, under the trees, on a hilltop—and that prayer was a very personal thing. "He always talked about respect and never making fun of people. He always said, 'You could be that person,' or, 'You could end up like that person.'"

Grace listened carefully to her father's teachings and reasoned that if you could pray anywhere, you could do good deeds anywhere too. Each month, when her parents received their family allowance cheques from the government, they turned them over to their children to spend as they pleased. Grace would buy dried peas and beans and chicken parts to make soup, or fruit and sugar to make preserves. She took her hearty soups and jars of fruit to the elders on the reserve because they often didn't have enough to eat while the young people were fishing or harvesting. One year the fishing was bad, and many of the family's crops had failed. When Christmas came, Norman gave each of his children a small amount of money so they could buy a present for themselves. Grace went into town and bought gifts for her brothers and sisters.

When Grace was six years old, Matilda and Norman went to town one day to buy groceries, leaving their nineteen-year-old son Edmond in charge of her. Grace was excited because she was especially close to Edmond, and he had promised her that she could come duck hunting with him in one of their canoes. But as they were about to leave he said, "No, you can't come."

Grace cried with disappointment and surprise. Edmond never went back on a promise. Hours later, when he hadn't returned, family and friends began to search for him. They found Edmond's shoes, gun, and neatly folded jacket on the shore, but they never found him. "That was something I carried with me for years," Grace says.

"I was heartbroken. I dreamt about him every night until I was about fourteen years old. I dreamt about him coming home."

No one understood what had happened. Edmond had been a good student, and he had seemed happy enough; although—like the rest of the Elliott children—he suffered from racism at the local school. Grace counts herself lucky that—thanks to her father's English ancestry—she didn't have to go to a residential school like the other Native children who had been sent to Kuper Island, where rows of small crosses marked the graves of those who had died there. Grace recalls that there was tremendous dysfunction in the Native community at that time because at the residential school, the children learned not to get attached to anyone since often they would go away or die. When they returned to their communities, they didn't know how to love or be good parents. The dysfunction was passed from generation to generation. Matilda had gone to the residential school on Kuper Island, but by some miracle she had not suffered as badly as some. Grace recalls that she was an affectionate and fiercely loving mother who put her children first. When she had extra money to spend, she spent it on clothing and food for them, and she always sent them to school with a nutritious lunch.

The Elliott children were the only Native children at Ladysmith Elementary School. Her older brothers, who attended the secondary school next door, tried to keep an eye out for Grace when she started Grade One, but they couldn't always be there. When they weren't around Grace was called a "Siwash" or a "dirty Indian" and was beaten and kicked by the other children. It was usually the older kids who beat her, preying on her vulnerability.

"How did you feel?" I ask her. "Were you angry? Did you try to fight back?"

"Yes, I was angry, and I fought back," she says. "I felt fear, but I don't ever remember hating any of them. I decided that no children should suffer what I was suffering—no matter who those children were—and I would do what I could so that they didn't."

Grace became more and more afraid of the school and begged her parents not to make her go. "I shut off the alarm clocks and did all kinds of things to avoid going," she laughs.

One day a child threatened her with a knife. She told her father, who went to the school with her and spoke to the teacher about the incident.

"That could not have happened," the teacher said. "Grace must have had a bad dream."

When she left the first grade and pleaded once again with her parents not to send her back the following year, they capitulated and enrolled their children in a correspondence program. When he was home, Norman supervised the children, and Matilda taught them the rest of the time. She was a hard taskmaster, making the children study their lessons from 8 a.m. until 5 p.m. Her father was a gentler tutor, who told the children stories and passed on the knowledge of his ancestors, along with the regular curriculum. "From him I learned respect for life," Grace says. "He taught me that people are people no matter what race they are. Some people are evil, but some people have a lack of knowledge. It's important to tell the difference. He said that we really needed to take care of the earth because all of it had been entrusted to us—the fishes, the birds, the animals ..."

"Look at the animals and how much time they spend with their young," Norman said. "If that doesn't happen, the young animals will just get crazy. They won't be able to learn anything." He then told his children that he and Matilda had learned how to be good parents by watching the animals.

"If a little child offers you a candy, never say no," he taught them. "And when you are a guest, always eat what is put before you. Never be disrespectful to the people whose homes you are in."

Grace put as much importance into her father's teachings as she did into her regular studies. Once when they were visiting her grandmother, Grace was served a bowl of applesauce that had been sitting in the pantry for a while. In the centre of her bowl was a dead cricket. Grace desperately wanted to push the applesauce away, but she remembered her father's words and dutifully ate everything on her plate except for the dead cricket, lying on a blob of applesauce in the centre.

"Why did you eat that?" her grandmother asked when she saw Grace's bowl.

Grace laughs at the memory. "I was just doing what I had been taught."

With the encouragement of her parents , Grace investigated religions and attended services at the Mormon, Seventh Day Adventist, Gospel, Protestant, and Catholic churches. Grace read the entire Bible through twice and bombarded her father with questions. "Why do religions hate each other when they all worship the same God?"

Norman told her religion had little to do with church. He incorporated spirituality and a love of God into the everyday events of life. For Norman, God was everywhere and in everything, and Grace believed what he told her. But she was enthralled with the music and ceremony of the Catholic Church, so when her parents told her that she would have to go back to school after she finished the eighth grade, she announced that she wanted to go to the convent in Nanaimo. Norman had doubts, but he respected her choice and took her to meet the nuns. "I was there for about an hour," Grace recalls. "And I decided, 'I'm not going there.'"

Instead, she attended John Barsby Community School in Nanaimo, boarding with her parents' friends, Dave and Mildred Simpson. She had always hated to be away from home and suffered agonizing bouts of homesickness. She cried every night, but she refused to go home to visit for two months because she was afraid that she would never come back. Much as she needed to be back home, she wanted an education more.

Grace wasn't called names in her new school, but she still felt racism as a constant and almost physical presence. "I was shy," she recalls. "And I was an average student, but I always had a holistic view. Education was just part of the learning."

As her classmates got to know her, they gave her the nickname "Miss Ethics" because she was so meticulous about telling the truth. "I'll never forget one girl telling me, 'You're going to go somewhere one day,'" Grace recalls.

She didn't graduate from John Barsby School. In her third year she contracted an infection and was so ill that she was hospitalized for two weeks. The doctors diagnosed tonsillitis, but the infection had spread so deeply that by the time she went to the hospital, she had temporarily lost her sight. When she was finally discharged, she was so weak that she couldn't go back to school. She completed her high school education through a correspondence course instead.

Grace wanted to be a practical nurse, so she applied to and was accepted at the Vocational Training School in Nanaimo. In the space of one year, she worked at the Nanaimo Native Hospital, the Nanaimo General Hospital, the Port Alberni Hospital, and the Ladysmith Hospital. She liked nursing, but with the exception of the Port Alberni Hospital, she once again found herself the target of racism. She was the only Native person in her class, and once when a doctor sat down beside her in the cafeteria of the Nanaimo Indian Hospital, she heard a nurse say, "I don't know why you would want to sit with that Indian."

Grace was constantly in trouble with her superiors because she spent too much time with the patients. Her instructions were to look after their physical needs, but she tried to look after their emotional needs as well. She spent time sitting and talking with them, especially those who were terminally ill.

When she graduated, she got a job at the Nanaimo Native Hospital, and that year she married Del Nielsen, a boy she had known and loved for years. Grace liked nursing, but she also felt drawn to do social work, so she enrolled in a counselling course at Malaspina College. Then she discovered yoga through Morag Renwick, a woman with whom she had briefly taken ballet lessons as a child and who had opened a yoga studio. "I liked yoga right away because it was so similar to the Native philosophy," she says.

She left nursing, and along with Renwick, founded the Yoga Council. She also began teaching yoga with the Nanaimo Department of Parks, Recreation and Culture and in the school system. Not surprisingly, Grace went beyond the yoga asanas, or postures, and taught her students the yoga philosophy of peace and tolerance and the interconnectedness between mind, body, and spirit. When the head of Parks, Recreation and Culture heard complaints from parents that Grace was teaching religion, he asked her to explain what she was doing. "No, I'm not teaching religion," she told him. "I'm teaching yoga."

"Well, I'm an Anglican, and what you're teaching is unacceptable," he said.

"Well then, I quit," Grace said, and left his office.

She continued to teach yoga in the schools, but she also opened her own studio in an empty apartment behind her father-in-law's grocery store. With so much space to work in, she decided to expand what she was doing. She purchased exercise equipment and turned the space into a holistic health studio that was open every day from 9:00 a.m. until 10.30 p.m. Five years later she sold the studio and went back to college to complete her counsellor training. A few months before graduating, she picked up a newspaper and saw that the Vancouver Island Training Program, located in Nanaimo, was advertising for someone to teach mildly handicapped youths to live independently. "Just for the heck of it I answered the ad," she laughs. Out of 132 applicants, eight were interviewed, and Grace got the job.

She told Mr. Curtis, the man who hired her, that she couldn't start until she had finished her courses; he agreed to wait. "What really interested me about your resumé is that you had so many varied interests," he told her. "I really believe that when you work with people you have to have an understanding and appreciation for many different areas and not to just be focussed on one thing."

Grace was so successful with the youths assigned to her that she was given the task of setting up the same program in Campbell River and then in Port Alberni. She believes she was good at her job because she loved the young people she worked with, and they returned her affection. "They come from a place of unconditional love," she says. "They appreciate everything you do for them. They know how to have fun, and they're not inhibited."

Grace's dream for the youths was not just for physical independence. She wanted to give them self-esteem, stability, and a deep sense of worth. Some of the youths came from difficult and dysfunctional backgrounds and some had problems with addictions, but Grace looked for their talents and abilities and worked to strengthen them. "Change is possible for anybody," she says.

Many of the youths went back to school, while others found jobs and careers. Some of the Native youths that came under her care were classified as mentally challenged, but Grace quickly saw that they were socially handicapped as a result of the time they had spent in residential schools, so she moved them out of her care into more appropriate programs.

In 1973, after working with the youth program for four years, Grace received a call from Mildred Simpson, the woman with whom she had boarded in high school. The Tillicum Haus Native Friendship Centre was in trouble, Mildred said. Could Grace help?

The Tillicum Native Friendship Centre (Tillicum Haus) in Nanaimo had been created to serve Native youths that had come from reserves to that city for an education. Grace agreed to attend a meeting to find out what the trouble was. She discovered that Tillicum Haus was in deep financial trouble and was on the verge of shutting down. She also detected friction between the Native band that made up the board and staff, and the off-reserve youths whom the centre was supposed to serve. The staff kept the centre open only two hours a day; furthermore, when money came in, it was not deposited in the bank and was never accounted for. "I thought, 'Oh my gosh, this is a real hornet's nest and I don't know if I want to be involved,'" Grace recalls.

She missed the next meeting, and when she walked into another meeting a week later, she was informed that the board had been elected at the previous meeting and she had been voted in as president. Nonplussed, Grace chaired the meeting. As the infighting and chaos began, one board member yelled at her, "You don't even know how to be a president."

"This is true," Grace said.

She laughs boisterously at the memory. "This was my first meeting and I didn't even know I was president!"

Grace headed the board of directors for six years, and during that time she practised what her father had taught her when she was a child: "In a bad situation, find out what is not working and get rid of it." Grace and the board removed some of the staff, and some left on their own. New board members were recruited; they hired a new executive director; and the Centre began to flourish.

While Grace was restaffing Tillicum Haus, she was also working at the Family Life Centre, dealing with suicidal teens and families at risk. She also performed group counselling in the local schools. One group was made up of what the school board considered the twelve most troubled boys in the system. Grace adhered to her philosophy of treating every human being with respect, even when confronted with a switchblade. "I can remember bringing them here to my home at Christmastime," she says. "I got them to help me make a special lunch and I'll always remember one boy saying, 'How come you're so good to us when we're so bad?' and I said, 'Because I know you're really not all that bad.' I thought it was really important to celebrate what was good in them." Many of them still telephone her from time to time to say, "Hey, I just got out of jail! I'm doing good now," or, "Hey, I'm working now!"

"I have one boy that phones me every Christmas," Grace says.

When Grace met the boys she remembered a piece of advice Mr. Curtis had given her: "You have access to all these people's files. Never look at those files until you've known your clients for some time. People tend to stereotype a kid, and then you might start to work with them from that perception. Always come to them with a fresh look. Look for their potential."

Grace approached her work at Tillicum Haus with her father's advice in mind: "Let go of what is there that is really evil and does not fit and keep what is there that you need to work with, even though it might not look so good." She met with the board or staff every day, and after two years Tillicum Haus was named the best Native Friendship Centre in B.C. "I was so happy," she says. "There were times when I thought, 'This is just impossible. This will never work!'" Several times she was close to walking out, but she stayed. She calls herself "tenacious" because if she starts a job, she has to see it through to the end. Her days were impossibly long. Without her mother's help she couldn't have done it, she says, because during this time she gave birth to two daughters, Tammie and Inga. Matilda looked after them while Grace worked, and when Norman died, she moved into the Nielsen household.

In 1979, after six years as president of Tillicum Haus, the executive director Tony Schachtel asked Grace to become the Centre's social worker. Although that was the position she would fill, the title of that position was "referral worker." According to federal law, Native organizations could not provide direct services. Grace had a tough decision to make. At the Family Life Centre she was intervening with teens in crisis, often saving their lives, and she deemed the work important. But if she took the job at Tillicum Haus, she believed she could make a valuable contribution to the Native community. "I was torn, and I cried for a week," she says.

"For goodness sake, if you don't want to leave your job, why are you going? Why are you applying?" her husband asked her.

"I don't know," Grace told him, and at the last hour of the last day for job applications, she submitted her resumé to Tony Schachtel. She won the job competition, and the first thing she did was write a letter to the government, protesting the title of referral worker. "I wouldn't stand for the fact that they felt we didn't have the skills to be social workers," she says.

Grace lobbied the Secretary of State and the Ministry of Children and Families and talked about the injustice at every government meeting she attended. Whenever she sent forms to the government, she filled in her title as social worker, not referral worker, and in her quiet, tenacious way, made her voice heard. Within two years, her official title became director of social services at Tillicum Haus.

Almost as soon as she had become a staff member, Grace began to attend the meetings of the provincial association of Native Friendship Centres, which operated under the auspices of the provincial Ministry of Children and Families. Grace wanted the centres to be governed by the Aboriginal community and to conform to Native traditions, so that the people who needed the services would feel comfortable accessing them. She found leaders in other Native Friendship Centres who shared her vision, and together they created a movement that quickly received support from all the centres in the province. They achieved the autonomy they wanted. Grace surmises that after the referral worker issue, the government wasn't too eager to challenge her again.

The Tillicum Haus Native Friendship Centre began initiatives such as the Aboriginal Health Council, which created its own criteria for drug and alcohol programs. One of Grace's passions was the creation of programs. She began the first program to deal with sexual abuse issues, which was quickly copied by the other centres. She also created the first program for male survivors of sexual abuse and the first program to train counsellors to deal with family violence. Drug and alcohol counsellors had been stymied for years because when issues of family violence had arisen, they had not been trained to deal with them.

Grace formed the first Aboriginal health centre in the province, and she was asked to sit on an advisory board in Vancouver to create a similar centre there—a daunting task considering the city had 68 urban Aboriginal associations, all fighting about who should be in charge of the centre.

In 1980 she became the executive director of Tillicum Haus and helped create the Building Better Babies program. When the building burned down, she moved the program into an old church owned by the City of Nanaimo. The added space suited her needs perfectly. In just one year the Centre's staff had increased from six to 58 people, including doctors, nurses, teachers, social workers, cooks, receptionists, therapists, and psychologists.

Grace told the City she wanted to buy the old church, and when they told her she could have it for $80,000, she offered them a dollar. They eventually compromised on $20,000.

I tell Grace that I had visited the Tillicum Haus Native Friendship Centre several times and each time, I noticed non-Native as well as Native people accessing services.

"The Native Friendship Centre was never limited to Natives," Grace says. "I saw that a lot of people were falling through the gaps, and those people's needs were not being addressed by social services. Either they didn't feel comfortable going there or they had just come into the community. If you come from one province to another you're not covered by a health plan for three months. We had pregnant women coming in who weren't well and couldn't see a doctor. The need was there."

The board agreed with Grace's vision and developed their mission statement, which promises justice and equality for all Aboriginal people and to meet the needs of all people in the community. Some staff members disagreed with helping non-Native people, but to them Grace said, "We serve whoever is in need."

Grace's influence began to be felt all across the province wherever Native health was at stake, whether that was physical, emotional, or mental health. She participated with the Provincial Aboriginal Health Council in developing criteria and policies with government. She also became involved in the B.C. Association of Aboriginal Friendship Centres, serving as president of that group for four years before stepping down in 1985 to become vice-president. The constitution stated that a president could not run for more than two terms; however, the association didn't want Grace to be vice-president, they wanted her as their leader. They solved their problem by changing the constitution. Once again, Grace became president and has been ever since. "I do love this work," she says. "I get to work with like-minded people, and we're working towards the same goals."

Their goals are to better the lives of Aboriginal people and to give them more control over their programs. The B.C. Aboriginal Friendship Centres have recently joined forces with the United Native Nations to form the Urban Aboriginal Policy Table, which created an agreement with the federal and provincial governments to work towards Native governance of Native health programs.

Tillicum Haus created a trade school for Natives, but for Grace, that is not enough. She is determined that the centre will one day also operate a college, where Native students can learn holistic life skills as well as the academic curriculum.

In 1990, Grace received a letter from Mikhail Gorbachev, inviting her to attend the annual State of the World Conference. Gorbachev, one of the chairs of the conference, wrote, "In humankind's search for a new, truly global and humane civilization the experience and the contributions of active leaders from all fields of human endeavor are indispensable. Together with the Forum's Co-Chairs, I request your participation in the development of this initiative ..." Grace's contribution in her field of holistic health was as valuable as the contributions of other world leaders present at that conference in San Francisco. Among them were Bishop Desmond Tutu, Elie Wiesel, Jane Goodall, and Ted Turner. There were actors, scientists, ministers, prime ministers, artists, and at least one king.

In 1998, Grace was once again invited to attend the State of the World Conference, where she remembers being especially inspired by Stephen Covey's workshop on building healthy organizations. She became increasingly bombarded with requests to attend conferences and seminars. In 2000 in Vancouver, she attended a United Nations conference on discrimination. "I was quite vocal," she recalls. She was so vocal on the subject of racism she assumed she would never hear from the United Nations again, but a few months later they asked her to attend another conference on racism in South Africa. This time Grace declined. "I don't know why," she says. "People told me to go, but I just had a real strong feeling not to."

That same summer, Grace received the Order of British Columbia. The certificate hangs on her wall next to her honorary Doctorate of Laws from Malaspina University College and the 125th Commemorative Award from the Governor General of Canada for outstanding contribution to the country.

Grace says that she has no immediate goals for the future. She continues to work as executive director of Tillicum Haus and sets new goals as the need arises. She wants to continue building a holistic community, and she has no doubt that her dream of a Native college will come true. When she eventually retires, she will leave behind a legacy of an enormous contribution to the culture, traditions, and spirituality of her people. For that, she thanks her father. "My dad lived that every day," she says. "So I try to live my spirituality every day. I always tell my students: you start from yourself, then your family, your community, your nation, and then the universe. You can't jump any of those steps."

When Grace started school, she was afraid to talk to anyone; now she is comfortable with heads of state. When she came to Nanaimo there were no Native treatment centres; today her community is growing strong and healthy and Tillicum Haus Native Friendship Centre is a shining example to the rest of the world. Native tradition states that how we live physically, mentally, emotionally, and environmentally affects seven generations after us. Grace Elliott-Nielsen has never forgotten that teaching or the words of her great-great-grandfather, Chief Seattle:

Your dead cease to love you
and the homes of their nativity
as soon as they pass the portals of the tomb.
They wander far off beyond the stars,
are soon forgotten, and never return.

Our dead never forget the beautiful world
that gave them being.
They still love its winding rivers,
its great mountains
and its sequestered vales,
and they ever yearn in tenderest affection
over the lonely hearted living
and often return to visit
and comfort them.

Dr. Roger Hayward Rogers, 2001

Dr. Roger Hayward Rogers:
The Gift of Healing

*I*t is no coincidence that the Centre for Integrated Healing in Vancouver has a logo in the shape of a heart: it is the embodiment of Dr. Roger Hayward Rogers' lifetime of dedication to health and healing and to his love of human beings. The centre, which Dr. Rogers founded, treats cancer patients using holistic methods that may include acupuncture, herbs, vitamins, diet, exercise, yoga, meditation, stress reduction, traditional Chinese medicine, and other therapies. Each of the staff, including four medical doctors, was hand-picked for skill as well as for a caring and loving manner. The Centre for Integrated Healing is the only one of its kind in Canada, and the only healing centre that is partially funded by the ministry of health.

Those whom traditional medicine had—in effect—given up on and who have regained their health at the centre, call the treatment methods miraculous. Dr. Rogers sees nothing miraculous in what he does for his patients. He steadfastly believes that human bodies were meant to be healthy, and he sees his job as restoring the body, mind, and spirit to its intended state.

Dr. Rogers spent all his life living and working in Vancouver, but in 2001 he and Marion, his wife, moved to Sidney on Vancouver Island to be near their daughter. There he has opened a small office on the second floor of a medical building on the main street. He divides his time between his Vancouver Island office and the clinic in Vancouver. I meet him in his Sidney office on a Saturday morning long before the shops and other offices will open. As I sit across the desk from him in his small, almost cramped office, I am impressed by his soft manner and his complete lack of self-consciousness. He is thin, and has a direct gaze that is not disconcerting but rather open and pleasant. We will have more what I would call a conversation than an interview, and it's a conversation I could have continued far longer than the two hours we had scheduled.

It is interesting that Roger chose to become a doctor because neither of his parents believed in them, but then, he adds, "Both my parents were more health minded than most people I knew. Going to a doctor or having a doctor come to your home was an expense they could well do without."

Roger was born in 1928, just prior to the Great Depression, into a family—like most families—that relied on a large reference book of illnesses and remedies when one of them came down with a cold or a headache. Roger recalls, "The favourite thing if you had a stomach upset was castor oil, which was a great motivating factor. If you know you're going to get treated with that vile stuff, you're not going to admit that you're sick."

The family was poor, but Roger considered himself one of the richest boys alive. "I lived in one of the most privileged locations I could have wished for," he says. Home was a big rambling house on West Hastings Street overlooking the CPR railway yard. He could spend hours prowling along the tracks behind the house or he could venture a bit farther and swim in the harbour. For 25 cents he could ride the ferry to the North Shore, where he could hike in the summer or ski during the winter. Percy, Roger's father, didn't work until the Second World War began because he had been in the trenches during the First World War and suffered from severe respiratory problems. Sarah Rogers made sure the family had enough money to pay the rent and buy groceries by letting out rooms to boarders and by buying and selling pianos. She was so shrewd in her acquisitions that even dealers came to the house to buy the pianos that Sarah had managed to find. Sometimes four or five pianos occupied various rooms in the house.

Having pianos available meant that Roger had to take lessons. Sarah loved music and had grand visions of her son as a concert pianist. Roger, on the other hand, hated the lessons because they meant he had to sit upright on the piano bench for an hour each day. Under protest he practised on the piano for ten years. "I had no illusions about my ability to become a concert pianist," he says. "I liked the music after a while; it was a very nice experience to share with other people, but I knew I could never reach the high standards required of a concert pianist."

If there was any tension at all in the Rogers household it was when Percy was in one of his bad tempers. "I guess he was still angry about things," Roger says. "Three years in the trenches—three years of watching people die and contributing to their deaths—it would throw anybody's perspective." Percy was a carpenter. When he was fixing things around the house Roger would follow him, watching and storing away all sorts of useful information about carpentry, plumbing, and electrical wiring.

He was also fascinated with the motley assortment of men who turned up at the front door begging for food. Sarah never turned anyone away. She brought the men into the warm hallway and fed them with whatever she had in her kitchen. Some of the boarders were as interesting and eccentric as the men who asked for food; they were old or young, seamen or skilled workers, lazy or industrious. For a while Roger adopted two young boarders as his heroes. They were athletic. They hiked and climbed and would regularly swim from the harbour around Stanley Park to English Bay. Sometimes one of them would place Roger on his back and swim out into the harbour while Roger hung on, feeling thrilled and full of admiration for the man's strength.

When Roger was eight years old he came down with mumps, an ailment Sarah considered serious enough to call the doctor. Roger recalls that Dr. Lyle Telford, who later became the mayor of Vancouver, was an exceptionally gentle man who did his best to make Roger comfortable, but because there was no cure for mumps he had to let disease run its course. Two years later Roger contracted double pneumonia. For three weeks Sarah tried every cure she knew, but no amount of steam inhalations or mustard plasters had any effect. So she finally called the doctor, and this time it was Lyle's brother, Dr. Douglas Telford, who visited the Rogers home. Douglas prescribed sulfa drugs, and within days Roger improved dramatically. "That was my first experience with success and the medical profession," he says. "Certainly my mother and I both attributed the recovery to the medicine."

In 1939 the Second World War broke out, and the failing economy recovered almost immediately. Everyone who was out of work got a job, including Percy, who left the family as soon as he got hired as a carpenter. Percy's desertion was not a traumatic event for Roger. His father had been a shadowy figure for so long that his leaving almost seemed inevitable. Sarah had meanwhile managed to save some of the money she had collected from the boarders' rents, so in 1940 she bought a big rambling house near English Bay for $1,200. She planned to renovate it and create some studio apartments. She had a problem getting the tradesmen she hired to complete the work. A plumber or a carpenter would turn up, work for a day or two, and then find a more lucrative position at the shipyards. Sarah became more and more frustrated. One day, when Roger found her in tears over yet another worker who had not completed a job, he said, "Never mind, I'll do it."

He was certain he could do the job. He had watched his father and the tradespeople who had come to the house. Percy had also left his large collection of tools behind; so despite his mother's deep skepticism, Roger set to work. "I had the dullest tools that had ever been created," he says. "But every spare moment when I wasn't at school I was working away. They'd already created a pattern of how to hang shelves on the walls and baseboards and sinks, and so I took on the whole thing."

He discovered he was a perfectionist. He did the plumbing, the electrical, and the carpentry; he hammered nails, screwed in cabinets, and rewired the house. Although he took great satisfaction in the work, he also got very frustrated when he made a mistake. If he cut a board too short, he would pound it with a hammer until he was exhausted; then, with his anger safely spent, he would get back to work.

Much to his mother's astonishment and his own satisfaction Roger built four very serviceable suites in the house. In 1946 Sarah sold the place for $8,000, and with $4,500 of the money she bought a property in North Vancouver that consisted of a small house and three storefronts. Roger renovated the shops, and Sarah opened a general store. That same year Roger graduated from high school with his senior matriculation. His sister Pamela had married, so he worked with his mother in the store because the business was so successful she couldn't run it on her own.

Roger recalls one incident while he worked in the store and one observation that impressed him. Making deliveries was one of his jobs. He would put the bags of groceries in the big carrier strapped to the handlebars of his bicycle and pedal through the neighbourhood, delivering the orders. One day he made a delivery to a regular customer named Fred, who invited Roger into his house and told him, "Something interesting has been happening." Fred raised champion Labrador retrievers. They were beautiful, intelligent dogs that he cared about dearly and sold for a great deal of money.

"I almost lost the whole kennel," Fred said, and told him the story. Food was still rationed in those days after the war and because Fred had a hard time finding meat to feed to his dogs he had made an agreement with a friend, who owned a bakery, to pick up the stale leftover bread at the end of the day. It was white bread made with bleached flour, because that was what people demanded in those days, and Fred fed it to his dogs. The animals became ill, some of them running around the kennel and throwing themselves against the wire, while others lay on their sides panting and drooling. Fred was afraid his dogs were dying from some strange disease and called the veterinarian, who came immediately. As Fred led the vet back to the kennels, the men passed by the sacks of stale bread. "Fred, what are you doing with all that?" the vet asked.

Fred told him he was feeding the bread to his dogs.

"How dare you give that dangerous food to these beautiful animals!" the vet shouted. "I don't need to see the animals. That's what's making them sick. Don't you ever give those animals that bread again!"

Roger left Fred's house, wondering, "What is so bad about white bread?"

Years later the scientific community began to answer that question. Recently, researchers at the University of British Columbia (UBC) discovered that the powerful chemical bleaching agent used to make white flour so white is extremely toxic to the brain and the cells of the nervous system and may be implicated in Lou Gehrig's disease and Parkinson's Disease.

Roger noticed something else while he worked in the grocery store. All the people in the neighbourhood shopped there for fresh meat, vegetables, fruit, canned goods, tobacco, sweets, and snacks, and Roger saw that the people who were ill most often and even looked sickly when they were not ill were the people who bought white bread, bologna, ice cream, and other processed foods. "There seemed to be a connection between diet and health," he says.

For three years Roger worked seven days a week from early morning until he fell into bed at night. "I had two days off in three years, and I slept through both of them," he recalls. "I was totally exhausted." He was so tired that one day he said to his mother, "I can't do this anymore. I just can't. The long hours, no time off—it's just too much."

Sarah was just as exhausted as her son and made no objection to selling the store. She bought another house in Vancouver's west end, and Roger felt like he was starting over. He had lost contact with all his friends except for one, his old high school friend, Bill Wynne, who had taken the ferry to North Vancouver to visit him every few weeks. Now that Roger was back in the city and not working, Bill urged him to continue his schooling at UBC, where Bill was studying. Roger needed little convincing. "This intense experience of working day and night for three years forced me to make up my mind to go back to school," he says.

His biggest decision was what to study. At that time newspapers and magazines were writing extensively about the wonders of nuclear power. The more Roger read about it, the more he was enthralled with the idea of building nuclear power plants, so he decided to enrol in the physics program at UBC. It helped that physics and mathematics had been his best subjects in high school.

When Bill saw what Roger was signing up for he pulled him aside and asked, "Roger, are you sure that's what you want to do?"

Roger told Bill about his ambition to build nuclear energy plants.

The next day Bill said to Roger, "Do you remember Gene Hess? He was in our class. He's completed his studies in nuclear physics and is teaching at the university. He's very bright. His family is German, and he's translating and correcting the work that is coming out of Germany."

Roger was impressed that a 22-year-old man was correcting the work of German physicists and scientists.

"Look, I've been in touch with Gene, and he's agreed to see you tomorrow."

Roger and Bill visited Gene Hess's laboratory in the physics building. The sun was streaming in through the tall windows and lighting up the blackboard that ran the full length of the wall. Written on the board was an incomprehensible formula that started on the left-hand side, continued across to the end, and then finished off about halfway across the blackboard on the next line down.

When Gene entered the room in his white lab coat with his face flushed, Roger thought, "This is what nuclear physics is about? I was thinking of building nuclear plants—the drama of working with this superior form of energy. I don't want to do this: wear a white coat and work on theoretical formulas."

The next day, Roger went back to the registrar and cancelled all the classes he had signed up for.

"What you need to do," Bill told him, "Is experience the luxury of an education."

Once again Roger listened to Bill's advice and signed up for economics, philosophy, psychology, English, and Russian. Only two hardships interfered with his luxury education: one was Russian, which Roger called "an absolute pig of a course," and the other was that Roger had to work hard to pay for his schooling. He took the toughest jobs he could find because they paid the most money.

Shortly after he started university Sarah's exhaustion from the years of working day and night at the store caught up with her; she became very ill. She was so weak and in such pain that she couldn't get out of bed. The doctor who came to see her didn't know what her illness was, and none of her friends' home remedies worked. Roger felt helpless as he watched his vital, dynamic mother grow weaker every day.

One day while Roger was pacing up and down the length of the living room, wondering what to do, he paused briefly in front of one of the bookshelves and noticed a book titled, *The Fast Way To Health.* Thinking the book was about a quick cure, he took it down from the shelf and opened it. It wasn't about a miracle cure, but was a compilation of articles written by a California physician, Dr. Frank McCoy, on the healing power of fasting. Roger was so astonished by the stories of Dr. McCoy's patients' miraculous recoveries that he couldn't put the book down until he had read it entirely in one weekend. The anecdotes described how people with life-threatening illnesses were restored to health by flushing the toxins from their bowels and drinking freshly squeezed grapefruit juice and water.

Roger was so sure that Dr. McCoy's cure would work that he convinced his mother to try it. On the first day of the fast, Sarah was able to get out of bed. On the second day she could sit and cross one leg over the other, and on the third day she was preparing dinner in the kitchen when Roger arrived home from school. "All her pain went away," he says. "So I watched this transformation with almost disbelief. I couldn't believe what was happening—that she suddenly changed from a very sick woman to a well woman."

Roger graduated with a Bachelor of Arts degree and asked himself, "Where do I go from here?" He was certain that he wanted to do something meaningful, perhaps something in service to mankind, but he didn't know what. His career counsellor suggested he choose between medicine, social work, and psychology.

Roger ruled out medical school because the veterans who had come back from the war were filling the universities, and competition was fierce. Besides, he didn't have the money or the medical school prerequisites of zoology and chemistry. He chose social work because he had met someone who was a social worker and seemed to like his work.

A few months into the program, Roger quit; he realized he wasn't interested in social work, he was fascinated with health and disease. While he was wrestling with the problem of his future career, a friend visited and said, "Why don't you go into naturopathy? I have a friend who is a naturopath, and I can arrange for you to see him and have an interview with him."

Roger was intrigued and began to research the subject. What he learned convinced him he should enrol in the naturopathic college in Oregon. Then he met with the naturopath, who spent three hours doing his best to discourage him from taking that route. "My advice to you is to become a medical doctor," he said. "Then you can practice the most natural medicine that you desire." He gave Roger a list of reasons not to become a naturopath: they could not admit a patient to the hospital, they couldn't sign death certificates, they couldn't prescribe medicines, no one listened to naturopaths, and they had no status in the community. There were only six naturopaths in all of B.C. at that time, and because no one really knew what they did, they were regarded with deep suspicion. "As a medical doctor people will listen to you and they'll respect what you do," the naturopath said.

Based on his advice, Roger booked an interview with the assistant dean of medicine at UBC. "Why do you want to go into medicine?" the assistant dean asked.

Roger told him that he believed there must be something useful he could do in the practice of medicine. He didn't tell the assistant dean about the Labrador retrievers or the pasty-looking people who used to shop at his mother's store or about his mother's miraculous recovery, but he did say that he had developed a strong interest in why people get sick.

"You're three courses short," the assistant dean said. "You need two chemistry courses and a zoology course. If you enrol in graduate studies and get satisfactory marks in those three subjects, I can assure you that you will be able to come in."

Roger couldn't believe what he was hearing. The field of medicine that had seemed so completely out of reach had suddenly become easily available to him. He passed his required courses and entered medical school. He had always enjoyed school and done well in his studies, but none of that could compare to medical school. "It was the most rewarding experience," he recalls. "Every day I looked forward to going and finding out something new and different."

He met Marion, a fellow medical student, at the start of a fall term. He had just come back from a summer of hard manual outdoor labour, was muscled and tanned, with his hair bleached blonde by the sun. Marion took a long look at him and said to her friend, "Who's the new guy?" Forty-two years later, Roger and Marion are still in love. They shared their internship and residency in pediatrics at St. Paul's Hospital in Vancouver. In the scant spare time they had, they built a boat and sailed away on it for their honeymoon. They started a family right away, and while Roger worked, Marion spent the first ten years after her internship raising their three children before returning to medicine part-time.

Roger opened his first practice in East Vancouver in 1960, where he incorporated all the holistic principles he had learned, advising his patients on diet and exercise and a healthy lifestyle. His patients spread the word that here was a different kind of doctor—one who listened and was open to new ideas. Soon Roger's patients began to bring him information they had read in magazines and books or had picked up somewhere, and from them Roger learned about things like acupuncture, healing touch, and many other practices. "My patients were a rich source of post-graduate training," he says. "They took me over and began to fill my mind with all sorts of interesting ideas and solutions."

At this point in Roger's narrative, I stop him. "But isn't that unusual? I've been to a doctor, who—when I told him about fasting or herbal medicine—wouldn't listen, and instead he referred to the big blue book of drugs and prescribed from that. But you listened to them!"

"This blue book is one of the most wearisome experiences that we should have in our work," Roger says. "In a lifetime you can't possibly be adequately informed of the products that are in that book. I had two or three experiences that shook me up and started me questioning, 'Why do people get ill in the first place? They must be making some mistakes.'"

As Roger treated his patients, he became more and more curious. He saw people who were weak and pale, disillusioned and unwell. He was sure that diet was one of the mistakes people were making. But what else? It took years before he would be more certain that he had an answer, but meanwhile he helped organize a medical/dental building in East Vancouver—the first comprehensive medical/dental facility in the east end of the city.

In 1969 Roger was invited to join the faculty of medicine at UBC and was on the faculty for 23 years. Shortly after being appointed, Roger met another faculty member, Robert Boese, who was a graduate of medical sociology from Berkley in California and one of two PhD doctors on the staff. Roger soon discovered that his colleague was a vegetarian and a fitness buff and that he had some definite opinions on the defects of the medical system. He encouraged Roger to attend various conferences in the U.S., one of them being the inaugural conference for the American Holistic Medical Association. "The people I heard and met at that conference just switched me on," Roger says. "There was one man, Norm Sheeley. When he comes into a room it's just like someone turning on the sun. He's just a beautiful personality, very caring, very knowledgeable, and the first president of the Holistic Association. I don't think I could have had a better introduction to holistic health." Everything Roger heard supported and vindicated his belief in holistic medicine.

After that conference, in the early 1970s, Robert and Roger decided to start a holistic centre in Vancouver. "We had such similar beliefs and ideas, it was just like looking into a mirror." The two men rented a small ground-floor apartment close to Vancouver General Hospital and opened their centre. When Roger told his colleagues what he was doing, they said, "Holistic? What the dickens does that mean?"

"I tried to interpret what it meant," he says. "And I sensed there was a great resistance to the name. Holistic was a bit too far off the centre line. It was sort of on the fringe of things."

Roger sat down with his partner. "Robert," he said. "We've got to change the name. I'm meeting a lot of resistance from my colleagues. If we want to make an impact, we have to make peace with them. If we want to contribute to the progress of medicine we have to use a name that isn't offensive. Why don't we call it the Thera Wellness Centre? Wellness tells people exactly what our objective is."

Robert agreed. They registered the Thera Wellness Centre as a non-profit society. It was successful in every way except financially because part of the premise of the centre was for the doctor to spend time with patients; Roger soon discovered that he couldn't spend an hour with a patient and still expect to make a living.

While he worked at the Wellness Centre Roger also continued to see people at his regular medical practice in the east end. One day a woman walked in, who was the sickest person he had ever seen. She had a large tumor on her neck, her feet and ankles were swollen, she was pale, in pain, and so weak that her husband had to help her sit down and stand up and walk the few steps from the waiting room to the examining room. She told Roger that she had been diagnosed with Hodgkin's disease and refused conventional treatment. Instead she went to Mexico and spent eighteen months in a cancer clinic, but after spending more than $100,000, she left the clinic worse instead of better. She told him that while she was in Mexico, she met a man from New York who said to her, "If they can't help you, here's the name of a doctor in Tennessee who cured himself when the Mayo Clinic refused to treat him for non-Hodgkins lymphona."

The woman left Mexico and went back to the cancer clinic in Vancouver, asking for help. They gave her four courses of chemotherapy, but it had no effect. As a last resort she contacted Dr. Cecil Pitard, the doctor in Tennessee. She showed Roger the three-page letter he had sent her in reply. Roger read it carefully.

"What do you think of his method of treatment?" she asked.

"Well, I'm seeing it for the first time. I really don't have an opinion."

"At my expense, will you phone this doctor and ask him anything you want to know about his method of treatment?" she asked.

Roger pondered the request. He was already running behind schedule. He considered the three-hour time difference, he worried about his patients in the waiting room, and he thought about the witch hunts in the U.S. that relentlessly tracked down any patient or doctor who dared to get involved in unorthodox cancer therapy. The woman had already asked Roger to promise never to mention her name. He knew he would be taking a great risk if he made the telephone call, but he cared about the young woman more. "If I'm ever going to phone this person, I'd better do it right away," he thought, and he dialed the number. Thirty minutes later he hung up.

He had heard the most extraordinary story about a cure for cancer. Dr. Cecil Pitard had had an advanced case of non-Hodgkins lymphona. The Mayo Clinic had turned him away. "Nothing we can give you will help you," they said. "Everything we give you will make you feel worse." When Pitard recovered from the shock of his death sentence, he decided to review every piece of medical information that had been written about cancer in the leading medical journals of the world during the previous ten years. From that information, he created a treatment that worked.

"Is this method of treatment safe?" Roger asked.

"It is."

"Does it have unpleasant side effects?"

"No."

"Is it compatible with any other treatments that might be in progress or that might be advocated?"

"Yes. In fact, if people need to have radiation or chemotherapy, this treatment will substantially reduce the side effects of both."

When Roger hung up, the young woman asked, "What do you think of his method of treatment now?"

114

"Well, it's safe, it's scientific, and it's probably something you should consider doing."

The woman handed Roger a brown paper bag containing the four components of the treatment that Dr. Cecil Pitard had sent to her. "Can we start today?" she asked.

"I suddenly felt trapped," Roger says. "I thought, 'Oh my gosh I told her it's a good idea, and now she wants me to step into the minefield of unorthodox cancer therapy.'"

But Dr. Pitard had just told him that the treatment was safe and free of side effects, and the young woman had no other chance at life. He weighed the risk and realized that even if the treatment didn't work, if all it gave her was comfort while she waited to die, he could not refuse her.

Roger began the treatment. That night his new patient slept for the first time in three months because for the first time in almost three years, she had hope. Six weeks later the large tumor on her neck disappeared, and her energy improved. She continued to heal and was eventually able to go back to work. "It was one of the most moving experiences of my life," Roger says. "To watch someone as sick as she was turn that disease around. That was a real eye-opener. I couldn't pretend it didn't happen. And so I thought, 'Well if this formulation will work for her, perhaps it will work for other patients in my medical practice who are struggling with cancer.'"

One by one, Roger invited his cancer patients into his office and told them about the treatment and about the results he had achieved with it. As he treated more and more patients, he watched more and more dramatic results take place. Then in 1985, two years and four months after treating his first patient, Roger received a letter from the College of Physicians and Surgeons: "We understand you are administering unorthodox cancer therapy. Please explain."

"I was shocked by this," Roger says. "This was incredibly threatening. I could foresee that I was going to be kicked out of the club."

Terrified as he was, Roger replied to the letter, giving what he thought was a good explanation of his activities. A few days later the registrar telephoned him, requesting the name of the first woman he had treated. "I couldn't believe my ears," he says, and even years later on the day of our interview, his voice was raised in surprise.

He explained that he had pledged to the woman that he would never tell her name. Within days, he received a formal invitation to an inquiry. "This is it," Roger thought, feeling doomed.

For a week, he couldn't sleep or eat a proper meal; he was overwhelmed with anxiety. Then one morning he woke up to bright sunlight flooding through the bedroom window, and he thought about his situation. He hadn't hurt anybody. Indeed, people were alive because of him. If the College of Physicians and Surgeons was to stop him from doing what he was doing, people were going to suffer and die. As soon as he stopped focussing on himself and his troubles, and considered the patients he cared about so deeply, he felt a new resolve. "I've got to get my act together," he thought.

He went to the head of the Cancer Agency and obtained every available cancer statistic. He learned that one-third of Canadians had cancer and one in five died as a result. Today more than one-third of Canadians get cancer and more than one in four die as a result. Roger gathered background information until he felt he was well prepared to defend his treatment. Two weeks after the inquiry where he presented his case, he received a letter from the College of Physicians and Surgeons, stating they had accepted his explanations and were encouraging him to work in association with the Cancer Agency. He was deeply relieved.

Roger had been seeing cancer patients at his own practice for some time. Shortly after The Thera Wellness Centre began to see cancer patients, Robert Boese died of non-Hodgkin's lymphoma—a cancer of the lymph nodes that is very difficult to control. It was a terrible loss. Losing Robert to cancer was not only a personal loss but also a professional one. Roger began to feel a bitter irony in his partner's death, as they were operating a wellness centre.

Since no one could fill Robert's role, Roger began to contemplate shutting the centre down. He changed its name to The Centre for Integrated Therapy, but that didn't seem to be right either because the word "therapy" implied that the centre was offering only a particular type of treatment. Two years later, the centre was still struggling along when Dr. Hal Gunn, a former student who had done part of his practicum with Roger, recognized Roger on national television in an interview about his work. He telephoned him. "Can we get together for lunch?" he asked.

Roger calls the chance meeting a remarkable stroke of luck. Dr. Hal Gunn had been working at UBC's Student Health Services for eight years and was deeply interested in the work Roger was doing. When Hal joined Roger at the centre, he brought some new energy and ideas. One of the first suggestions he made was a name change to The Centre for Integrated Healing. Roger marvelled that he had not thought of the name himself because it reflected his original inspiration for creating the centre. "We are born to heal," he says. "At the moment of conception, when we are invisible, the master plan for everything we will become is all in place. The colour of our eyes, skin, and hair, the shape of our nose, ears and teeth, the height to which we will grow, whether we are left or right handed, our blood type, and every conceivable thing that we are going to be is already in place. Even our talent, our intuition, everything. And the really interesting thing is that at that moment of the beginning of life we have the most elaborate, the most precise, extraordinary, exquisite capacity to heal from every possible hazard. We were never intended to be ill. It doesn't make sense. Why would we have this elaborate defense system if we were also intended to be compromised by illness?"

It was this realization—this knowledge that humans were meant to be well and that they were capable of healing—which illuminated all the work he continued to do. It was this knowledge that kept him working long past retirement, and it is what keeps him working today. The centre's purpose, Roger says, is to alert people to what is happening all around them. For example, it is there to tell people that tobacco and alcohol are the number one and two killers in the Western world. In 1996 more than half of all the people who died from all causes in B.C. died from diseases directly associated with tobacco.

Hal Gunn's intense energy and a boundless capacity for leadership and organization helped the centre to expand rapidly. Much of the centre's work involves educating people about risk factors for cancer that are not common knowledge and to offer a different kind of treatment. Roger explains that the tendency in Western medicine is to treat the disease and not the patient, which means that people continue to live the same way after their diagnosis. They continue to smoke and eat the same foods that may have caused their illness. The centre empowers people to take charge of their lives and encourages them to look at the way they eat, at their exercise, their quality of sleep, their use of chlorinated water, and at the stress in their lives. The centre has a large file of testimonials from people cured of cancer. It was also recently asked by the National Institute of Health in the U.S. to submit a best-case series of outstanding recoveries. Roger says that complying with the request won't be a difficult task.

Roger worked long, hard hours, but it was by choice. His passion for his work sustained him, as does his relationship with his wife Marion. "She has been my greatest help and support. I feel privileged." His deep spirituality also shaped his philosophy. "You can't worship a loving, forgiving genius of a God and believe that that same God would betray us with illness. We have to take away any guilt or blame about illness. If we were in our right minds we wouldn't allow ourselves to get ill, and if we're not in our right minds we're innocent anyway. Illness is the result of innocent mismanagement."

If there is a culprit in the illness game it is the effective marketing systems that convince people to buy products that are detrimental to health, Roger says. As his wellness example, he points to the wild mammals that die violent deaths or die of starvation: They do not die of human diseases because they do not eat refined foods or foods with additives. He has never forgotten his first observation of the relationship between food and health when Fred's Labrador retrievers suffered on a diet of white bread.

In 2001 Roger received a telephone call from Government House in Victoria, informing him that he had been awarded the Order of British Columbia. He was surprised, and he also felt uneasy. "Of all the people in the province doing such worthwhile work, why me?" he wondered. And then he resolved to live up to the honour bestowed on him. "When you get the Order of B.C., you feel like you want to devote the rest of your life to making as much progress as you can."

And that might explain why Dr. Roger Hayward Rogers still works when most of his colleagues have long since retired. "I've led a privileged life," he says, and then he asks me to be sure I write that the greatest of those privileges is knowing and loving his wife, Marion.

Rick Hansen:
Man in Motion

*R*ick Hansen is the only person in this book that I was not able to interview face to face. The logistics of getting together proved insurmountable, due to Rick's formidable schedule. Sarah Sugiyama, his assistant, and I communicated for at least two months before she was able to slot in even one hour. During one of my conversations with Sarah, when I was trying to negotiate an extra half-hour and she was listing some of his commitments, I said something like, "Wow, he's awfully busy!"

Sarah chuckled and said, "They don't call him the 'Man in Motion' for nothing." She later explained to me that there is a double meaning to the epithet. Yes, he is always moving, but "Man in Motion" also refers to the way he inspires his staff to keep looking to the future.

While talking to Rick on the telephone I quickly come to the conclusion that he is a man with a lifelong mission—a man who is passionate about life and about being in service to others. He says that he is an adventurer and a pioneer. After listening to his story I'd say the description is accurate.

Rick was born in Port Alberni on August 26, 1957, and grew up in Williams Lake, as the oldest of four children. "In my early years I felt like I was a kid in a candy shop," he says. "I was born and raised in rural British Columbia, and I loved the outdoors. It just seemed like I was in an adventure playground. No matter where I was I was surrounded by family, and I was engaged in one adventure after another."

119

Rick Hansen, 1989

His father, Marvin, was a lineman for the B.C. Telephone Company. His job kept him moving from town to town. Every new move meant new places for Rick to discover. He explored the forests surrounding the towns, swam or fished in the rivers and lakes, and hiked on the wilderness trails. In school he was also an accomplished athlete. "I think sports really helped define my character and shape my life," he says. "Sport helped me learn a lot about myself, my body, my mind, my team mates. Sport is really a metaphor for life. It reflects back all the difficult qualities that we deal with." His coaches became some of his earliest role models and continued to be his heroes all his life.

He was fifteen and had just completed Grade Ten in Williams Lake when his life changed. Instead of going to volleyball camp to train for the provincial championships, he had decided to go fishing with two friends. They hitchhiked home and got a ride in a pickup truck. The driver had had a couple of drinks, lost control on a sharp turn, and crashed. Rick's spine was shattered in the accident. "The magnitude of the injury was just inconceivable," he says. "You can imagine: if you're athletic and in good shape, and then all of a sudden the first thing you notice is that your legs are numb and when you touch them they jiggle like jelly and you can't feel anything … It's a dramatic moment for a child at the age of fifteen."

He refused to believe that his injury was permanent. Surely he would run again and play volleyball and hike in the woods. After all, he had only had an accident and he had seen other people with injuries or even broken legs and they recovered in time. But the weeks passed, and no matter how much willpower Rick exerted, he could not move his legs or wiggle his toes. "I had some moments of real depression. At first, I felt angry with the driver, and I had to move through that and take personal responsibility and forgive him because I was the one who decided to get in the back of the pickup truck. I was the one who decided to take the risk."

Even in his anger Rick noticed the kindness and dedication of the doctors, nurses, and physiotherapists who worked with him. Family members left their jobs in Williams Lake to come to Vancouver and spend time with him in the hospital. "I was lying there, flat on my back, totally devastated and incapacitated, traumatized and in shock, and all I was exposed to were great people."

When he said cruel things in frustration or anger, his family just listened to him. Other people, who had lost the use of their legs in accidents, visited him and urged him to change his mind about how his life could be in the future. "Don't give up your dreams," they said.

"At the end of the day, if I would have carried that anger around, then I would truly have been a victim," Rick says. "So I decided to let it go."

After four months in the hospital he transferred to the G.F. Strong Rehabilitation Centre, where he learned to walk on crutches and braces and to use hand controls to drive a four-wheel-drive Bronco. After three months of rehabilitation, he returned to Williams Lake. His high school had no wheelchair ramps or elevators. "If I had not mastered the use of crutches and braces, I would not have been able to go back," Rick says. "I was fortunate that I worked very, very hard to achieve that goal. It gave me the ability to go back to school, catch my second semester of Grade Eleven and graduate on time. Going back home was probably a bigger challenge than I would have imagined, but not physically."

Rick still thought of himself as an athlete. His accident suddenly forced him to question what was really important to him. "Most people begin to ask those questions as adults," he says. "I faced them at age sixteen. I used to define myself by how powerful I was physically and how fiercely independent I was. What I came to realize was that life is not about your legs—it's about your heart and your passion and your experience. It's about being connected to the quality of life, about ultimately being able to make a difference in your life and the lives of others."

It was difficult for him to stop comparing life in a wheelchair to how it had been before the accident. Because he hated to ask for help and refused it when it was offered, Rick stopped doing the things that had given him so much pleasure. For example, he stopped fishing because he couldn't negotiate the rocky paths and steep cliffs that led to the river. One day his brother convinced Rick to be carried on his brother's back while he climbed down the cliff to the shores of the Thompson River. His brother carried him partway, and when he couldn't manage it further, he and other family members lowered

Rick on a rope. "I had a life jacket strapped to me, and I was sitting there, catching big fish and having a great time again," Rick recalls.

When he picked up his friends to drive them to the swimming hole, Rick would sit in the hot, stuffy cab of the truck while the others dove into the water. "I'd sit there and pout because I didn't want to ask them for help. Finally I realized that it wasn't my physical disability that was causing the problem: it was my mental disability—my attitude. So I started accepting help and reaching out and engaging again. I started realizing that I was the same person I was before my injury, with the same passions and interests, all of which could still be a reality. I just had to do them a little differently."

Rick assumed he would have to sit on the sidelines and watch his former teammates play volleyball and basketball, but his high school coach, Bob Redford, challenged him. "You're a born athlete," he said. "You can still be an athlete, but in a different way."

Bob suggested that Rick try coaching, and Rick discovered excitement and joy in training other athletes. Then Bob introduced Rick to wheelchair sports. "The definition of an athlete is not whether or not you use your legs," he told him. At first Rick was reluctant, but with Bob's encouragement, he began to play wheelchair volleyball.

"As a result of his inspiration every athletic dream I had ever dreamt came true," Rick says. "It's amazing to think it was all pivotal on a choice. It's amazing when someone is there for you and gives you perspective. We have a choice of paths in life, and I often wonder what might have happened if I had not made that choice."

Bob Redford also urged Rick to pursue his dream of being a physical education teacher. It wasn't important that there were no disabled physical education teachers in Canada, he said. Rick could be the first. "By getting me into coaching he was essentially building my confidence and making me believe I could teach and coach," Rick says.

When Rick was in Grade Twelve, the school's principal, Dave Shore, and the vice-principal, Jim Longridge, also helped build his self-esteem by asking him to substitute for the Grade Eleven math teacher. "It was amazing," Rick says. "The experiences I had in high school gave me an incredible sense of hope and optimism that I could be a good teacher and that I could teach in classrooms."

Rick applied to the physical education department at the University of British Columbia (UBC). When his application was rejected, Bob Redford encouraged Rick to approach the faculty at UBC and convince them that he was the right person to break precedent and be accepted in the program. "And so I did, and I did convince them," Rick says. "It was another pivotal choice. Bob didn't let me give up on myself."

Rick continued to play wheelchair volleyball at UBC. Through the athletic community he heard of a young coach named Tim Frick, who was helping athletes achieve remarkable goals. He met Tim in 1977, when they were both assigned to a committee that was helping to organize the Canada Summer Wheelchair Games. Rick was convinced that Tim was the person his team needed. They had a lot of heart and enthusiasm, but they were rough and ready and lacked finesse. Tim was busy and reluctant to get involved; besides, what did he know about wheelchair sports?

"Just come by and watch a practice," Rick said.

Tim watched and gave the team some tips, but he recognized so much untapped potential in them that he agreed to become their coach. Tim had a natural talent for bringing out the best in people and that was especially true when he worked with Rick. He created a program to help Rick train for wheelchair track and marathon events. Early in their partnership they prepared for the Vancouver marathon, which was classified as a "fun" event. Rick came in fourth, so they began an intense training program for his first competitive race at the Orange Bowl Marathon in Miami, Florida. Because it was winter and they only had six months to get ready, Tim and Rick decided they would have to train indoors. They bought wood, lengths of pipe, and roller bearings at the hardware store and built a set of rollers for the wheelchair in Tim's basement. Rick trained intensely on the improvised rollers through days of rain, sleet, and snow. When he won the Miami marathon by an enormous margin, he shocked himself and the athletic world. "That was the beginning of our success together."

In early 1984 he took part in the World Wheelchair Games and won the marathon. His next goal was to compete in the first Olympic exhibition wheelchair race scheduled to take place that summer at the Los Angeles Olympic Games. In April of that year, Rick crashed and dislocated his left shoulder. His doctors told him it would not be healed sufficiently to allow him to participate in sports until the fall. But the Olympics were taking place that summer, and Rick was determined to be there.

Amanda Reid, who is now Rick's wife, was the physiotherapist assigned to him. She worked with him aggressively and with such care and encouragement that Rick decided to defy the doctors' warnings. He did just well enough in the qualifying rounds to win one of eight starting positions, so he flew to Los Angeles to compete. Out of a field of eight in the 1500-metre race, Rick came in seventh. "Considering the circumstances, just to be there was a thrill," he says.

Although I can't see Rick's face because he's on the other end of a telephone line, when he says, "Yes, it was a thrill," his voice slows and lowers, and I am sure I detect a note of regret that he had not been at his physical peak and had not won that race.

Neither the injury nor the loss prevented him from playing sports or competing or from embarking on his new goal to inspire others. "When you have so many incredible people rally around you to help you out, you become totally convinced of how powerful that human trait of helping is, and you become motivated to give it back to them," he says. "You start to evolve your life's mission around service."

Rick's mission became clear as he and Tim Frick staged demonstration games against able-bodied volleyball teams at schools in the Lower Mainland. They were undefeated. "We were showing a new generation of Canadians that people with disabilities can achieve their potential," Rick says. "But as I travelled the world and represented my country, I was constantly bombarded with the stark reality that we had a long way to go because there were many physical and attitudinal barriers that stopped people from achieving their potential."

Whenever Rick was not able to enter a building or participate in an event, or when his friends told him similar stories of exclusion, he filed the information away in his mind. He knew that one of the major obstacles he had to overcome was attitude. Once when he was late for class at UBC and wheeling up a hill as fast as he could, a girl who was also late came jogging up behind him. When she noticed Rick she ran faster, and when she reached him, she was gasping for breath. "Can I help push you up the hill?" she asked.

"Well, actually, you're the one who's out of breath," he said. "Maybe you want to sit on my lap and I'll give you a ride."

Other friends with disabilities had similar experiences. Rick started to think seriously about an idea that had first occurred to him while he was still at G.F. Strong Rehabilitation Centre. "It was the germ of an idea that evolved over fifteen years or so. It started when I was trying to picture my life again. Because I was an adventurer and a pioneer, I was trying to conceive of new adventures in my new world, and one of the ideas I thought of—even though it was so far out of the realm of possibility—was taking my buddies on their bikes, and I would have a trailer behind my wheelchair, and we'd cruise the world."

He knew the idea was outrageous, but instead of forgetting about it, he let it sit in the back of his mind, bringing it to fore now and then, modifying it, and polishing it until it began to seem possible. The idea took on the shape of a practical reality when he met Terry Fox, who had lost his leg to cancer. An acquaintance suggested that he invite Terry to play wheelchair basketball, and they became good friends who trained and roomed together. He watched Terry run across Canada to raise money for cancer research. As he followed Terry's journey, Rick saw people's attitudes about disabilities change. They stopped viewing Terry as someone who was unable to do things and began to realize that he was achieving something that very few people with two healthy legs could even begin to accomplish. Rick thought, "Maybe I can take that childhood dream of wheeling around the world, and maybe I can change attitudes. Maybe I can shock their perceptions. Maybe I can use it as an example, and maybe I can help remove some barriers."

Tim Frick was one of the first people Rick called when he decided to stop dreaming and actually go around the world in his wheelchair. On March 21, 1985, Rick left Vancouver with his friends, Tim Frick and Don Alder, and his cousin, Lee Gibson, on the Man in Motion World Tour. They had enough money to get them to Texas. After that they figured they would have to go on faith, hope, and trust. In his mind, Rick had pictured the adventures they would have along the way. He could not possibly have imagined the rigors of the journey. "It was about as intense and brutal as you can imagine," he says. "In a sense the team that came back were the survivors of a very difficult battle."

Each day the team struggled with organizational logistics, the weather, and Rick's physical pain. "Just going from point A to point B—trying to communicate the message and get people to respond, and on top of that to raise money, and then dealing with the things that were required with rooms and transport and wheelchair equipment and injuries and physiotherapy and flying back home and having to stay close to it, and the only way I was able to survive was to think, 'Oh, when it gets better, all I'll have to deal with are the interviews.'" He laughs because it never got easy.

Despite the physical hardships he never lost sight of the purpose. He was carrying a message to the world even though at times it seemed the world didn't want to listen. When they were crossing impossible stretches of country, it took every ounce of strength just to find a reason to keep going. "If you look at it analytically we probably never should have started," Rick says. "But then, in reality, the only way it could have been done was to just get started. We were fortunate enough to make the decision to go in spite of the fact that we weren't ready."

When Amanda joined the tour she brought a spirit and determination that helped everyone to continue, especially Rick. Although the first days and weeks were the most difficult time, the European tour was the most intense part of the journey. The team had been on the road for six months, and they were exhausted. "We were tired and not much was happening," Rick says. "So far to go—so far from home."

Some countries wouldn't let the team cross their borders, and in others, no one seemed to know why they were there. There were a few inspirational moments, but they didn't make up for the disappointments. For Rick the toughest time was when Tim Frick decided to leave the tour. The team had made a vow to stick together no matter how hard the going got, and letting go of that piece of the dream almost ended it. "One of the hardest things for me was to let go of that fantasy. But he had given so much that he finally realized he couldn't give to anyone if he didn't take care of himself. And yet, that vow was the last thing we had to hang on to. I was pretty devastated by that. It took me a while to recognize what a courageous act it was. I wouldn't have got through the most difficult time if it wasn't for him." Rick knew that their friendship would survive Tim's departure, but he also recognized that the tour was too important to put in jeopardy for any reason. It had to go on, with or without Tim.

The Man in Motion World Tour wound its way through Europe and Asia. When they arrived back in the U.S., they hit another low point. There was no fanfare and no excitement anywhere. Rick was so close to home, but he was so discouraged he decided to quit. Amanda was the one who refused to give in; she wouldn't let Rick stop. So, mile by mile and day by day, he continued. When the team crossed the border into Canada the magic began. "It was one highlight after another," Rick says. "It was just the most privileged experience I could imagine."

It seemed like every person in the country had dropped whatever they were doing to line city streets and rural roads to cheer for Rick Hansen. He was their hero. The Man in Motion World Tour became a magic carpet ride from east to west, and the money poured in to the Legacy Fund for spinal cord injury research.

The euphoria was tempered somewhat by a physically gruelling trip across the prairies and the Rocky Mountains in subzero temperatures and raging winter storms. The team had to modify Rick's wheelchair to four-wheel-drive, and they attached heat sensors to Rick's legs to make sure he wouldn't accidentally succumb to frostbite. Rick remembers it as one of the most physically brutal legs of the trip.

When the Tour arrived back in Vancouver two years, two months, and two days after setting out, the line between dreams and reality blurred and disappeared. "It became one and the same," Rick says. "It was a phenomenal moment—one that I will always remember and appreciate. It was magic. I'd had this sort of recurring fear that after all that work, I'd come home and just wheel through an empty street, and I'd be up in this empty office room with my crew, trying to find some moments to celebrate."

Crowds lined the streets ten deep; they hung out of office windows, shouted themselves hoarse, and wept with joy and awe. Rick Hansen had wheeled 40,072 kilometres through 34 countries on four continents. At the finish line a banner declared "Welcome Home Rick!" Printed underneath in small letters were the words, "The end is just the beginning." It may not have been what Rick wanted to hear at that point, but in retrospect, he says it was prophetic.

The Man in Motion World Tour was Rick's first attempt to resolve the issues in society that limit people with disabilities and to find a cure for spinal cord injuries. When they had set off in 1985, Rick and the team had hoped to raise $1 million. Then they reconsidered because it was, after all, a big adventure and decided to aim for $10 million. When the tour ended, they had raised $24 million. In 1985 most scientists believed a cure was impossible, but Rick knew nothing was impossible if you believed.

When the tour was over, and after a brief rest, Rick tried to train for another marathon, but his body rebelled. "I had to recognize that my life was profoundly changed by the experience of the road. I would never be the same. Essentially, I didn't have the strength to even do a workout simply because my priorities and my passions had changed. It wasn't in sports anymore; it was in hunting the dream—that's where your strength comes from—by aligning your dreams and your goals with your actions. When I realized what my dreams were, I started embracing that slogan, 'The end is just the beginning.'"

Rick's new goals were to find a cure for spinal cord injuries and to make changes in the global community that would benefit the physically disabled. Along with a dedicated team, he built the legacy fund and a leadership fund of tens of millions of dollars. About 65 percent of the monies go to spinal cord research while the other 35 percent supports wheelchair sports, rehabilitation, and injury prevention.

In the years since the Man in Motion World Tour, Rick has become an inspirational speaker and a role model for the disabled and for children all across Canada. He has received seven honorary law degrees from McMaster University and the Universities of Western Ontario, Toronto, Regina, Victoria, Calgary, and British Columbia. He has been named athlete of the week, year, and century by various organizations and the media. In 1986, the Canadian Press named him "Newsmaker of the Year." His list of awards and offices is impressive.

Many members of his Man in Motion team, including his wife Amanda, work with him and share his dream. He calls Amanda his biggest role model. "She's had an amazing impact on my life," he says. "She was my physiotherapist when I was dealing with my injury. She was also the spiritual team leader and my friend and confidant. As my wife, partner, and mother of our three daughters, she is now involved in our school program, taking our story to a new generation of Canadians."

The Rick Hansen Foundation has also set up a Rick Hansen Awards program, recognizing young Canadians who make a difference in the lives of others. Nancy Thompson, who was the Man In Motion World Tour manager, is now the head of the Rick Hansen Wheels in Motion event, whose purpose is to bring people together to help find a cure for spinal cord injures. In 1997 Rick founded the Rick Hansen Institute, which is dedicated to finding a cure because where scientists once believed there was no cure, there is now hope.

Awareness has to be ongoing, Rick says, "So that someone won't have to wheel around the world in a wheelchair again, and more importantly, so someone in a wheel chair will be able to stand up and walk away. That's the dream."

When Rick was injured, he was told to lower his expectations so that he would not be disappointed. He was told not to use crutches and braces, and he was told not to dream of having a family or a successful career. People like Christopher Reeve with severe spinal cord injuries were lucky to survive, Rick says, and if they did, their prognosis was to spend their lives in a hospital bed. Today, people like Christopher Reeve live in the community. They are married and they have careers as actors, producers, educators, or engineers. "They're just getting on with life. And even though they are inspirational in the way they conduct themselves, not many people know there is still an incredible burden that they bear everyday. They have physical pain, and in one day they put in more effort than a lot of us would in a lifetime. It takes incredible courage and determination."

It's little wonder that some disabled people give up and that they see no hope or opportunity for themselves, he says. Some commit suicide or live a life feeling trapped and helpless. "If you're the kind of person who has lived that and experienced that, you become pretty motivated to try to help somebody out. My motivation for focussing exclusively on finding a cure for spinal cord injuries is that I believe anything is possible. I demonstrated that before, and I think I can demonstrate it again by making a difference in the field and helping to accelerate the pace of finding a cure. And also, I want to make a difference. I want to see a difference in the quality of life in this generation or the next."

In 1987 Rick was made a Companion of the Order of Canada. In 1989 the Province of British Columbia created a new award—the Order of British Columbia—in recognition of excellence and achievement by British Columbians for the benefit of others. Rick Hansen was among the first to receive it in 1990. "It was a tremendous honour that I was considered part of the first of those amazing British Columbians," he says. "When you get awards like the Order of Canada and the Order of B.C., you get pretty humble. In a way it's not fair. How do you choose among the great people? And I'm up there, receiving this thing, but in reality I was receiving it on behalf of a whole team of people who gave their all. I was very grateful."

Today Rick works harder than ever to make his dreams and the dreams of thousands of others come true. The Rick Hansen Man in Motion Foundation and Institute are building on the legacy by finding new ways to raise money and create awareness and by accelerating the search for a cure.

The Rick Hansen Institute, in partnership with the University of British Columbia and the Vancouver Coastal Health Authority, is building a spinal cord research centre at the Vancouver General Hospital, which will bring together the top researchers in the world to study spinal cord injuries and possibly find a cure. The Rick Hansen Institute has also established centres of excellence across the country that work together as a collaborative network in a search for a cure. It is also part of a larger global network of research centres such as the Christopher Reeve Group because the search and the dream is global in scope.

"My tour was worldwide," Rick says. "The cure will be global, too. Our Foundation, our Institute, and our legacy are pointed that way."

Our hour was finished too soon, and though I was reluctant to end a conversation that had so inspired me. I felt marvelously energized. It's easy to understand how the "Man in Motion" continues to inspire so many people, even those who weren't yet born, when he persevered to complete his famous world tour.

Tim Frick, 1998

Tim Frick:
For Love of Sports

*O*f all the places I interviewed people for this book, perhaps Tim Frick's meeting deserves the "most unusual place" award. In endeavouring to coordinate our schedules, Tim had determined that the most convenient place for us to meet would be in the parking lot of the Swartz Bay ferry terminal near Victoria, while he waited to board a ferry bound for one of the Gulf Islands. We decide to sit in my car, and I give him the driver's seat. He protests, saying that he doesn't mind sitting in the passenger seat, which is perpetually covered by fallout from my dog, but I explain that politeness is not my motive. I need room to manoeuvre my notebook, and the steering wheel will get in the way.

As we talk, the car's windows fog up and the skies threaten rain. Tim has thick dark hair and is very muscular. He's a natural athlete, he says, blessed with perfect hand-eye coordination and a passion for sports. From the time he was a young boy he could do anything well: run marathons, play cricket, or get a wicked slapshot past the goalie.

His mother, Mary, gave birth to Tim in her bedroom in a little house in Aldershot, England, on November 23, 1952. Both his parents had been in the war: his father Tony as an aircraft mechanic, and Mary had done something so "top secret" she never revealed it in her lifetime, no matter how much her children pestered her to tell.

After the war, Tony joined the police force, and in June 1957 he applied to immigrate to Canada. Like so many people in those post-war years, Tony wanted a better life for his family. He intended to go to Kitimat, where he had heard there was a construction boom, but first he stopped in Sudbury, Ontario, to visit a friend in the Copper Cliff police force, and signed up with it instead. Six months later he sent for his family.

They lived on the shores of Long Lake, surrounded by endless miles of wilderness that were young Tim's idea of paradise. In the winter the children skated across the lake and organized games of ice hockey. In the summer they hiked, played baseball, and spent every waking minute outdoors.

But in 1965 Mary and Tony, tired of the northern Ontario winters, moved to Parksville on Vancouver Island. Tim had been about to enter Grade Eight and it was to be his glorious senior year; instead, he entered a junior high school where his grade was the bottom rung of the class ladder.

"Back in those days there were never any hockey rinks anywhere in Parksville," Tim recalls. "At the high school, one of the favourite things to do during the lunch hour was to play indoor hockey. They actually played with hockey sticks and a leather tape-wrapped puck. Well, I had spent hours and hours and hours working on my slapshot. In Ontario, during the summer, I'd put out a four- by eight-foot sheet of plywood and a bucket of pucks, and I'd shoot pucks against the brick wall of the house, which is probably why they had to sell it. So there I am at Parksville Junior High—and I'm a little guy to begin with—and apprehensive, and I go out to play hockey because it's the one thing I know I can do … and I put a slap shot through the gyprock of the gym wall. I was first pick for the team."

I laugh and Tim joins in. "I never suffered any major trauma."

When his father, who was a member of Legion #49, convinced the organization to fund a soccer program, Tim excelled there as well. He was only thirteen years old when his soccer coach asked him to coach a group of six-year-olds that were just starting their first season. "I'll never forget that," he says. "At a practice, I was demonstrating a certain drill that involved running along and tapping the ball back to the guy behind you, and as I was looking back to make sure the kids were doing the drill right, I actually ran into the goal post and knocked myself out."

We both laugh again. "I certainly know now how it feels to be Gulliver. I woke up and looked up at all these little kids." Since that year, 1965, Tim has coached either a team or an individual every year.

I ask, "Did you immediately like coaching?"

"I don't know," Tim says. "In high school I coached little boy's soccer and I coached minor softball. In senior high I coached the junior girl's basketball team. Yet all the time I was playing on all the teams."

He played senior men's softball and community soccer and was a member of the Nanaimo Track and Field Club. "I just loved sports," he explains. "I remember in high school reading absolutely every coach biography I could get my hands on just so that I could learn how to be a coach. I never had any grandiose plans—I just happened to like it at the time."

Tim didn't concentrate on his academic work as much as sports, but he did well and went to college to study forensic science. During his first year at Malaspina College in Nanaimo he restricted his sports activities to the college soccer team and the community team. He passed with a phenomenal 90-plus percent average, and he could have gone on to study anything he wanted to. "But, you know, at the end of that first summer I thought, 'My life is sports. I've got to do something in sports.'"

He switched his studies to physical education and entered the University of British Columbia, where he played on the university volleyball team and went on to win the national championship in his last year. While he was at university, Tim coached high school teams and the junior varsity women's team. In 1976 he graduated and went on to study for his Master of Physical Education degree. While doing his postgraduate work, he coached the men's volleyball team at Langara College. In his third and final year of coaching, the Langara team won the first Canadian College Volleyball Championship. That same year Tim coached a community senior women's team to the national title.

During that time, Tim met and worked with Vic Lindal, a coach and mentor who encouraged him to tap into his creativity, to be open to new ideas, and to constantly challenge himself and his beliefs. "He was a real catalyst for me to want to continue coaching," Tim says.

In 1977 Glen Burrell, a volleyball player on the provincial team, introduced Tim to Rick Hansen. After the accident that had left him a paraplegic, Rick had gone from his rehabilitation to his hometown of Williams Lake to finish high school and help coach the school volleyball team. Rick was passionate about volleyball, so when he enrolled at UBC, he organized a wheelchair volleyball team. All they lacked was a coach. "So naturally, the guy he knew through Glen Burrell was me, so he hounded me," Tim recalls.

"He hounded you?" I ask.

"Essentially, yes. Well, he asked a few times. I managed to find excuses for a while, but eventually I said that I would do it, but that since I knew nothing about wheelchairs or paraplegia, I would just coach the way I coach, and at the end of two weeks they could decide whether that was okay or not. But I was coaching volleyball, so I knew about that, and I figured, how hard can it be to wheel your chair?"

Tim used his creativity to adapt his drills and game plan but essentially he kept the game the same. "After the two-week period they didn't kick me off," he chuckles. "So we ended up winning the National Volleyball Championship in 1977, '78, '79, and '80. We won the first year, which was amazing. I thought it would take us a couple of years to get up to speed."

In 1981 the league folded, but by then Tim's team was literally toying with the other teams. His coaching methods worked. The others were hitting the ball back across the net the first time. Tim, by not compromising for the wheelchairs, encouraged his players to hit the ball three times and go for accuracy of placement. It took more skill, but it won games.

Tim decided early on that if he was going to coach wheelchair sports, he wanted the experience of playing. When the men's wheelchair basketball team was short a man for practice, he filled in. The first time he sat in a chair was the day the men went on a ten-kilometre training push around Stanley Park. "I remember I counted the blisters on my hands when I was finished," Tim says. "I think I had 40 or 50. I'd wheel for a while, and then I'd change my grip a little bit. And I was covering my hands with my shirt. By the end my hands were just covered—they were like raw hamburger. The boys thought that was pretty funny."

But he had earned his spot as a stand-in wheelchair basketball player. "So I'd go to practice," he says. "I'd played basketball in high school, of course. I loved basketball. I loved any sport really." From filling in, he went on to being the basketball equipment manager, then assistant coach, and then in 1989 he coached the provincial team for the first time.

During the summer of 1977 Rick Hansen also met Terry Fox and asked him to join the wheelchair basketball team and the volleyball team. With his knowledge of physiology, Tim helped Terry with his running training. Rick was also getting involved in track at about the same time. He loved volleyball and basketball, but he realized that as long as he played team sports he would have to rely on other people for his success. If he went into track, road racing, and marathon he could be successful on his own. "So he dragged me along as his track and road racing coach," Tim says. "My knowledge of phys ed and my career as a runner with the Nanaimo Track and Field Club and the general jogging I did on the side helped me. In fact, the first thing I did in this coaching was to look up some methods for cross-country skiing and cycling because those are the two areas where you get glide."

In 1980 Tim left Vancouver to teach at Selkirk College in the Kootenays and adopted Castlegar as his second home. He loved the wild and beautiful country that in many ways reminded him of his childhood in Sudbury. He hiked and skied and played all the sports he loved. He taught physical education for three years and adult special education for one year.

Meanwhile, Rick Hansen had decided to go on his world Man In Motion World Tour to raise awareness of spinal cord injuries. As his coach, it was simply understood that Tim would come back to Vancouver, help Rick train intensively, and go with him. In 1984 Tim went back, and in March 1985 Rick, Tim, and a very small entourage set off from Oakridge in south Vancouver towards Bellingham in Washington state. Despite their lengthy training, neither Tim nor Rick really knew what the following weeks and months held in store. "I think we both had these grandiose dreams of this huge welcome home and maybe a million dollars or something like that as a legacy," Tim recalls. "I think the cause was not as important to me at the time as the friendship with Rick and the coaching challenge. It was my belief in Rick's character. The spinal cord research stuff—that was nice—but I was a young man. I thought I was invincible. I don't think I really appreciated the need for spinal cord research. I understood the need for more rehabilitation and wheelchair sports, but the concept of a cure was so remotely possible I felt, 'Let's get it started and make rehab a bit better and maybe one day, but not in our lifetimes.' Simply stated, I was his coach."

Rick held to his belief that a wheelchair would one day be a curiosity in a museum—a relic of the past. For him, that was what the world tour was about.

Tim, Rick, Rick's cousin Lee Gibson, and Don Alder, Rick's old childhood friend, set off down Oak Street, their heads and hearts full of excitement. People were lining the streets. Tim was in tears. In his mind was a picture of coming back home to Vancouver with the streets lined with people. "Rick and I had had this idea that maybe we'd have to stay in the back of my truck and that's how we'd get around the world—sleep in the back. It wasn't even a camper; it was a canopy. But we'd do it. We had this dream that he would wheel and I would cycle around the world, and we'd have this great adventure. We got smacked right in the face in the first few days."

The weather was awful. No matter which way they faced, they were wheeling into the wind and the rain. Every day Rick got a new, nagging injury. "It was a bit of a shocker," Tim recalls. "But you know, we were committed. We were in for the long haul."

The schedule called for Rick to wheel 70 miles for each of three days and then take one day off. Each day of wheeling, Rick would take a break after every 23 miles. The days started at six in the morning and finished at eight at night. Each new ache or pain meant seat or wheel adjustments, but they never found the right position. "It's just so demanding on the body to do that much," Tim says. "It was really tough—really tough."

The crew rotated through the jobs of driving the truck, doing advance route reconnaissance, chair repairs, and being with Rick. At the end of the day, everyone was exhausted and collapsed into his hotel room except Don and Tim, who stayed up late every night, trying to make the right adjustments to Rick's chair. They were lucky if they slept three hours.

It was somewhere in Oregon, early on in the campaign, that Amanda Reid, Rick's physiotherapist, joined the team. "We were bloody thrilled when she joined us," Tim says. "We were phoning the sports medicine guys all the time, and she agreed to come down for a few days. It was somewhere in California that she decided to come on full-time, and Don and Lee and I just jumped for joy. We had to provide Rick with his emotional support as well as the food and the ice and all the information, and it was overwhelming. When she came, we thought, 'Oh man, we've got it made. She can give him the caring he needs and we can get on with fixing the chairs.'"

They wheeled down to San Diego and across to Florida. Wherever they went, they collected money for the cause, and on a good day they might get $100. "One day we didn't get anything," Tim recalls. "I actually put money in so that Rick wouldn't know we didn't get anything that day—then we could at least have a record of having gotten some money every day."

When they arrived in Florida, Tim flew ahead to England to make advance arrangements for the arrival of the rest of the party. But the first thing he did was fall into bed and sleep for twenty hours. From England they travelled to the Continent. In Europe, the team member responsible for reconnaissance and route planning dropped out of the tour, and Tim took over that duty as well. On his day off, Tim would drive ahead and chart the course for the next three days. "I got really, really tired," he says. "And I started making little mistakes. I didn't even know they were mistakes because I was so sleep deprived."

Somewhere in Germany, eight months after setting out, Tim and Rick realized that Tim could no longer carry on. "I was really exhausted," Tim says. "We looked at some possible solutions, but I had one of these epiphanies, which really—honest to God—just changed my life incredibly. All throughout this time I was doing it all for Rick, because I really believed in the guy. I felt that my job as a coach is essentially a helping profession. I put my needs aside to look after his needs. He was the show. Without him, we had no tour, but he was also a great guy, so I was 100 percent committed. And when you're a sports guy, the idea of quitting something is just the worst thing you could ever imagine … But at some point I had this epiphany, where I realized that Rick was more important to me than I was. And I realized that he was more important to himself than I was. And at some point I realized if I'm not more important to myself than anyone else, then I can't care for those other people effectively. It was a tremendous turning point in my life, and I decided, 'Okay, I've done my job.'"

He had stuck by Rick through all the training and planning and through the earliest and most gruelling days of the tour. He had done everything he could to help him, and he knew Rick would be fine: he would survive and finish the tour. "I had to start looking at *my* goals," Tim says.

He went to Switzerland for a few weeks to recuperate. Years before, his father had told him that prior to going to England, the Fricks had come from the little Swiss town of Frick, so it suddenly seemed as good a place as any to rest and kick back. Tim quickly became known as Herr Frick from Frick. He kept a journal and explored his thoughts and feelings. But he soon heard that there was a local men's volleyball team in town and he dropped in to a practice session. The team was pleased to have him; for Tim, it was just fun to play again.

He flew back home from Switzerland and after a brief stay, travelled to Australia and New Zealand, where he knew he could join Rick again. In New Zealand he bought a bicycle and cycled along with Rick for a while and then joined him again briefly in Australia.

Six months later, Tim came back home and looked for work. It was the spring of Expo '86 and Vancouver was buzzing with excitement. He applied for a one-year job at Douglas College as a replacement for a physical-education teacher on leave, and the year stretched on. He's still there and thinks of Douglas College as his home. "This is a great job," he says. "I'm working with talented young people who want to be phys ed teachers and coaches. I have the freedom to be creative and try exciting innovative things in the way of teaching. I can really be responsible for my own area. I can't imagine doing anything else. My party line now is, 'They pay me to go to meetings; teaching I do for free.'"

That same year, 1986, Tim became reacquainted with Gerry Phillips, a former classmate from UBC. Within two years they had formed a permanent and lasting relationship.

In March 1987, the Man in Motion World Tour came back to Canada. Tim met Rick and his entourage at the B.C./Alberta border and travelled with them for a few days. When Rick toured up through Williams Lake, Tim joined him again for the celebration of Rick arriving in his hometown. When he travelled through the Kootenays, Tim joined him again, and on the last day, when Rick returned to the city that he had left two years earlier, Tim drove the motor home. Rick wanted the crew that had toured with him to ride outside with him and to savour every second of that incredible time.

"Do you remember what that was like?" I ask.

"It was just unbelievable," Tim says. "In my wildest dream I had seen the streets packed with people. I had not pictured them hanging out of the windows and just being armed to the street. I think on the last day they figured there were over 200,000 people lining the streets. Vancouver has never had anything like that. It was like déjà vu all over again: it was just like I had pictured. I wasn't emotional or anything. It was like, yes, this is what we figured would happen and nobody believed us."

The Man in Motion World Tour raised $24 million. They'd come a long way from the day Tim tossed his own money in the hat so that Rick wouldn't have to know no one had donated to his cause that day of the tour. "Those were very special times," Tim says. "To go back to Rick's home town, and my adopted area, and the B.C. border, and then the last day—for me, that was what I needed to bring closure to it."

In 1989, Tim was on the B.C. senior men's championship volleyball team as a player/coach because he had decided the only coaching he would do was in that capacity. In December of that year he was asked to do an interview for a book by the provincial sport branch on the success of B.C. coaches. "I can't remember the name of the lady who interviewed me," he says. "But she interviewed me for eight hours, and after eight hours talking about coaching and how I loved it, the next morning—and this is coincidence here—I got a call from a lady named Mary Jane Waugh, who was in charge of the National Women's Wheelchair Basketball program. She asked, 'Are you interested in coaching the women's national wheelchair basketball team?'"

"Oh, man, you've gotta be kidding me," Tim said. "I'm retired. I've coached Rick Hansen, I've coached Terry Fox. I quit now! What more can I possibly do?" Mary Jane refused to hang up until Tim had said, "Okay, I'll think about it."

She called back and explained that the women's program had had major problems after the Paralympics in Seoul, Korea. Tim didn't care about the details. All he knew was that the team had broken up and there literally was no women's wheelchair basketball program. The World Championships were in August 1990, which was less than a year away. If Canada was to compete, they needed someone to put the program back together.

"Okay, here's what I'll do for you," Tim said. "I'll run all the camps and events. I'll promise you we'll have a fantastically positive experience, put the program back on it's feet again, and you can get a coach to take it from there." He told Mary Jane Waugh the same thing in 1991 and in 1992 and every year until 1996, when he said, "Okay, I'll go until 1998." In 1998 he said, "Okay, 2000." In 2000 he said, "Look, I'll stay on until you and the team are tired of me."

It's doubtful they'll ever get "tired" of him: He is the winningest coach in the history of the game. Since late 1990, his team has not lost a sanctioned game. At the first World Championship, less than a year after Tim started working with the team, they entered the tournament as the underdog and won the bronze medal. "I still thought we played pretty crummy," he says. "But the team was back in positive territory in terms of attitudes and commitments." The semifinal game they lost, which preceded their winning the bronze medal, was the last sanctioned game the team has lost. That record was true as of the day I interviewed Tim in spring 2002.

In 1991 Tim's team played in a sanctioned tournament and finished with a record of 8–0. In 1992, at the Paralympics in Barcelona, Spain, the team squeaked by Australia, Germany, and the Netherlands by a point or two to meet the heavily favoured U.S. team in the final game. The U.S. team had trounced the Canadians the previous year. "They had a heckuva good team," Tim says. "They were the reigning world champions, and we beat them."

Tim had two assistant coaches: Joe Higgins and Barb Griffin. "They were one of the major reasons we won that game," Tim says.

"They did the strategy and the planning. I knew that I wasn't technically good enough at that point to lead the team to victory. I figured my only chance was to bring in a guy like Joe, who was a technical genius, and sort of give up some of that control that coaches often get carried away with—and so, we won. It was an unbelievable upset—a huge upset!"

"Did it feel good?" I ask.

"I think Joe and I were emotionally exhausted. We were happy, no question about that, but we were absolutely—well, tears of joy would be the correct phrase."

In 1994, at the World Championships in England, Tim's team once again beat the Americans in the final. "We weren't beating teams because we deserved to beat them," he says. "We were just mentally better prepared. With my physiology knowledge I knew I could have the team fit. Technically, I was still growing in the sport, and I wasn't as confident, and the team wasn't as technically good as the rest of the world. But the one thing I can do better than anybody is mentally prepare my team. Psychology was my second major in university. I know sports psychology. I knew, guaranteed, that I would have the best mentally prepared team anywhere and that's what carried us through in 1994."

In 1996 the Canadian team was the favourite in the Paralympics and continued their winning streak. In 1997, the American's Qualifying Tournaments were added to the circuit, and Tim's team won. In 1998, they travelled to Australia to compete in the Gold Cup, and once again the Canadian team met the Americans in the final. At half time, the U.S. team was up by one point. "My normal half-time speech, I go into the locker room, look around, and I say, 'I don't see a guy here handing out the gold medals,'" Tim says. "This time I go into the locker room. We're playing great. They're playing great. I'm out of ideas. I say to my team, 'Look you guys, we're not going to make any major changes here. We're playing great. They're playing great. If they can keep that up for the whole game, then there's nothing we can do about it.'"

Tim decided to be just a bit more aggressive on defense when they started the second half. The Americans continued to play flawlessly. Within minutes, Tim's team was down by five points and the score was 35–30. "What the hell do I do now?" Tim asked his assistant coach, Jo Anne Burleigh. "We're doing everything we should do, and the Americans are still bloody winning."

Jo Anne had no magic answer. "Don't panic," she said. "Just stay with it."

Tim did the only thing he could do: he remained mentally focussed, and he stayed with the program. Then, somehow, his team began to score. With five minutes left in the game, they were ahead by eleven points, and Tim decided to prepare his team for the obvious opposition strategy. He expected the other team to foul his players, force them to the foul line, hope for a miss, get the ball back, and come back to score. He called a time out and huddled with the team. "Look, here's the press break."

"But they're not pressing," the team said.

"Yes, but they're going to. Look at the score. They're going to start fouling you."

The team turned to look at the scoreboard.

"They couldn't believe they were ahead," he recalls. "They have no idea they're ahead. They're just playing the game for the love of the game. They're in 'the zone.' So we end up winning 54–36. It was just incredible."

In 1999, Tim's team won the America's Qualifying Tournament again. In the 2000 Paralympics in Sydney, the Canadian women were favoured to win, and they were counting on it. Most teams would have been afraid to play against Australia in their hometown but not the Canadians. "This is why mentally we're so tough," Tim says. "You know there's going to be a packed gym, and they're going to be pumped. But our dream was to play Australia in the final game. Then nobody could say, 'Well they got lucky this time or they got lucky that time.' If we play the top team in their home gym in the last game ... if we can win this one, then we are truly the best. That was our goal."

The dream came true. They won most of their games by margins of fifteen to twenty points and faced Australia in the last game. By half time they were up 23–13 and won by a margin of nineteen points. "It was a fabulous win," Tim says. "Everybody got to play, and everybody played well. It was a tremendous victory."

As the years went by, it became financially easier for Tim to teach and coach. There is now a series of National Sport Centres across Canada sponsored by Sport Canada, the Canadian Olympic Association, the Coaching Association of Canada, and various levels of government. The sports centres provide support and funding for athletes and coaches. The National Sport Centre in Greater Vancouver has also formed a partnership with the B.C. Wheelchair Basketball Society, the B.C. Wheelchair Sports Association, and the Canadian Wheelchair Basketball Association; funding from these organizations pays for Douglas College to release Tim for part-time coaching. Douglas College provides the facilities. Tim says the funding made all the difference. "To be honest, you can't coach at that level and still work. I worked full-time for a couple of years and still did the coaching, and man, it just about killed me."

Tim's strategy was to take a year's leave of absence and spread it over two years, which in effect meant taking a pay cut so that he could coach the national team. There was a small honorarium available of $3,000 a year, which Tim would use to buy something useful like a new video camera. When the coaching honorarium went up to $8,000, he banked the money and used it to buy time off during the critical weeks of the season.

"The National Sport Centre was my salvation," he says "They brought some more money to the table, so now I teach approximately half-time and I coach full-time. Now it's more like a normal lifestyle. It's rejuvenated my life as a coach, and it's given me tremendous joy in coaching. I can't wait to get to practice. After all these years—after having retired—most people my age are giving it up or are burned out, and I'm just absolutely loving it. At some point in my life I realized coaching was something I was okay at, and so the opportunity to coach virtually as my job is unbelievable. Some of the courses I teach are coaching courses. What more could a guy ask for?"

Tim also teaches an adapted physical education course for people with disabilities. "And that's become another passion: the whole area of disability awareness. You're hanging around with guys like Rick, and you go to these events with blind guys, and you get to know people and start talking and discussing social issues and medical issues—all kinds of issues. And at some point I decided that would be the field I would devote some time and energy to. If I can contribute to society somehow—that's a good way to do it." Tim believes that coaching itself is a social issue because a coach can be a powerful role model. It's a responsibility he takes seriously.

Tim played such a large role in so many people's lives that in 1998 he received the Order of British Columbia. He was cited for his contribution to wheelchair sports, including his many hours of volunteer work coaching wheelchair athletes in volleyball, basketball, and track and field. Even during his busiest times with the women's national team, he always found time to volunteer in many of the other wheelchair sports events. "It was an incredible honour," Tim says. "And I was awfully young and I was thinking, 'Are you sure?' And the other people who get it are these famous people who do these famous things. But on the other hand, I was also thinking, 'Isn't it neat that they recognize a guy like me in the trenches?' That makes the Order of B.C. even more meaningful. Usually it's the big names that get the press—the Rick Hansens and so on, and deservedly so—but for a little guy in the trenches to receive the honour and get recognized for those contributions that aren't so public and spectacular, I thought that was very meaningful and neat."

Tim's father, Tony, went to the ceremony at Government House in his military uniform, wearing the medals he had earned during his years of service during the Second World War. "He was a huge sensation," Tim recalls.

When it was Tim's turn to take the stage and his biography was read out, including his team's winning streak, the audience broke into spontaneous applause and cheering. "I thought, 'Isn't that typical of Canadians? We don't put a lot into sport, but we really do love sport.' That's what really got people excited: a sporting achievement, and in women's wheelchair basketball, which none of them had probably ever seen."

Tim has made a conscious decision to stay with women's wheelchair basketball even though he could easily have switched to the men's team years ago. "These women athletes are under-served. This is another chance to contribute to the social fabric."

One of his rules is that his assistant coaches must be women. There have been times when for unforeseen circumstances he has hired a male coach, but generally he works hard to give the job to women. Like the other causes Tim champions, he says he did not set out to be an advocate for women, but he couldn't work with them day after day or coach them for so many years and not become a believer.

"It seems to me you started off a jock and became a social advocate," I say.

Tim laughs. "You know, it's funny. When I read those coaching biographies in high school, I wanted to find out what made a successful coach. How can I win? I was looking for techniques or a magical recipe. And you know what it was? It boiled down to one thing: the coaches had an intense personal interest in the well being of their players on and off the court. That was the recipe for success." Tim has been working with the same recipe for more than 30 years.

Several years ago he picked up the newspaper and read about a high school coach who had just taken his team to the provincial championship. The coach was one of Tim's former students, and he was quoted as saying that it was his intense personal interest in his players that made him a successful coach. "I think it was the greatest thing that ever happened to me," Tim says. "Seeing that same concept. You could read between the lines and see what the quote was—he had taken that intense personal interest in his players."

Over the years Tim has developed deep friendships with his coaches and players, and sometimes it's hard, he says. "You have to select the teams. You have to cut people, and when you're cutting people who are fabulous friends of yours—that's difficult. But you know what? I'd rather do that than have the nagging feeling that someone was cut from a team and thought I didn't care. I couldn't live with that."

Through all the hard work, it's Gerry that Tim credits with making it all possible. She supported him without question and brought him the peace of mind he needed off the court and track. "Without her I would have self-destructed," he says.

In March 1998, Tim's mother died of cancer. His father died in the summer of 2000, but before he died, Tim and Tony set up the Mary and Tony Frick Memorial Scholarship. With money donated by friends and family, and matched by the college, scholarships worth $3,000 were given to future coaches in 2002.

The first year of the scholarship, Tony was still alive. Each year Tim hopes to manage to give the scholarships away and not lose his composure. He has not yet been successful at keeping the tears inside. "Establishing that scholarship fund is what I am most proud of. I remember being in university, and I remember how much a dollar is worth. Seeing those students getting those cheques for $500 or $1,000 is just the thrill of a lifetime. You know these kids are good kids. You know they aren't going to spend it on drugs or booze. It's going to go to living and to becoming what they can be in life. It's a great feeling."

Dr. Roger Tonkin:
Advocate for Youth

I didn't choose to interview Dr. Roger Tonkin just because he is well known for his work with teenagers with eating disorders, but I'm sure it was a factor. It's a subject in which I have a personal interest, because I suffered from anorexia nervosa when I was much younger and I know how difficult it is to treat.

I take the ferry from Nanaimo to Gabriola Island and drive to Dr. Tonkin's waterfront home. It's a chilly, early spring day, but the sun is shining through the windows of his "West Coast" home with its high ceilings, hardwood floors, and northeast view of Georgia Strait. When I meet Roger I notice that his face, although lined, is youthful. Perhaps his many years of working with youths has kept him young, I think as we shake hands.

Roger Tonkin was just a kid himself—eleven years old—when he chose to become a doctor. He didn't make the decision because he wanted to help people or because he wanted recognition and awards. "I picked medicine because it was the hardest and best thing I could think of to do." Eleven-year-old Roger could not have predicted how hard or how good that choice would turn out to be, but it seems he was determined to find out.

Roger was born on October 31, 1936, in Montreal, where he and his younger sister grew up in the city's Anglophone community. His mother stayed home to look after the family while his father worked for the same insurance company all his life, retiring with a gold watch. Roger's parents had come to Canada from Cornwall,

Dr. Roger Tonkin

England, before the Second World War broke out. They had promised themselves that they would return "home" regularly—a promise they didn't fulfil until 1948, when they travelled to Cornwall. Roger, his mother, and his sister stayed for a year, and his father returned to Montreal to work. Roger had hoped that the year in England would be one long, extended holiday, but his mother quickly shattered his expectations. "They didn't just put me into school; they put me into an English school to boot," he laughs. "And I have to confess that up until that time I was a rather mediocre student. I have memories of sitting in the back of the class and not being very appreciated by my teachers. But I went to school, and I surprised myself by doing very well."

Roger believes he did well because at his new school he discovered a talent for mental arithmetic. He also remembers that he wanted to prove to his parents that he was good, at least as good as his sister. He also wanted to live up to or surpass the achievements of his father, who had competed for and won a coveted scholarship to the local grammar school when he was a boy. Roger's teachers gave him only the slimmest chance of winning such a scholarship because he was the youngest admissible age and because he was Canadian. "In fact, I fooled them all and got the scholarship, and everyone was quite titillated with that," Roger recalls. "I was very proud. I remember my grandfather, a very austere man, giving me a shilling, which is the only time he ever gave me anything. I guess it was quite an accomplishment. That taught me that if I worked hard I could do stuff, and that's when I decided to be a doctor. I didn't know what being a doctor involved. If I'd know then, I would have done what my grandfather did, which was to become a fisherman on the boats." He laughs at the memory, and I notice how easily his face falls into these deep crease lines, as though laughter were the expression with which his face is most familiar.

At the end of a year in Cornwall, Roger's parents gave him the choice of remaining in England to go to school or returning home with his mother and sister. He chose to go home because, Roger says with a chuckle, "I'm a Canadian. To put it bluntly—I knew I wasn't a little Brit." They returned to one of many unprepossessing flats his parents rented and moved into every three years. Like so many Montreal families, the Tonkins would sign a three-year lease, at which time the landlord inevitably raised the rent, and the family would move to a flat with a more reasonable rent for another three years, at which time the cycle was repeated. Because of the frequent moves Roger's parents accumulated few possessions. They did not own a stereo or a television—only the bare necessities they could pack quickly and move easily to another flat.

Roger completed Grade Seven, but instead of attending West Hill High School with his friends, he chose to enrol in the High School of Montreal, across the street from McGill University, because it had a better academic standing. He planned to finish his four years of high school and go straight into medicine at the university across the road. "Whatever happened in England must have spilled over," he says. "I did quite well through the rest of my secondary education, taking several prizes. I was never one to take the top prize, but I would always come a strong second."

The year Roger graduated, the school created a new award to recognize a student for his all-around contributions, and he received that first award. "I really didn't understand the import of it at the time," Roger says. "I was embarrassed. I can remember standing up on stage, and then when I got back down to my seat, my best buddy said to me, 'Roger, your face was sure red.'"

Overall, he recalls his high school years as "very seminal." He remembers an English essay assignment on The Group of Seven, and although he knows that he didn't fully appreciate how revolutionary these artists were, he felt deeply drawn to their work. When he received excellent marks for his project, he realized he had the ability to be creative as well as persistent and that imagination could take him farther than hard work alone.

Roger graduated from high school at age sixteen. One hot sunny day during the summer break before entering university, he was sitting on the porch with his best buddy talking about the future. He doesn't recall who had the idea first but one of them said, "To heck with school. Let's get jobs and then go and tour Britain."

"Part of the lure for me was that I wanted to go back to Cornwall," Roger laughs. "I loved Cornish cream."

He worked for a year in the quality-assurance department of a local textile mill, and though he thought of the job as "mind-numbingly boring," he liked being in the work environment. At the end of the year he and his friend had saved enough money, so they travelled to England, where they bicycled through the countryside.

While he was away, his father's company moved him to Toronto. When Roger returned from his trip, he came back to a suburban house near Burnhamthorpe and Highway 27 in the west end of the city. For Roger, who considered himself a Montrealer through and through, being stuck in one of the remotest suburbs of a city he didn't like was an enormous disappointment. What made him even more frustrated was that Ontario required five years of high school and Roger had to go back for one more year after having graduated near the top of his class in Montreal.

As the months went by, his dislike of Toronto grew. Then his mother was diagnosed with renal tuberculosis and was sent to the sanatorium in Weston, a northern suburb almost ridiculously impossible to reach if one didn't own a car, which the Tonkins did not.

Roger found it hard to apply himself to his schoolwork, but near the end of a year of mediocrity he decided to prove how well he could do if he wanted to. One day, while he was working at a lab table, he said to the other students near him, "I'm going to be in the top ten come graduation time."

"Oh sure," they said.

Regardless of their scepticism, he studied diligently for six weeks before exam time and graduated third in his school. "For me, the take-home message was, if you work hard enough and you're realistic, you can get your goals," he says.

With good marks, Roger entered premed at the University of Toronto (U of T), and he should have done well, but he found himself struggling to keep up. "It was something about my schooling or about me as an adolescent," he says. "I didn't like being a student, and I particularly didn't like being a student at U of T. In fact, I had to write supplemental exams, and I had never failed an exam in my life. Part of it was that I was working, but part of it was that I had reached a level where power-braining my way through wasn't enough."

While he struggled with school, his mother was released from the sanatorium and his father was transferred back to Montreal. Roger could have stayed in Toronto, but for him the move back was an opportunity to study at McGill University, which had a reputation for teaching the Oslerian tradition of medicine, named after the humanist doctor William Osler. Roger thought of McGill as a humanist medical school and U of T as a technical institution. He applied to study medicine at McGill and was accepted, but almost immediately afterwards he failed another exam in Toronto and lost his place. He went back to Montreal anyway, determined to reapply to McGill the following year.

While he waited, he took various courses at McGill, including a first-year introductory course in sociology. He did so well that his professor pulled him into his office and said, "Why are you wasting your time going into medicine?"

"I thought about that a bit during the course of that year," Roger recalls. "Was I making a mistake? And I thought, 'No, this is what I wanted to do—I wanted to go into medicine.' And a piece of that was the eleven-year-old boy saying, 'You set your goal and you're going to get it.'"

Roger finally entered McGill's medical school in 1957 and discovered that he enjoyed working with patients. He also liked anatomy and histology and was so good in those subjects that he could have chosen a career in research. The McGill School of Medicine trained specialists. Roger had originally planned to become a neurosurgeon, but after watching several operations he realized he would never have the patience to do such painstaking work, so he ruled out surgery. His other options were internal medicine, pediatrics, psychiatry, or obstetrics/gynecology He chose pediatrics because during his second year he discovered he had an affinity for children.

He had moved out of his parents' house and did odd jobs to support himself until he got a position at the Montreal Children's Hospital that gave him a small salary and a room. For the next two years he worked every second night; during his fourth year he also did ward duty. There were weeks when he rarely slept. His schoolwork suffered, but he had found his niche with the children.

Because of the long hours he worked, Roger knew he wouldn't be in the top of his class, but he also knew he was too smart to be in the bottom, so he aimed for the middle. Near the end of his last year, he had to make a presentation before the fellow in medicine and the resident in medicine. The students had been assigned into teams with each member taking one part of the assignment. Roger was to handle the lab report for his team, so he worked right through the night before the presentation and in the morning he was exhausted.

"I came to the presentation ill prepared, and it showed. I had done enough work to cover my butt on the part I was assigned, but I should have known better. These two guys were terrors. They started pushing me in related aspects that I hadn't covered. At the end of the discussion, in front of all my classmates, they said 'We don't understand how you ever got into med school, and we're not sure you should graduate.'"

Roger was distressed and embarrassed, but he turned his anger into a determination to prove them wrong. He didn't graduate with great distinction, but he did finish his four years. Since he had worked so hard, he decided to intern at a non-teaching hospital where the pace was less demanding, preferably on the West Coast. He had externed one summer at Lion's Gate Hospital in North Vancouver and had liked it so much, he had come home imagining a future that included a beautiful waterfront home in West Vancouver and a pediatric consulting practice.

Roger went to St. Joseph's Hospital in Victoria in 1962, where he met his first wife, Patricia. He was the only single male intern at the hospital, and he remembers that the nuns and his fiancé's family spoiled him rotten. He had never been so well fed or offered so many chocolates at the nursing stations. Within a few months he had gained 30 pounds. He was happy, not just with the attention, but also with the work he was doing.

"I used to do rounds of all the patients at the hospital with the night nurse. The night supervisor was a very experienced nurse. She could have run the place. She didn't need me. But when we were on rounds I would come out of a patient's room and I'd say, 'That one is going to be okay,' or I'd say, 'That one you're going to have to watch.' And I was just a first-year intern."

"Roger, how do you know that about the patient?" the nurse asked him during one round.

"I don't know," he replied. "I just know."

These days physicians rely on lab tests, Roger says, because it's the safe way. "Relying on your intuition is not playing safe. But in my opinion, if your intuition is good, it's safer for the patient."

At the end of his internship, he and Patricia moved back east, where he worked for three years as a pediatric resident at Montreal Children's Hospital. He would often get home at eight o'clock at night and be back on the ward at seven in the morning. Patricia worked as an operating-room nurse in the same hospital, and sometimes it seemed that all she did was feed him and put him to bed. There are whole sections of those years that Roger doesn't remember, except that he loved the work despite the long hours. What he loved best were the kids. "I didn't know it at the time, but when I think about it now ... you don't get very many chances in the practice of medicine to save a life, but you do when you're a resident at a place like Montreal Children's," he says. "Saving a life is a gift."

He adds that helping someone leave their life is just as important; it also takes compassion and humanity. When he was eleven years old, he may not have fully understood that being a good doctor required care, dedication, and humanity, but in retrospect, he suspects it was those elements that drew him to the profession.

At the end of his residency, Roger returned to the West Coast. He needed one more year to become a fellow of medicine, so he did six months as an adult neurology resident at St. Paul's Hospital in Vancouver and six months as a teaching fellow at the Health Centre for Children. He received his fellowship in the Royal College of Medicine and became an academic at the University of B.C. (UBC). Shortly after he took up his position, Dr. Sydney Israels, the department head, said to him, "I want you to apply for the Markle Scholar Award."

"I thought he had taken leave of his senses," Roger says. "Not only did I know people who had failed the fellowship time and time again, but I knew people from my training at Montreal Children's Hospital who were Markle scholars, and I knew I wasn't in their league. People who were Markle scholars went on to become deans and presidents of universities."

The Markle Scholar Award was instituted after the Second World War because the universities felt they needed to have some incentive to lure bright young men and women doctors into choosing an academic career. The award offered a way to top up the salary provided by the university. It was also a mark of prestige and distinction. The university department received the funding, and the bright young doctor got tenure at the end of five years.

Roger had doubts, but the medical school insisted on sponsoring him for the award, so he agreed to apply. He flew to Colorado Springs for the interview, and he won the award, becoming its last recipient. The

Markle foundation shifted its attention to children's television and communication in the following years.

A requirement of winning the Markle Scholar Award was for the recipient to present a plan for the allocation of the scholarship funds. Roger had given this some thought, so he proposed to create something that had never previously been tried: a community-based teaching unit of the hospital, which he called the REACH Centre (Research and Educational Attack on Community Health). The name "Attac" was taken from an existing group of young people who were activists on behalf of community health. REACH passed through the various approval levels of UBC, but when doctors in the community heard about it, they objected strongly, asking, "What right does this pediatrician have to get involved in primary care?"

The university went ahead regardless and gave Roger a choice of opening the teaching clinic in Kitsilano or the Grandview/Woodlands area on the east side of town. It was 1969, the height of Vancouver's hippie era, and Kitsilano was the city's version of San Francisco's Haight-Ashbury district. It was here that the men in their beards and beads and the young women in their flowing tie-dyed dresses sat for long hours in coffee shops or panhandled on the sidewalks. Roger didn't understand hippies. He wanted to get as far away from them as possible, so he chose to open his clinic on Vancouver's east side. He involved the family doctors in the community, who gradually came to see the value of having a teaching clinic in their neighbourhood.

Roger designed REACH to fill a void. In Montreal, families and children had always crowded the waiting rooms of the hospitals, which meant the residents there got plenty of experience treating them. In Vancouver, there was no emergency clinic for children. Pediatricians had private practices, so doctors had little opportunity to learn about caring for children. But his vision for REACH extended beyond dispensing basic medical care. He created a multi-disciplinary practice that involved social workers, psychologists, and public health officials, as well as medical staff. The waiting room of the clinic was always full, and although he did his best to remove it from the hippie neighbourhood, the young men and women found it and arrived in overwhelming numbers. There were so many of them that Roger had to set up a special Tuesday evening clinic to accommodate them in order to remove them from his daytime family clinics. He called the Tuesday night clinic "the youth clinic."

"In those days it was a bad scene for young people," he says. "We had a lot of draft dodgers who wouldn't get care because they were afraid they'd get picked up. We had a situation where the emergency department at VGH [Vancouver General Hospital] didn't want to take them because they had no medical insurance."

REACH took them. Roger may not have had much sympathy for hippies, but he cared about people, especially young people—and some of them were no older than thirteen or fourteen. "We didn't set up with them in mind," he says. "But we got them anyway, and as was typical with me I said, 'Well, we may as well adjust and adapt.' And we evolved one of the most exciting experiments—the people who were involved still talk about it."

The staff gathered every Tuesday night at one of the area restaurants before the clinic opened to discuss cases and strategies, and—in effect—became the de facto coordinating committee that eventually influenced the City of Vancouver to open the Pine Free Clinic. "We said it wasn't our job to do the City's job for them," Roger says. "Finally they actually agreed that that was the case."

At the same time, community health centres were beginning to open all across the country, and the downtown east side looked to REACH as a model for a clinic in their own neighbourhood. The East Side Clinic asked Roger to run their centre too, but he declined. "I'll give you advice," he said, "But I'm not going to run another community health centre."

In 1974 Roger left the clinic to look for new challenges. Dr. Israels suggested he consider the possibility of creating a child development centre. Roger visited various prestigious centres around the U.S. and came up with a proposal for a centre devoted to the study of childhood that would fall under the auspices of the graduate faculty of medicine at UBC. Roger and Dr. Israels obtained approval for the centre from the faculty and the board of governors at UBC and named it the Jack McCreary Centre, after the former dean of medicine at UBC, who was well-known for his interest in children.

Shortly afterwards, Dr. Israels asked Roger to take on adolescent medicine for a year while the chair of that department was on a sabbatical. Roger was reluctant. He had tried to avoid the hippies at

REACH, and here they were again; but, of course, that was Israels' argument. He said that Roger had worked with youths at REACH and knew what he was doing. Roger finally capitulated to Dr. Israels' request and agreed to look after adolescent medicine for a year; however, when his colleague came back from his sabbatical and went on to other things, Roger kept the brief.

He also kept himself informed on the developments of the McCreary Centre Society, which was beginning to make good progress when Dr. Sydney Israels died. His death was a big loss to everyone on the faculty of medicine. It was also a loss to the Jack McCreary Centre itself because without him as its champion, the child development centre became a low priority with the university. Roger, the United Way, and a small group of supporters managed to open the centre anyway through hard work and arduous fundraising.

In 1977 Roger took time to stop and question his future. He was working harder than ever while at the same time looking after five children and going through a divorce. "I made a career decision that I was to stay in Vancouver," he says. "But I took myself off the academic ladder in the sense that I was not going to be competitive for headships or deanships. You take yourself off the ladder, and they stop asking."

The adolescent medicine chairship that Roger had been so reluctant to take on soon became his passion. He did not consider himself an expert in the field of adolescent medicine. In fact, he says, "I had no training. When I started working with youths, I had no clue about who did what. I was told, here's the ward, do the rounds. And I didn't even want to do it." His practice was in the old Children's Hospital on 59th Street in cramped, inadequate quarters that were always full. When he did a survey of the city hospitals, he found there were enough adolescents to fill a ward, so he began to lobby for a purpose-built adolescent unit at the new Children's Hospital. "The basis of adolescent medicine is developmental," he argued. "It's a significant phase of the life cycle. It's the last phase in the cycle where there are major biological changes and the beginnings of major psychosocial changes. So it's a unique period."

He received little support in his fight to create an adolescent unit in the new hospital and came to the conclusion that adolescent health was the underdog of the health care system. He also noticed that although the medical and surgical care given to youths was excellent, it was not always humane or respectful, and definitely not multi-disciplinary. He soon became frustrated with the system that dictated that although he was the ward chief he had no right to interfere in the care given to the youths by their primary physicians. For him, protocol took second place to the kids. Love is too strong a word to describe his feelings for his young patients—he reserved love for his own children—but he cared about them deeply. He would do the rounds of the ward with the head nurse just to talk to the kids. One day he walked into a room where a young girl had had surgery to correct a curvature of the spine. "You don't look quite right," Roger said to her. The girl burst into tears, and the nurse gathered her into her arms and cuddled her into her bosom. And this was not an isolated incident; it was the sort of thing that happened almost every day.

Roger believed that if these youths were to get the care they needed, he would have to create his own adolescent unit, where he and his team could treat the patients holistically. He set up a Tuesday night youth clinic in a trailer on the hospital grounds with a nurse, an endocrinologist, a social worker, a psychologist, a nutritionist, and an occupational therapist, all of them working as volunteers. He took the concept of "holistic" care one step further when he said, "If we're going to have young people as clients, we need to have young people as greeters," and created a peer-helping program in the belief that youth helping youth would enormously benefit his patients.

The clinic ran on a shoestring budget for several years while the staff held onto a dream of a spacious unit in the new Children's Hospital. When the hospital was ready to open, the adolescent program was one of two teams that was ready to start immediately. But at that crucial moment the administration decided it didn't have enough money to run all its proposed programs and moved the youth clinic into a tiny room that was barely big enough to swing a stethoscope.

The team was demoralized. Roger's nurse left to take another position, and the rest of his staff moved into the little room in the new hospital. The conditions were deplorable. One day Roger was in the room with a gynecologist who was examining a young girl with her feet up in stirrups. Without even a knock on the door, the janitor walked in. That incident was symptomatic of the value placed on adolescent care. Roger felt he was fighting a constant uphill battle to have the youths' rights and confidentiality respected. Twenty-five years later he says, "I'd love to tell you that battle has been won, but it hasn't. It's getting better and it will get better, but it took a long, long time."

The new Children's Hospital had a 22-bed adolescent ward that quickly became the place where doctors put patients who didn't seem to fit in anywhere else. One of the youths sent to the unit was a young girl from Gabriola Island who had been referred by a top anorexia nervosa specialist. Soon more anorexia patients began to fill the beds, many of them as young as twelve or thirteen years old. The ward became the centre for anorexia nervosa in B.C. and soon Roger's youth clinic became an eating-disorders program.

Roger was supervising the ward and still running the clinic when the hospital decided it needed the little room and moved the clinic to a trailer on the grounds of Sunnyhill Hospital. Ironically, the trailer was the same one that the clinic had previously occupied on the site of the old Children's Hospital. Roger carried on with his work, and because he was still the executive director of the McCreary Society, he was able to interest them in eating disorders and get some support. "We began to stimulate people to look at the services for people of all ages with eating disorders in the province. We held seminars. It was a self-started multi-disciplinary kind of thing," he recalls.

He continued to struggle at the Children's Hospital. It seemed that whenever it was necessary to move a nurse, or a ward, or to free up space, the adolescent unit suffered. "We'd had a string of these closures, and it really didn't work very well," Roger says. "And I was convinced that we would have an accident sooner or later."

In an effort to find a solution to treat his young patients effectively, he came up with an unorthodox plan. He and Carrol, his new partner and wife-to-be, had recently bought a piece of oceanfront property on Gabriola Island, one of the southern Gulf Islands easily accessed from Nanaimo on Vancouver Island. Roger and Carrol thought, "Instead of commuting to Vancouver all summer, why not set up a camp here for the kids?"

They ran their first camp in 1988, putting the camp counsellors in a small, white cabin on the property, and setting up tents on the lawn by the ocean for the six anorexic girls they had brought from the hospital.

The girls did not go willingly, and their parents were anxious about what was going to happen to their children. Roger wanted to give the girls an ordinary camp experience to take them away from the anxieties and stresses that may have caused or contributed to their disease. One rule he made was, "No parent visits."

The first night of the camp, all six girls disappeared. Roger and Carrol were worried, but they also knew that they couldn't have gone far. The ferries had stopped running for the night, and with no streetlights to guide them, they would probably be stumbling around in the dark. Carrol and Roger found them within a couple of hours, and though they didn't try to run away again, they wrote letters home describing the harsh life they were living. Their parents began to telephone, demanding to know what was happening; so three weeks after the start of the program, Roger allowed one mother to visit. She arrived, expecting the worst, and saw exactly what Roger and Carrol had been watching from the windows of their house: a group of young teen-age girls laughing and giggling together and having a marvelous time. She went home, phoned all the other mothers, and said, "Stop worrying. They're doing fine."

At the end of six weeks, Roger decided the camp had had a positive effect on the girls. He believed he saw a change in them, and as a bonus, they had not been occupying expensive hospital beds while they were at the camp. The only problem was the location, because the lawn where they had pitched the tents faced northeast. When the winds blew, they brought a chill even on otherwise warm, summer days, and it was often much too cold for an anorexic teen with no body fat to protect her.

Roger convinced the hospital, various levels of government, and the Vancouver Foundation to carry on with the experiment. He bought an old six-bedroom farmhouse on Gabriola Island with his own money—his ultimate goal being to create the camp as a year-round residential treatment centre for eating disorders. He envisioned this as a place for youths whose families were so dysfunctional that they could not be treated successfully at home. But running the centre year-round required government funding, which Roger applied for but didn't receive. Still, he got enough funding to continue running the program each summer for eight years. It was not just for anorexics and bulimics, but also for obese youths, because Roger recognized obesity as an eating disorder despite the criticisms of his contemporaries in adult medicine, who believed obese people just had to shape up and eat less.

After the camp closed in 1996, Roger evaluated the results. Within three weeks of arriving at the camp, the girls would begin to shed their stress and relax. Their day-to-day contact was with counsellors, who treated them like any other camper, not like someone with a problem; Roger believed that attitude contributed significantly to the healing process. But the biggest thing that emerged out of the experiment was the importance of empowering parents in dealing with their children's anorexia. "The trouble with anorexia when it occurs in teenagers is that it disempowers the parents," he says. "The parents are demoralized and immobilized and don't know how they can get their children to eat. Ghandi brought a major nation to the table by starving himself. It's an incredibly powerful tool. What we learned in the process was that by empowering parents and de-emphasizing the hospital as a place to treat these kids, you could make a difference. You put kids into the hospital, and when they leave they're in great shape. Six weeks later they're back; it's like a revolving door. We didn't completely put a stop to that with the camp, but we greatly reduced the length of hospital stays and frequency of admissions."

Roger and Carrol made no money with the camp in eight years. In fact, they lost some, but Roger didn't care—what mattered was that it helped the kids. Some results of the camp couldn't be measured. Four of the original six girls still keep in touch with him, and every one of them is better and functioning well as an adult.

In March 1995 the Jack McCreary Centre hosted a meeting of the International Association of Adolescent Health and the Society of Adolescent Medicine. It was the largest international meeting in adolescent health ever held, with 1,600 delegates attending, including 500 youths from Canada and other countries. At the end of that conference, Roger's energy was drained, and in the fall of that year, he had an emergency bypass operation. "When you have emergency surgery you get a sense of your own vulnerability," he says. "You can't sit around and think you're going to die the next day, but you have to be prepared for dying."

His mother's death earlier that year had also brought him closer to a sense of mortality, and his grief over her loss probably contributed to his stress. He decided to leave his position with UBC to reduce his workload and to free up the funds to replace him. But it took six years to find that replacement, and even then it was only part-time.

In 1979 Roger had began another controversial project. Through the Jack McCreary Centre, he had created a Child Health Profile that was sent to the schools in the province and received major coverage in newspapers, radio, and television. In 1981, McCreary's "Violence in Adolescence" survey received similar attention. The research showed that 350 youths had died in one year in motor vehicle accidents and most of those accidents were preventable. As a result of the survey, the Jack McCreary Centre held a conference on risky behaviour and worked with the motor vehicle branch and the Insurance Corporation of B.C. to produce the *Co-Pilot Manual* for parents, which introduced the concept of a graduated licence and taught parents how to train towards one with their children.

By 1987 Roger had learned quite a bit about the adolescent health field when he attended a conference in Australia at which a Minnesota survey was presented on the connection between adolescent health status and misbehavior. "That's what we're going to do in B.C.," he promised himself. In 1990 the Jack McCreary Centre brought Dr. Bob Blum from Minnesota to Vancouver to talk about his survey. Then in 1992, with funding from the Vancouver Foundation, the Lions Gate Medical Research Foundation, and the B.C. Health Research Foundation, the centre designed its own survey, hired staff, and sent questionnaires to high schools across the province. No government money was involved.

A reporter from *The Vancouver Sun* somehow managed to get a copy of the Centre's survey and wrote a sensational story on the "sex and drugs" study. The story was the focus of a major debate in provincial legislature. The minister of education disavowed it, but Paul Ramsey, the minister of health, stood up in the House and said, "We believe this is important and we support it."

The 1992 survey involved 16,000 youths. In 1998 the Jack McCreary Centre survey included 26,000 youths. "It's become one of the best data sources on adolescents anywhere in Canada," Roger says. "What we learned from that was that it's safe to ask kids, and they take it seriously."

The surveys, he says, contained invaluable data about adolescents that will allow doctors to care for their young patients more effectively. Adolescent medicine is still on the bottom rung of the medical ladder, he adds, but that is beginning to change. "It's gone from not even being on the map to being at least in the bottom of the window."

Roger did everything he could to make people understand the importance of adolescent health. From the women's movement he learned that words are important, and for many years he campaigned to include the phrase "and youth" in programs aimed towards children. In June 2001, when the Canadian Pediatric Society issued a revised vision statement that used the words "children and youths," he considered those words a major triumph.

In July 1996 Roger retired from the university as the only full professor in adolescent medicine in English speaking Canada. In 1998 he was awarded the Order of British Columbia in recognition of his work. "You can't not feel honoured," he says. "But I've never seen myself as anybody extraordinary. You don't go into medicine to get medals."

In 1999, when Roger was on the advisory committee that selected that year's recipients for the Order of British Columbia, he understood the true import of the award. "Some of the people who were nominated were outstanding, and I began to realize how many outstanding people there are in this province who never get nominated. But what I also realized, and what I like about the Order of B.C., is that we didn't award people who just did their jobs. We awarded people who chose the path less travelled."

At the end of our interview, after I have put on my jacket and gathered up my notes and am walking towards the door, I say to him, "I was so interested in hearing you talking about those anorexic girls. I was anorexic years ago when I was young."

He doesn't pause or give any indication that he is surprised, but he asks me, "What made you stop?"

"I don't know," I say. "I think one day I just decided to start eating again."

"You know, that's the darn thing," he says. "That's what happens: sometimes they just decide to start eating all on their own." I don't think his acknowledgement that—to a large extent—anorexia nervosa remains an enigma somehow negates the years he worked with patients who were afflicted by it. It is the efforts of people like Dr. Roger Tonkin that significantly influence these adolescents to make such a life-saving choice.

Hilda Gregory, 1998

Hilda Gregory:
A Person of Faith and Action

*I*n 1999, 35 years after founding the Vancouver Oral Centre for Deaf Children, Hilda Gregory retired as its principal, but that doesn't mean she's idle. She fills her days by working to increase affordable housing in Vancouver and by volunteering as a peer mentor for the Kidney Foundation of Canada. Still, she admits that she does have more time to read and to enjoy the peace and solitude of her own company, and this is time alone she treasures.

I can see right away how reading must be important to her. When we sit at her small dining room table for our interview, she has to push aside a stack of papers and books to make room for my notepad. Her living room contains a lot of shelves crammed with so many books they have spilled out and are sitting in stacks on various end tables.

Hilda says that she never gets lonely. In fact, she doesn't understand people who are bored. She also says that she loves her apartment, and I can understand why, when she describes the crowded house she grew up in. She was born in Liverpool, England, on August 19, 1936, as the third of nine children. The family lived in a row house with three rooms on the ground floor, three bedrooms on the second floor, and a privy at the foot of the yard. Hilda shared a tiny bedroom with her two older sisters; the boys were in another bedroom. At one time or another the younger children shared with their parents. There was no privacy in the little row house and precious little quiet.

Alfred, her father, was a dock labourer. Each morning he went to the waterfront and stood in the crowd of men, hoping to be selected to work that day. The foreman would stand in front of the crowd and point his finger, "You … you … and you … you …" The men he pointed to worked that day. Because Hilda's father was a hard and conscientious worker, he rarely missed a day.

Her mother, Hilda, worked hard too: cooking, cleaning, shopping, doing laundry, tidying up, and urging her children to make something of themselves.

Hilda grew up being acutely aware of being poor. "I didn't like it," she says. "I can remember waiting for my father to come home on a Thursday with his pay packet before we could have a meal because my mother had no money left. So, it was fish and chips on a Thursday night."

The girls in the neighbourhood were expected to leave school at age fifteen or sixteen, get a job, and contribute to the family income. Then they would get married to a neighbourhood boy and move into a row house and have children of their own, repeating the cycle. "I wasn't interested in the typical things they would get involved in," Hilda says. "Somehow I felt that the other children accepted it and followed in their parents' footsteps. I didn't feel I fit in with the neighbourhood families. I know my eldest sister felt the same way—that there was something different. It didn't have to be this way."

Her mother was also not interested in having her children follow the usual pattern. She kept them busy by enrolling them in a host of after school activities. On Monday nights the girls went to a church club, where they participated in gymnastics and dancing. On Tuesday nights they attended Christian Endeavour, where they learned about God, the Bible, and the Christian faith. On Thursday nights they went to Brownies and Girl Guides, and on Friday nights the children went to the little "Free Church" church around the corner for more Christian studies.

Alfred was not a religious man, but Hilda's mother belonged to the Church of England. Although she rarely had time to go to services, she made sure her children attended regularly. She also sent them to the "Free Church" for Sunday school. What was important to the elder Hilda was not so much which faith her children believed in, but that they should grow up having one. Hilda experienced no great revelations in Sunday school, although she recalls that she always had a faith in God that came quite naturally to her.

Alfred and Hilda's children were too busy to get into trouble, but keeping them occupied wasn't enough for Hilda. She knew that if her children were to rise out of the poverty cycle, they would have to have a good education. She was prepared to continue to scrimp and cut corners if it meant her children could stay in school. There were two educational routes open to children in England. They went either to a secondary school to learn a trade, or to grammar school in preparation for college or university. Hilda was eleven years old when she took the eleven-plus exam that would determine whether she might go on to grammar school. She passed easily and attended a school that was a combination technical/ grammar school for two years before enrolling in the Holly Lodge Grammar School at age thirteen.

Holly Lodge drew its student population from many neighborhoods in Liverpool. Hilda's oldest sister, Joan, had also gone to school there. Like her sister, Hilda took the bus each day, leaving her own neighbourhood for the first time in her life. "There was a much wider cross-section of students at the school, so that helped emphasize that many of them came from much more comfortable or middle class families than we did," Hilda recalls. "It was hard in many ways. It wasn't anything I talked about at that time. Joan and I talked about it much later—we both felt different."

Alfred and Hilda had barely managed to get the money to buy uniforms for the girls, and there was no money for extras. When the other children at school talked about their holidays, Hilda could not add to the conversation because the idea of going on a family holiday was unthinkable. She received no pocket money like most of the other students; but at the same time, she never heard either parent say, "No you cannot go on because we can't afford to have you stay in school."

Hilda earned a bit of pocket money by delivering newspapers every morning before school and every afternoon when she arrived home. She used the money to treat herself to an occasional movie or play. "I can remember—when I was about fifteen or sixteen—running around, delivering the papers on a Saturday because I had arranged with a friend that we would go to the repertory theatre at the Liverpool Playhouse," she recalls. "I raced to get my paper route done, so I could catch the bus. For a shilling, we could stand at the back to see the play."

When she was sixteen, Hilda went to see a film called *Mandy,* starring the actor Jack Hawkins. Hilda usually didn't care much about the story line as long as she could sit in the darkened theatre and gaze dreamily at her favourite movie idol. The film was based on a true story about a young couple who had had their first baby and discovered that the child was deaf. The mother was determined that her child should have an education and embarked on a search for a school that could help her, but the father and grandparents were protective of the child and afraid of exposing her to the world. The mother disregarded her husband's fears and found a school in Manchester, affiliated with the university and doing work with deaf children. She met with the headmaster—this was when the dreamy Jack Hawkins made his appearance—and learned that her toddler could learn to talk. So, she enrolled her child in the school and left her home to go to Manchester, despite the conflict it caused in the family. The film ended dramatically and tearfully when the little girl spoke her first word.

When the lights in the theatre came back on, Hilda thought, "That's what I want to do. I want to teach deaf children to talk."

At school the next week she talked to her English teacher, Miss Bufton, about her desire to teach deaf children. Miss Bufton said, "Why don't you contact the Liverpool School for the Deaf and go and visit them?"

Hilda went to the school and watched the teachers in action. "Yes," she thought. "This is what I want to do." Her next question was, "What do I have to do in order to become a teacher of deaf children?" Miss Bufton advised her to first become a teacher, and then go to Manchester University for specialized training.

When Hilda graduated from grammar school at age eighteen, she left home to enter Alsager Teachers College in Cheshire, where she lived in residence. For the first time in her life she had a room of her own. She recalls that being able to study with no noise surrounding her was absolutely heavenly! At home she had to either study at the noisy and crowded kitchen table or retreat to her bedroom, which was freezing cold in the winter because there was no central heating. "I've had a room of my own ever since," she laughs. "I don't share with anybody. I love my own space!"

Hilda did well at school, but she did not consider herself an academic because she didn't enjoying learning for the pure sake of increasing her knowledge; she had to have an application for studies. "One of the things I've discovered about myself," she says, "is that if I have a goal in mind, I'm very tenacious. I don't give up easily. If I have an idea or a goal and I get the strong sense that something can be achieved, I'll go after it. When I need to be, I'm a very focussed person, and I can be very disciplined."

When she graduated and qualified as a teacher, Hilda's advisor said, "Don't go straight on to Manchester University to specialize. Teach hearing children before you get into deaf education so that you have a base to work from."

Looking back, Hilda says the advice was invaluable. In August 1956 she started teaching her first class of five-year-olds in a regular school. She enjoyed it so much that in her third year she realized she had better apply to Manchester University before she became too comfortable and was tempted to stay where she was. She sent for the application forms, went through the interview process, and took up residency at the school.

The head of the department, Professor Alexander Ewing, who later received a British knighthood, was a pioneer in the methods of teaching deaf children to talk. He recognized that although they were deaf, they did not inhabit a silent world. Ewing believed that each child had a unique degree of hearing ability and could be taught to use whatever residual hearing he or she had so that they were not solely dependent on lip reading. He also believed that hearing aids were an important factor in teaching them to speak.

Hilda graduated in 1960 and went back to Liverpool. Even though it was not the best school, she felt an obligation to teach at the Liverpool School for the Deaf for two years because the Education Authority had sponsored her to study at Manchester. At her interview, the Liverpool school told her she would be teaching five-year-olds, the age in which she had specialized; but when the school term began, she found herself with a class of seven- and eight-year-olds. She was surprised but didn't complain.

Hilda had just come from Manchester, where she had learned from the recognized master in the field, and felt that she was on a mission to make a difference in her students' lives. "I enjoyed the teaching," she says. "But I was not enamoured by what was going on in that school. I was idealistic, and I didn't feel they were doing all that could be done. They weren't achieving the goal."

She became dissatisfied and restless. She was living with her parents again because in those days the only reason girls left home was to get married. She had no intention of marrying, but she wanted her independence and had no idea how to explain that to her parents without upsetting them. The only solution she could think of was to get a job in a different town, but the town would have to be far enough away that she couldn't commute.

As she pondered her dilemma she remembered her sister Joan's words when she was preparing to move to Vancouver, Canada, with her husband and two small boys: "You'll always be able to come and visit us. Maybe you can get an exchange year and see what it's like." Hilda wrote to her sister and asked if there was a school for the deaf in Vancouver. Joan investigated and sent information about the Jericho Hill School for the Deaf. Hilda wrote to them, and within days she received an application form in the mail.

Now she had a new dilemma. "Do I really want to go that far?" she wondered. "It's 6,000 miles. It's a new country, and even though my sister is there, she's married and has children. What will it be like?"

She laid the application aside. A few weeks later she received a letter from the school superintendent with another application. "Perhaps the previous application form didn't arrive or perhaps you mislaid it," the letter said. "So we're sending you another one."

"This is telling me something," Hilda thought. "I'd better do something about this."

She filled out the form and sent it to the Jericho Hill School. Within days they sent a cable with a prepaid reply, offering her the job. Hilda then realized that the Jericho Hill School needed her badly. "So I plucked up the courage and wrote back and said, 'Yes.'"

After an exhausting thirteen-hour flight, at about midnight on August 10, 1962, Hilda's plane from England landed at the Vancouver airport. Joan and her husband picked her up and took her to their home in East Vancouver, near the Pacific National Exhibition grounds. Hilda fell asleep and awoke the next morning to what sounded like the world's largest nest of hornets buzzing angrily outside her window.

Later that morning she learned that she had had her first encounter with an electric lawn mower.

On the Tuesday after Labour Day, she reported to her new school. To her delight she recognized two teachers from the Manchester school where she had trained. Her second surprise was not nearly as pleasant because although she had been promised a class of five-year-olds, she was given a small group of children between the ages of seven and nine, who had missed a good deal of schooling and needed to catch up to their peers. Her classroom was another shock; she had been assigned the old principal's office, which had not previously been used as a classroom and contained a few desks, a cupboard with almost no supplies, and some very antiquated audio equipment. "So," she thought. "I suppose I shall have to teach them to talk with nothing."

She created her own visual aids and taught the children with the methods she had learned at Manchester. One day another teacher walked into her classroom and looked at what Hilda had written on the blackboard. "Why are you teaching them the present participle when they haven't got the more basic grammar yet?" the teacher asked.

"Because they need it," Hilda replied.

She thought the question was silly. "You don't teach grammar sequentially," she says. "You don't give toddlers long, complicated sentences, but you don't break down the grammar and say I'll only teach them the present and then I'll start teaching them the future."

Hilda had disagreements with the system. The Jericho Hill School was a primary school that was teaching oral language, but when the children graduated to the intermediate and the senior levels they were introduced to signing. She wanted to know, "Why are we working hard to develop their oral communication skills, when the minute they get into the intermediate school they're introduced to signing, so that they all resort just to signing and lose their ability to use their speech skills?"

"That was one thing that bothered me," Hilda says. "But then I noticed that while the program was oral, it wasn't being taught the way I understood it should be. I was young and idealistic. I'd been to Manchester, and I knew how to do it."

The method Hilda used was strongly visual, and at Jericho Hill School the teachers tended to say things and then write what they had said on the blackboard. "I didn't see that as a vehicle for developing good oral skills. People thought you could teach it through reading. No, the oral comes before reading. You've got to have a good base in language to be able to understand what you're reading; otherwise it's what I call 'barking at print.' You can teach children to sound out those words or know visually what to say, but ask them what a word means and they haven't a clue. You can teach the mechanics of reading, but if you don't understand what you're reading, what's the point?"

Another thing that bothered her was that the children were coming to the school at age five with no prior training. They were not learning any oral skills in their preschool years, and because Jericho Hill School was a provincial school, it had no programs for young children. The importance of those early years was simply not recognized at that time, she says. She began to have second thoughts about her decision to come to Canada and thought about returning to England. And then she argued, "I've only been out here a short time. I'm only partway through my first year."

"I always felt obligated to people," she says. "You don't just walk away from things. So I was having this sort of dialogue with myself, 'Well, what are you going to do?'" Should she stay at Jericho Hill for another year and then go back? But if she stayed, would she compromise her standards? Would she get used to the status quo and gradually believe it wasn't so bad after all? She was deeply involved in this internal debate when she heard about a small group of parents whose children had been diagnosed as deaf by the diagnostic team at the Speech and Hearing Clinic. The team had told the parents that they should think about starting a school because their children were too young for Jericho Hill School and they should begin their education early.

Hilda thought there could be no harm in finding out how serious these parents were, so she made a few inquiries and discovered that the team had told the parents that if they could support the school financially, they would recruit a qualified teacher. Feeling encouraged, Hilda called the clinic and booked an interview with Dr. Ken Cambon— the ear, nose, and throat specialist. Dr. Cambon, the parents, and the rest of the team at the clinic thought Hilda—with her specialty in early childhood education—could be just the person they were looking for. The job solved Hilda's dilemma over staying at Jericho Hill School for another year, and the parents solved their problem of teaching their children to talk.

Hilda finished off the year with Jericho Hill School and started hunting for a space to put the new school. She found three unused rooms in the back wing of Sunnyhill Hospital, which the administration offered to rent to the group. But before the school could open, Hilda had to make the space suitable for teaching deaf children. She had learned at Manchester that the acoustics of a classroom for deaf children were crucial and there should be as little reverberation and external noise as possible. She called the University of British Columbia and asked if someone from the acoustical engineering department could look at the rooms. They put in acoustic tiles, sealed the doors as tightly as possible, and renovated the space. Hilda can recall sweeping the floors shortly before Labour Day and saying to the parents, "I'm not opening this class until everything is ready because if I open it and things aren't ready, they'll never get done."

One affluent couple who had taken their child to a summer program at the John Tracy Clinic in the U.S. had come back full of enthusiasm about the methods taught there. They asked Hilda to teach their child using that system. She listened to the parents' request and said, "I don't think that's the best way to teach young deaf children to talk. I won't do it that way. I have to do it in the way I think it should be done, and if you want someone to do it this other way, you're going to have to find somebody else."

"In spite of the fact that I didn't always speak up in terms of myself, I was never afraid to speak up about what I thought were appropriate things to do for others," Hilda says.

She got her way. She had her own school, her classrooms were completed, and she was using her own methods. She taught eight three-year-olds in the mornings, and in the afternoons she went to the Speech and Hearing Clinic to do individual work with two-year-old children, who had also been diagnosed as deaf.

The parents called their group The Society for Children with a Hearing Handicap. They received no government funding for the school; in fact, Hilda was never quite sure at the end of each month if there would be enough money to pay her. But the parents raised funds through local service groups and bake sales, and after a few months, the Kinsmen Club gave the parents a guarantee for Hilda's salary for the first year.

When the two-year-olds at the clinic turned three, Hilda brought them to the school at Sunnyhill, and by January she had two groups: one in the morning and one in the afternoon. The following year, Hilda told the parents that the first group of children, who were now four, should be in an all-day program.

"Can children that age cope with a full school day?" they asked.

"Of course they can," Hilda said. "They do it in England all the time."

I laugh at Hilda's statement, delivered in such a matter-of-fact way. She laughs too, and then explains, "I've always felt that parents here have been very overprotective and underestimate what their children can do. I'm very opinionated about that."

Meanwhile another group of three-year-olds was ready to enrol in the school, and Hilda realized that she would need another teacher to help her. The parents' society and Hilda talked to the provincial government and convinced them that they had some responsibility to educate these children. When Hilda proved to them that education in the early years was critical because those were the years when children learned to talk, the government gave them enough funding so that they could hire another teacher.

The next year, they increased their enrolment again and had to hire yet another teacher. Finding a good, trained teacher was a challenge, as there were no training programs for teachers of the deaf in B.C. The first teacher Hilda hired was a Canadian woman, who had received her training in the U.S. The second teacher she hired was from England.

When the original group of eight children reached Kindergarten age they were eligible to enrol at the Jericho Hill School for the Deaf. Hilda wasn't pleased to see them go because she knew the methods Jericho Hill used and didn't approve of them. The parents weren't pleased either. "Why should we send them to the provincial school for the deaf to be incorporated with children who are just coming into school with no prior education?" they asked. In effect, their children would be set back two years. So they asked the Jericho Hill School to have their children put into a separate off-campus class with their own teacher, who would continue to use the instruction methods Hilda had employed. Even the couple who had wanted Hilda to teach by the methods used at the John Tracy Clinic now supported her methods fully.

"Does that mean your methods were working?" I ask. Hilda answers simply, saying, "Yes."

After long discussions, the Jericho Hill School agreed to the parents' demands. Although they believed they had won, Hilda was still not happy. "Who knows about bureaucracies and large organizations?" she says. "My concern was that they would say one thing and do it for a while, but once they had control they could do their own thing, and you would have no say in it. My concern was that, 'Oh yes, they'll do that to begin with but they'll find some reason why they should not keep on running it and then absorb the children into the rest of the school.'"

Within two or three years—Hilda isn't sure of the exact time— that is exactly what happened. When the parents of the children who were then in Hilda's school saw what had occurred, they said they had no intention of giving over control of their children's education to the provincial government. One couple, Brenda and Michael O'Keefe, was particularly adamant. "We don't want that to happen. We've got to push ahead and create not just a preschool program. We've got to create a school," they said. The O'Keefes proposed that the Society for Children with a Hearing Handicap should stop running the school. Instead, they created a non-profit organization that would operate a school, encompassing all the primary grades.

In 1970 Hilda's preschool became the Vancouver Oral Centre for Deaf Children, an independent school that operated under a board made up of community members, business people, special educators, medical specialists, and some parents. Michael O'Keefe had seen the flaw in having Hilda and the teachers under the authority of the children's parents and wrote the constitution so that parents would never be in a majority.

Hilda became the principal of the new school, which grew so rapidly it had to add portable classrooms to the grounds. In 1972 Sunnyhill Hospital asked the school to vacate the building because they wanted to tear down that section of the building. The board searched for another location and found a building on the east side of town owned by the Holy Family Catholic parish. It had been used as a school but had shut down when enrolment declined. The archdiocese was delighted to rent it to the Vancouver Oral Centre for Deaf Children because they considered it a worthy organization.

The school continued to expand to include an off-campus class in a school run by the Vancouver School Board. The Oral Centre supplied the instructor and teaching materials, and the children had the advantage of being able to participate in extracurricular school activities. As the reputation of the Oral Centre for Deaf Children grew and gained international recognition, it became clear that what Hilda Gregory was doing worked. She taught the children to listen. She had each child's ears plotted individually so that she would know exactly how much hearing each child had, how loud the sounds had to be for the child to hear them, and how loud those sounds had to be before the child could discriminate differences and nuances. Hilda's school was the first in B.C. to use two hearing aids with separate controls for each ear. Over the years, she incorporated new knowledge and technology as it became available. When she worked with children individually, she used earphones that she could attune to the exact level each child needed to allow them to discriminate between sounds with the goal of teaching them to listen and to use whatever hearing they had to the best of their ability. "If they could hear sounds and if they could discriminate between speech sounds, they could imitate those sounds and learn to speak," she says.

The goal of the Oral Centre for Deaf Children was to get the children to the stage where they had a high enough language level and could speak well enough to be understood by others and integrated into a regular classroom with support teachers. The Oral Centre for Deaf Children supplied support teachers to various classrooms in the city to give the students individual tutoring up to the end of their high school education. Hilda believed that it was only by giving the students continued support that the Oral Centre for Deaf Children could prove its methods were working. If they simply integrated them in the school system without support and the children did not do well, there was no way of knowing whether it was the training they had received at the Oral Centre or the education they had received afterwards that was at fault. "We've got to follow students through to Grade Twelve," she argued. "Only then will we be able to say, 'Look at our product.'"

"And how was your product?" I ask. By this time I'm not surprised by her blunt reply: "We had a very good success rate." Most of the high school graduates continued on to college or university. Many of them learned sign language after they learned to talk, and Hilda didn't mind that as long as they mastered oral skills first.

While Hilda was establishing the Oral Centre for Deaf Children, she was also an active member of Christ Church Cathedral. In 1981 she had chaired a program at the Vancouver School of Theology called *The Journey of Discovery*, which focussed on the group's journey as a Christian community. She also served on the board of the Alexander Graham Bell Association of the Deaf and was travelling to Washington, D.C., for a committee meeting when a worker at the cathedral asked her to take an extra day to meet with Dr. Conrad Hoover, who was doing some work with the poor in the inner city and who had been recommended to be a speaker for the final *Journey of Discovery* event. "So I did that," Hilda says. "And I came back all enthusiastic and said, 'Yes, we should have him.'"

Dr. Hoover flew to Vancouver and talked about the projects his community groups were working on. The one that caught Hilda's imagination was housing for the poor, and she felt exactly the same sense of being "called" as she had when she saw the film *Mandy* at age sixteen. She recalls, "Just like that I stood up and said, 'Is there anybody else in the group interested in getting together with me to look at the issue of housing in Vancouver?'"

About six people agreed to start meeting with her. They formed a non-profit society called the 127 Society for Housing, taking the name from Psalm 127: "Unless the Lord builds the house the labourers build in vain." The small group had no idea what they were going to do beyond meeting regularly and investigating the housing situation. They discovered that there was an acute shortage of affordable rental housing in Vancouver, and landlords could charge whatever they wanted. The only accommodation many people could afford was in seedy, filthy, firetrap hotels, and those who couldn't even pay for those dingy rooms slept on the streets. "We thought we were dreaming when we said that maybe the most we could do was put a down payment on a house in Kits and do it up and rent it out to a few people at a reasonable rent," Hilda says.

In their search for a house they found a group that operated a drop-in centre on the downtown south side and they asked them, "What do these people need?"

"Housing," they replied. "No one in this area is doing anything for them. They're all living in old hotels and rooming houses."

"Well our interest is housing," Hilda said. "We've never done anything like this before, but would you be interested in working with us?"

"We have no experience in housing either," they said. "But you just go ahead and do it, and we'll support you."

Hilda had never owned property or even an apartment. "I didn't know anything about it," she says. "But one of the things I'd learned in my life was: You don't have to know—you just have to know how to find out."

The group walked the streets, looked at property, and eventually found a vacant lot downtown at Seymour and Helmcken, which the City of Vancouver owned. When they asked about it, they were told that the lot was designated for parking, so Hilda said, "If we find another site in that area, and if you don't already own it, would you consider purchasing it and banking it so that we can go to Canada Mortgage and Housing Corporation and apply for units?" The City said yes.

Using a small grant of $2,000 from the Anglican Church, they hired a consultant who referred them to a firm of architects that had previously designed social housing units. One of the architects showed them a site at the corner of Richards and Helmcken that was owned by an oil company.

The group went back to the City, which kept its word, and purchased it for just over $1 million. Hilda then convinced the Canada Mortgage and Housing Corporation (CMHC) to give them units under the social housing program, allowing them to qualify for a subsidy.

In June 1986 the 127 Society for Housing had its first building, consisting of 86 apartments. The outrageous dream of a renovated house in Kitsilano had become a $3-million building—and it was only the first one. In 1989 the society completed the construction of a second building of 78 units. Besides merely constructing the buildings, the society also obtained a long-term lease with the City to operate them. In 1997 the society got its third building, creating a grand total of 254 units of affordable housing. These housing projects are especially remarkable, as they were begun by six people with $2,000 and some faith that they put into action. "And that's where my tenacity comes in," Hilda says. "When I believe something can happen, I go after it, and I don't give up easily. I think it's because I have such strong faith that what I'm doing is meant to be done."

In 1995 the Catholic archdiocese informed the Oral Centre for Deaf Children that they were going to take back possession of their building to create a school and community centre for the large Spanish population that had recently moved into the area. They gave the centre six month's notice to vacate the building.

"Impossible!" the board said. They needed time to either find a building they could adapt to a school for the deaf, or to build a brand new school. When their search for an older building proved futile, Hilda drew upon her work with the 127 Society for Housing. She called the architect she had been working with and said, "Help! You might know where there are sites. Can you do something?"

Once again Hilda talked to the City, and one day a friend—who was a social worker—said to her, "Hilda, have you thought of going to Sunnyhill Hospital? They own quite a bit of land around the hospital, and there's been a change in their mission. They want to extend into the community and establish partnerships."

Hilda called the hospital's chief executive officer, asked for a meeting, and told him who she was and why she was there. "I like to come straight to the point," she explains, and I can't help smiling because by now I've noticed her penchant for doing just that. "And as I was telling him about our problem, his eyes began to sparkle and he got very excited."

"That's perfect," the CEO said. "That fits right in with our mandate."

The long bureaucratic negotiating process for a long-term lease with the hospital began, so while the board dealt with it, Hilda called in acquaintances to form a committee and work with the architects. Then she called on other people and asked them to work on a fundraising committee because she knew the building was going to be expensive and she did not want to involve the board, as they already had a big enough job to do. The fundraising committee went to the Variety Club, who agreed to partner with and support the school.

By 1997 the hard work was done, and all Hilda had to do was sit back and watch the construction begin. A few days before Thanksgiving she became ill with what she thought was a bad bout of the flu, but that weekend a neighbour found her collapsed in her apartment and called an ambulance. Her kidneys had failed, and for a while the doctors didn't think she would survive. But she did. As part of her recovery she began using renal dialysis equipment. With her usual no-nonsense approach, she trained to do her own dialysis and was back at work in January 1998, carrying her equipment with her. "I did dialysis in my office, in meetings, at hearings. I wasn't going to let the disease control me," Hilda says. "I was going to control it."

In 1998 the Vancouver Oral Centre for Deaf Children moved into its new building. Those who know Hilda Gregory say the building is a perfect reflection of her. The building is simple but elegant with four airy classrooms, an audiological suite, a room for the family support worker, a gathering room for parents, a large activity room, observation rooms off the classrooms, a central atrium, a staff room, kitchen, boardroom, offices, an outdoor playground, and all the latest technology—it has everything Hilda had ever dreamed for a school for deaf children.

She moved into her beautiful new office, but one year later, she moved out.

"Did you mind leaving?" I asked.

"No, I knew it was right," she said. "It was my 35th anniversary; I had achieved the goal. I had a brand new building and that had always been my dream: to have a building designed for the purposes of teaching young deaf children. So I had achieved my dream. I was coming up to a new century, and someone else could take it on." She says that she never looked back, and she rarely drops in to the school to visit. "The new principal doesn't need me looking over her shoulder," she said.

In 1998, the year the new building was completed, Hilda Gregory was awarded the Order of British Columbia. A year later she received the Order of Canada. "I felt very honoured and humbled," she says. "Here I was: somebody who had come to Canada. It was my adopted country, and I think for me it was a greater honour because of that. I felt honoured, humbled, and I had a sense of satisfaction that I had given something to the country."

Hilda's greatest sense of satisfaction comes from seeing the success of the graduates from the centre and from feeling that she has fulfilled her calling. "I am definitely a person of faith," she says. "I don't know if it happens for everybody, but I get this strong sense from within that I've got to act on something. I have no choice but to act. I happen to be religious as well, but it is my faith that has made the difference. It is what has always been there as the rock or the centre. It has held me stable, and it has got me through things. My tenacity has come from my strong sense from within that I'm meant to do something."

There are many things Hilda has yet to do. She is president of the board of the 127 Society for Housing, but she believes housing is only the first step in establishing a different lifestyle for the residents. She believes they can change their way of living and can be helped to make such a change. The society has a part-time community worker in each of its three buildings. Two of the buildings have low-cost stores that are managed by the tenants, and one building houses a workshop room for crafts and hobbies. She continues to raise funds for the continuation of the workshop and the community work program in each of the buildings, and she also continues to look for opportunities to create more social housing projects.

In 2001 Hilda received a kidney transplant, and today she is a mentor to others undergoing dialysis. She also serves on the patient education committee of the hospital renal clinic. "I think the more you give to your community, the more you receive," she says. "I've never had a five-year-plan. I don't need to plan my life. It's likely to be thrown out of the window, anyway, by some little twist that comes along."

As we reach the end of the interview, I ask her, "Is there anything we've left out? Is there anything you wish I had asked that I haven't?"

She laughs. "That's what I always say at the end of interviews: 'Is there anything you want to tell me that hasn't been covered by the questions?' I don't think so. I suppose in some ways I'm amazed at my life and the direction it's taken. If anyone had told me this is what you'll do with your life, I wouldn't have believed it. And here I am. I think my proudest moment was being able to call my mother in England to tell her I got the Order of B.C."

Although the Order of British Columbia carries the province's recognition of her accomplishments, Hilda was most proud to receive her mother's recognition: a fitting tribute to a woman who instilled in her daughter the will to succeed, and to always have faith.

Takao Tanabe, 1993

Takao Tanabe:
Capturing Quintessential Nature

*T*akao Tanabe's landscapes of Canada's misty West Coast and the vast dry lands of B.C.'s Interior evoke the expansiveness of their beauty and something more—something primal, often something barren and lonely, and always a sense of wonder. In an interview with Roger H. Broulet, the author of the catalogue for Takao's exhibition *wet coasts and dry lands*, Takao was asked about his transition from a modernist to a romantic landscape artist. Takao says that when he answered, he had his tongue planted firmly in his cheek. "I wanted to paint the sublime!" But to my eyes, his paintings are indeed sublime. They arouse in me a profound sense of solitude. It may be fanciful to suggest that his landscapes, largely free of any sign of human alteration, reflect an early disillusionment with people—or perhaps not.

Takao Tanabe was born on September 16, 1926, in Seal Cove, a small village near Prince Rupert that was almost exclusively Japanese. Like most of the inhabitants, Takao's father worked as a fisherman and his mother was employed at the local cannery. Takao was the fifth of seven children. The family was very poor, and Takao remembers their poverty as being "bloody awful." Poor families like his lived beside the bay, and the white people, who were the managers of the fish plant, lived on a ridge on the edge of the town.

"We lived in a Japanese community—that's what this was," Takao says. "There was no interchange, and in elementary school—up to about Grade Three—there were very few occidentals."

"Was there prejudice?" I ask.

"We didn't know about prejudice because it was all around us. We didn't call it racism. We were Japs, and there were a lot of other people in the same boat. There were Chinks, as they were called, and there were some turbaned Sikhs, and we were all in the same underclass. We knew that the whites were there and they were the boss."

"Did it bother you?" I ask.

Takao's voice rises. "When you're six, seven, or eight years old—how can it bother you? That's the normal way of life. It doesn't bother you until you read books and newspapers, and eventually in the war, you come face to face with it when the Japs are segregated, put into gathering camps, and eventually shipped off into the Interior."

In 1937, Takao's family moved to Vancouver, where he made a couple of non-Japanese friends, but they never spoke outside of the schoolyard. Then, in 1941, Japan bombed Pearl Harbour, and the Canadian government instituted a curfew on the Japanese.

Takao pauses in his narrative, and then he says, "Geez, I don't know why I have to relive all this. But I was in Grade Ten, and I was completely angry with the government and with Canada. I had put my faith in the government being fair and that we were all equal—we believed what they were saying—but on the other hand, here we were being told, 'You can't go out after six because you're a Jap. You have to hand in all your radios. All the Japanese who are on the coast have to hand over their boats.' Then the government decided we should all be moved from the coast."

A temporary camp was constructed in Vancouver's Hastings Park. The adult males were housed in the ice rink, while the women and children were assigned to the horse arena. Another large building served as the mess hall. When a family was signed in to the camp, they were not allowed to leave except to go to internment camps in the Interior.

In late July, the Tanabe family was ordered to the camp, but three of Takao's older siblings and a brother-in-law decided instead to take advantage of their option to go to Manitoba to work as indentured farm labourers for eighteen months. Meanwhile, another brother-in-law became involved in a movement to protest the separation of Japanese families. The Royal Canadian Mounted Police rounded up the troublemakers and sent them to northern Ontario, where they were put into camps adjacent to the prisoner of war camps. Takao's brother-in-law was one of the dissidents who was caught and sent away. Takao's father escaped capture. "So my father and my thirteen-year-old brother and I slept in what would be the ice rink. We slept in the bleachers. My mother and younger sister slept in the horse barns with my oldest sister and her two children—in the smelly horse barn. It hadn't been cleaned properly, and the smell was horrendous."

As the government rounded up the Japanese on the coast, they shipped them to old abandoned mining towns or deserted villages in the Interior. When there weren't enough buildings to house everyone, the Japanese were put to work building makeshift huts, receiving between eight and seventeen cents per hour.

Takao's family was assigned to Lemon Creek, a Doukhobor farmer's field near Slocan in the West Kootenays. Takao described the houses he helped build as about the size of a modern two-car garage. There was no insulation for the buildings, and the roof was made of tarpaper. The interior was divided into three rooms with a sink and a stove in one. Each hut was designed to house a minimum of six or seven people, so because there were only five in the Tanabe family, they shared their hut with another family of three. "We soon realized, of course, that it would be impossible to have five sleep in one room," Takao says. "There just wasn't room in this dinky little shack, so my father and my brother and I added a room on to it. Using four- or five-inch [diameter] small trees that we could carry from the forest we built a little log-type addition. And that was luxury because we were able to build it ourselves. The government certainly wasn't going to give us the wood or allow it to be built."

A two-seat outhouse served every two huts, and the camp also had a bathhouse and a couple of grocery stores, where people could buy food with the small stipend the government allotted them. There was no fence around the camp, but no one left because there was nowhere to go. The inhabitants could walk to other camps within a few miles of their own; however they had to have a permit from the RCMP to travel farther. "They had us pretty well cowed," Takao says.

There were many teens and small children among the 1,000 people at the Lemon Creek camp, so at the end of the summer, the adults who were qualified as teachers started an elementary school, and the older children were enrolled in the government correspondence course. Takao had no interest in school.

"How did you feel through all this?" I ask.

"I was angry for twenty years—for thirty years. I may still be angry. That's why I find it very hard to talk about this sort of thing. I'm reluctantly telling you all this. I would rather not talk about it because all it does is put my back up and make me very angry."

In 1943, the government began disbanding the internment camps. They encouraged Japanese families either to be repatriated to Japan or to leave—as long as they did not go back to the coast. Takao joined his brothers and sister, who had finished their eighteen-month stint on a farm in Manitoba and had moved to Winnipeg. He got a job in a warehouse, and after a year, when the family had saved up enough money to afford a bigger house, Takao's parents and younger brother and sister joined them.

Takao was eighteen years old. "I had no idea what art was," he says. "But I knew I didn't want to be a warehousing hand all my life. I thought I'd go to school, and since I had totally ignored the whole idea of doing correspondence courses in the camp I had only managed to finish Grade Ten in Vancouver. I thought about getting my high school degree and going to university, which is what my mother wanted, but I didn't think I could handle going to high school for a couple of years. So I hunted around and went to the art school to see if I could get in without a high school degree."

The Winnipeg School of Art accepted him. The principal of the school was Lemoine Fitzgerald, one of The Group of Seven. To Takao, the name meant nothing. He left the warehouse and got a job in the peat fields east of Winnipeg. The work was physically exhausting, but the pay enough to allow him to attend school in the fall.

The school had five instructors; Fitzgerald taught only second- and third-year students. In his first year, Takao learned drawing, design, sign lettering, and other basics. In his second year, he was scheduled to take painting classes with Lemoine Fitzgerald, but Fitgerald took a sabbatical. The school hired a young man named Joseph Plaskett to take his place.

Takao recalls one encounter with Fitzgerald. "Mr. Fitzgerald was this remote person, and the only time he ever spoke to me was as three or four of us were sneaking down the stairs in the spring of 1947 to go for a hike somewhere—we were skipping classes—and he—this light-footed gentlemen—leaned over the balustrade and said, 'Yes, it's very lovely weather. Have a good time, boys.'"

Takao laughs, "He didn't say, 'Come back to class.' Just, 'Have a good time.' That was the only contact I had with him. Lemoine Fitzgerald, I subsequently found out, was one of the last members of The Group of Seven, who did wonderful paintings and wonderful etchings, none of which we knew about."

Joseph Plaskett was a native of Canada's West Coast. He had returned to Canada after a year of studies in San Francisco and New York, full of enthusiasm for the new abstract expressionism. Plaskett's students had never seen so much as one reproduction of an abstract expressionist painting, but Plaskett, undeterred, described the work he had seen that had fired his imagination. He talked about the paintings of Hans Hofmann, the famous abstract expressionist in New York, and he described some of his own work that he had done under the master's tutelage. The school had no art history course and no library, so with only descriptions to go by, Plaskett's students attempted to paint in the abstract expressionist style. "I'm sure we painted bloody awful paintings—oils and watercolours—but we had a good time," Takao says.

"Were you getting turned on to painting?" I ask.

"How would I know," Takao says. "We were painting. You get a board, you squeeze out the paint, and you have three brushes—because that's all you could afford—and you're told to paint. It's very inhibiting, or it could be very liberating for those who have that kind of personality. It took me some time to get started."

To make extra money during the school year, Takao had taken the job of janitor at the school, so each day he would knock on Plaskett's door to ask permission to sweep and empty the garbage. Plaskett, who used his office as a studio, would usually be working on a painting, and Takao caught his first glimpse of abstract art. "So this gave me some idea of what abstract painting was about," he says. "You could see examples of late nineteenth century romantic paintings and figurative paintings at the Winnipeg Art Gallery—they had a few English and a few French on display—but we certainly had no idea what abstract art looked like."

In his third year, the Winnipeg School of Art brought in American art magazines that featured reproductions of some of the early work of abstract expressionist painters such as Hans Hofmann, so the students finally had some visual reference. "In my third year I was a bit more enthusiastic about my painting," Takao recalls. "It seemed like a nice thing, but of course, we all knew there was no way we could make a living at it. In Winnipeg there was no place one could exhibit stuff like this, so my view was still to be a show card sign writer—not that I was very good at it, but I could see that it could be one way to make a few dollars. And a constant background noise was that I had to make a few bucks because there was nothing else to fall back on, and nobody else was going to support me."

At the end of the three-year program, Takao and a few of his classmates decided to put on an exhibition. The daughter of the manager of the Hudson's Bay store was a second-year student at the school; the group promised to include one of her paintings if she would ask her father for exhibition space. The manager gave them permission, so Takao and his classmates invited students who had graduated the previous year to participate in their exhibition.

The one-week show was well attended, and although none of the young people sold their art, they were still pleased with the exposure. Buoyed by their success Takao and two of his classmates, who had helped stage the exhibit, said, "Let's run a summer school." Lots of people wanted to sketch in nature, they reasoned, and they could charge a fee and perhaps make a good profit.

For their venue they chose the Icelandic community and summer resort at Gimli Lake. They asked Carol, a university professor who taught art history and was a member of the Icelandic community, to be in charge of the school and to find space to house the classroom and dormitory. Carol liked the idea. She obtained permission to use the second floor of the local elementary school and the small community hall. Only twelve students enrolled, however, which was barely enough to support two teachers. Takao's classmates dropped out of the project, and the summer school opened with Takao teaching drawing in the mornings while Carol took them on sketching trips in the afternoons.

At the end of the four-week session, after adding up their expenses and taking into account the small tuition fees, Carol and Takao just managed to break even. "It never crossed our minds to try for a second year," he says.

Takao now was faced with the decision of what to do with the rest of his life. "I decided that if I was going to be serious about painting I had to go to study in the United States—somewhere where this new wonderful art was being made. I had to go and see some of it."

After the summer school experiment, Takao and a friend hitchhiked to Banff, Alberta for a brief holiday. They stayed with friends who were working at the Banff School of Fine Arts. When Takao realized that work was available, he found a job washing dishes and then later, cleaning up the school grounds. At the end of the summer, he went back to Winnipeg. When he couldn't find a job, he applied for unemployment insurance.

In 1950, the Winnipeg School of Art was incorporated into the University of Manitoba, and the new administration hired a faculty of four teachers from the American Midwest. Takao, jobless and aimless, introduced himself to the principal, John McCloy, who allowed him to use one of the rooms as a studio when there were no classes in session. Takao painted three days a week and in time began to meet the new instructors. One of them, John Kacere, became a friend.

Kacere was an abstract expressionist painter who had studied in Chicago. He told Takao about Paul Brach, with whom he had gone to school and who was a very good painter. Brach had moved to New York, so when Takao confessed his ambition to study there, Kacere gave him Paul Brach's phone number. "Be sure to look him up," he said.

Takao got a job in Banff again the following summer, saved his money, and travelled to New York in the winter of 1951. When he contacted Hans Hofmann's art school and was told that his painting classes were already full, he enrolled in an evening drawing class. "It was a wonderful studio school that he had," Takao recalls. "It was on Eighth Street in the middle of Greenwich Village."

He also registered for painting classes at the Brooklyn Museum Art School. "It was a good choice," Takao recalls. "Although Reuben Tam, the teacher, was not an abstract expressionist painter, he was very sympathetic to it. And every week, the school invited one of the painters prominent in abstract expressionism in New York to come in and lecture."

Takao found a room in a flat on the far lower East Side near the river, which he shared with three roommates who were happy to let him use the living room as a studio. When he was settled, he called Paul Brach. Paul lived in the "village," near Hans Hofmann's school. "Come for a drink after class," Paul said.

So at 9:30 p.m. Takao walked to the studio that Paul shared with his wife, Mimi Shapiro. They took him to the Cedar Bar, New York's most important gathering place for abstract expressionist artists. Paul introduced Takao to the famous people he had read about, whom he had never expected to meet and whose paintings he had admired in the pages of art magazines. "I could just listen in on conversations," he says. "These men were all ten or twelve years older. They had been around a longer time. They were all painting and in the news; they were big shots. So it was all very interesting to listen to their conversations and their arguments. It was all very exhilarating."

On subsequent visits to Paul and Mimi's studio, Takao met Philip Guston, one of the leading painters in New York at the time, and Joan Mitchell, another well-known artist. "Then I decided that being a painter wasn't such a bad idea and I could give it a try," Takao says. "It was an interesting way to get through life, and I had decided I had a bit of talent. Looking around at exhibitions and at the work of other students around me, I decided I had enough talent to give it a try."

Once or twice a month, on Saturdays, Hofmann held an open studio where any of his students could bring one or two paintings for a critique. While the students and Hofmann sat in chairs facing the model's platform, each person's painting would be placed on the easel set up there. Hofmann would look, comment, and call, "Next!"

One Saturday Takao brought in one of his paintings. When it was Takao's turn a monitor placed it on the easel. Hofmann sat in the middle of the crowd, and for a minute there was silence. "Whose painting is that?" Hofmann asked.

Takao put up his hand.

"Oh yes," Hofmann said.

"I'm in one of your drawing classes at night," Takao explained.

"Oh yes," Hofmann said and looked at the painting again. "Very good. Very good. Next."

Takao was not pleased with the praise. He wanted feedback. "Is it too red? Is it too yellow? Is the movement controlled enough or is it uncontrolled? I mean—no comment!"

Two weeks later, Takao brought another painting to the open studio and waited in the audience. Once again it was placed on the easel.

"Whose painting is that?" Hofmann asked.

Takao raised his hand.

"Oh yes," Hofmann nodded. "Very good. Next."

Takao laughs. "So I thought, 'That's it. There's no point. I don't need to go anymore.' So I continued taking his drawing class, but I stopped taking paintings in for his critique."

When summer came he went back to the Banff School of Fine Arts to work. One of Takao's jobs was monitor for the art department. While he moved easels around or did other odd jobs for the instructors, he talked to the painters and became quite friendly with some of them. Each summer the school brought in painters from England, and that year Takao met William Townsend, who became a good friend.

At the end of the summer school session, Takao travelled to Vancouver to visit his former home. While he was there he contacted Joseph Plaskett, who had settled in the city after a couple of years in Paris. One day Takao accompanied Plaskett to the printing house that was designing and printing the invitations for the opening of Plaskett's upcoming exhibition.

Robert R. Reid, who was later to become a fine book designer, operated the small shop. While Joseph and Robert discussed design ideas, Takao explored. Robert had one automatic press, a hand-operated platen press, and a bank of hand set types. Takao watched while Robert set the type for the job. "I couldn't take my eyes off what he was doing," he says. "I found it such a fascinating thing to see how pages were actually being printed." He asked Robert if he could see something he had printed, so Robert showed him a couple of announcements.

"That's really fascinating," Takao said.

"Well, come on down, and I'll give you a lesson or two."

Takao went to the shop every day. Robert showed him the basics of setting type and eventually allowed him to operate the platen press. He stayed in Vancouver the rest of the winter, dividing his time between setting type at Robert's shop and painting in his small rented room.

In the spring of 1953, a couple of artists he had met told him he should apply for the Emily Carr scholarship run by Lawren Harris, one of The Group of Seven. The scholarship was worth $1,200. Takao could live for almost a year on that amount of money, so he sent in his application and promptly forgot about it.

One day Robert gave Takao a message: "Please call Lawren Harris."

Takao knew that Robert was a great practical joker. "Okay, I will," he said.

The next day Robert asked him, "Did you phone?"

"No, it's a joke. You're just pulling my leg."

"No, it's not a joke. I'm serious."

"Sure, Bob. Okay, I will."

For two more days Robert asked Takao, "Have you called Lawren Harris yet?"

Finally Takao said, "Okay. I'll call. But I'm going to kill you if this is a joke."

When he telephoned the number, Lawren Harris said, "I have been waiting for you to call. You are the winner of the 1953 Emily Carr Scholarship."

"Great," Takao said. "I'm off to Europe in the fall."

That summer Takao went back to the Banff School of Fine Arts. He met another English painter, William Scott, whose work was very well regarded. Takao had seen some reproductions of Scott's paintings and had been impressed. He asked the director of the school, Donald Cameron, for a brief leave of absence from his job so that he could attend Scott's classes. Cameron gave him permission and allowed him to attend classes free of charge. "So I managed to take this class with Scott, which was wonderful," Takao says. "He was a very kind fellow, and I kept in touch with him for many years."

When Takao arrived in London that fall, he enrolled in the Central School of Arts and Crafts to learn printmaking and fulfil the terms of his scholarship. He also called on William Scott, who introduced him to some of the leading artists in the city. He contacted William Townsend, who taught at the Slade Academy.

Takao was reluctant to leave after his year in London, but he could not afford to stay. Fortuitously, an art teacher and his wife, who Takao knew from Vancouver, were on an exchange visit to London. The man was teaching art at a girl's grammar school in East London, and their flat in St. John's Wood, which belonged to a Royal Academician, was large enough to accommodate Takao in the artist's studio in the attic room. "It was a wonderful room," Takao says.

All he needed then was money. Shortly after the fall semester began, his friend told him that another art teacher at the grammar school was ill. Would Takao be interested in filling in two days a week? "And I said, 'Yes of course, that would be great.' I could get enough money to live on."

The job paid ten pounds a week and that—plus a small loan from his mother—allowed him to stay in London for another year. "It was quite a good time," Takao says. "I learned a lot. I saw a lot of art. I travelled a lot and saw some of the major museums in Europe. In between all of these things, I was painting in oils in this former studio of a Royal Academician."

When he had about twelve paintings he was happy with, Takao says he "worked up the courage" to ask one of the owners at the Gimpel Gallery—one of London's leading abstract galleries—if he would come to his studio to look at them. The owner, Peter Gimpel, came on the appointed day, and after looking at the paintings and asking Takao about where he had studied and what his plans were, said, "I'm very impressed. I will send my brother, Charles. Then we will discuss it again."

Charles was as impressed as was his brother. Takao hoped their praise would mean an exhibition, but Charles shattered his hopes. "We're very interested in what you are doing," he said. "But we'd like to see more work. If you did these paintings in the last year, I suggest you paint for another year so that you have twice as many or more from which we might make a selection for a show. At the present time there is nothing we can do. You should somehow manage to paint for another year; then we shall see."

"I don't have the resources to stay for another year. I wish I did, but I don't," Takao said. "Thank you very much for your time."

"I was thinking that if I could manage to get a show or two I would see whether I could be a proper, professional artist," Takao says.

He flew back to Winnipeg with his paintings. During his absence, enrolments had increased at the University of Manitoba art school, and two Canadians had been added to the faculty. Takao introduced himself to some of the instructors and told them he was looking for exhibition space. They suggested a show at the school: the hallways had been freshly painted and could provide a suitable area to hang his work. So in late 1955 Takao had an exhibition of his London paintings.

"How did that show go?" I ask.

He shrugs. "How do all shows go?"

He had recently married, and they had moved to Vancouver together. He contacted Robert Reid and proposed that he use his printing equipment to do a few jobs that would help him earn a living while he painted. Robert agreed, and Takao and his wife settled down in Vancouver's west end.

While he painted in the evenings, he listened to CBC on his radio. One of his favourite shows was a program of classical music. The announcer always signed off with, "Good night. This is Bill Reid."

One night Takao met Bill at a party and said, "It's you! I listen to you every night!" The two men became friends. Bill was trying to make the decision to leave broadcasting and become a full-time Haida artist. He worked on his art during the day and at the radio station at night. Some evenings, Bill would sign off and Takao's phone would ring. "Hello," Bill would say.

"Want to come for coffee?" Takao would ask.

"Yes."

Half an hour later Bill would arrive, Takao would make coffee, and the two men would sit in the living room having quiet conversations punctuated by long silences. The two men remained close friends until Bill Reid died in 1998.

In 1959 Takao received a Canada Council grant to study art in Japan. "I spent almost two years in Japan, which was a really good thing for me," he says. "To see that I was not really Japanese. I was a westerner. Although people here call me Japanese, I am not—I am a westerner. I have nothing in common with them except for the way I look. The whole Japanese way of life—the ritual—is completely foreign to me. I could not fit in."

Takao returned to Vancouver in 1961 committed to being an artist. "I had deliberately stayed away from trying to get teaching jobs," he says. "I knew in my own mind what I was doing, but eventually—in 1963—I thought it would be interesting to try teaching."

He obtained a part-time position at the Vancouver School of Art, but even with the reduced hours, he found the work too time-consuming and intense. "The energy that one needs to be a good teacher is the same kind of energy that one needs to be a good painter," Takao says. "I just found I was doing very little of my own work in the school year."

After three years, Takao gave up teaching. In 1968 he left Vancouver, moving briefly to Philadelphia. He and his wife separated, and he moved to New York, which was still the centre of the art world. He found an empty loft in the then burgeoning SoHo area, where he stayed for the next four years. He became reacquainted with his friend, John Kacere, who had become a successful artist and who also had a studio nearby. Takao helped John renovate his loft, and through him he met other people who gave him odd jobs.

The Mira Godard Gallery in Montreal had discovered Takao's art and had made an arrangement to present him with a monthly cheque. At the end of the year they totalled up the cheques and the paintings that had sold, and usually the two came out even. His odd jobs and the gallery payments allowed Takao to pursue his painting, which at this time was undergoing an important evolution. "In about 1970 I slowly came around to the idea of painting the landscape," he says. "It was a complete break from being an abstract painter."

After four years in New York, Takao decided to go back to Canada to paint the landscape and to find a part-time teaching job to support himself. While he was investigating various schools, the Banff School of Fine Arts (The Banff Centre) invited him to teach in its summer program. "It worked out very nicely with my plans to paint the prairie landscape," he says.

During the six-week program, director Dr. David Leighton asked Takao to head the school's art department and revitalize it. Takao's old friend, William Townsend, who was also teaching at Banff School of Fine Arts that summer, urged him to take the position; but Takao turned it down. "I don't want a full-time job," he said.

David Leighton continued to negotiate with Takao, and between them they arrived at a solution. Takao would be head of the department and artist in residence, which gave the school the leeway to allow him the freedom to paint while organizing the summer and winter schools and performing his other duties. Before taking up his new position in the spring of 1973, Takao went back to New York to pack up and dispose of his loft. He also made arrangements for an exhibition at the Mira Godard Gallery. Studios were in great demand in SoHo, and his friends suggested he to put the studio up for sale and make a tidy profit. "No," he said. "I want it to go to some young artist coming in from outside, just the way I was. It would have been nice if someone had been around who could have given me a hand up." He found a promising young painter and turned over his studio to him for what it had cost him: $4,000.

In Banff, Takao established the school's first winter program. He was determined to attract only serious painters to the summer program and said, "I'm not inviting anyone who was here before back to be a faculty member." Locally, Takao's policy created some consternation, and several faculty members were completely incensed that they were not being hired back after teaching there for fifteen years or more.

"The kind of school I wanted was not a degree-granting school or anything like that," Takao says. "I wanted people who were past the undergraduate level of study. This would be a time for them to work out their problems and get on the first step to being an artist. We managed to attract enough students that the idea seemed sound."

When he was not working at the school, Takao tried to capture the essence of the prairie landscape. It was a challenging subject—the simple division of the canvas with a strong horizontal line separating land and sky, very few trees, and ploughed furrows in the fields to animate the land, however slightly. As much as possible, Takao eliminated the marks left by man: the power poles, the grain elevators, and the roads. He looked for the pristine, unspoiled landscape, leaving only the patterns in the fields as evidence of human interaction with the land.

The Banff school's reputation grew while Takao had more and more exhibitions and became increasingly successful. The list of Takao's exhibitions fills many pages in a recent catalogue: *The Dark Land* at the Art Gallery of Hamilton, *Flatlands* at the Canada House Gallery in London, England, *wet coasts and dry lands* at the Kelowna Art Gallery, *Reflecting Paradise* at the University of Lethbridge, *The Crisis of Abstractionism in Canada* circulated by the National Gallery of Canada, and many, many more.

After seven years at Banff School of Fine Arts, Takao felt he had accomplished everything he had set out to do and that it was time to become a full-time artist again. "And I decided that after all these years that I didn't mind living in the country," he says. "It keeps me away from people, and it allows me time to think and paint."

He knew he wanted to live on the West Coast, so he began exploring. He eventually found a secluded property on Vancouver Island, near the small resort town of Parksville. He built a house and studio and has been living and painting there ever since.

In moving to the coast, Takao was in a sense, returning to his roots. It was the fog-shrouded beauty of the West Coast that was to be his next major subject; he became as obsessive about the misty, wet coastal land as he had been about the grand sweep of the prairies. The Inside Passage and the Queen Charlotte Islands, in particular, captivated him. He also travelled to the Arctic, the Northwest Territories, Resolute Bay, and Labrador, awed by majestic landscapes just waiting to be painted.

In 1993 Takao Tanabe was awarded the Order of British Columbia. "The Order of B.C. was a complete surprise," he says. "I knew nothing about it, and so when the phone call came, I thought. 'My God! Why me?' One of the things I have managed to do is keep my head down so low that in the twenty years I have lived there, there are very few people who know who I am. I'm anonymous."

He stretches his anonymity to include what he does for others. Takao did not receive the award only for his paintings that so perfectly capture the glorious B.C. landscape, but for his mentoring and encouragement of young artists. He has given and continues to give much, all of it quietly and without fanfare. "I'm trying to be supportive of younger artists because I remember how hard it was," he says.

In 1999 Takao was awarded the Order of Canada, which he viewed as an elevation of stature that might help him make a difference to other artists. "Visual arts are not as valued as other art forms," he says. "Composers of serious music are probably the worst off in Canadian society for public recognition. Visual artists aren't quite as badly off, but society as a whole is rather neglectful, and perhaps it's because the history of art is not taught in schools."

Takao began to campaign to establish a Governor General's Award for the Visual Arts. Prizes had long been awarded to literature and the performing arts, he said, and he wanted to achieve similar recognition of visual artists for lifetime achievements and great bodies of work. For four years he worked on his campaign. He approached the Governor General Romeo LeBlanc, and he met with various gallery directors, including Dr. Shirley Thomson, who was then the director of the National Gallery in Ottawa. She later became the director of the Canada Council. Takao was eventually successful, although the end result fell short of his vision. Thanks to Dr. Thomson's personal interest in the project, the Canada Council espoused Takao's cause, and the first Governor General's Awards for the visual and media arts were presented in 1999. "This is one step in the process of getting better respect for art. It's one more step in the process of the government and we as a society honouring visual artists," Takao says.

As we end our conversation, I become more aware of the busy, noisy coffee shop on the harbourfront in Nanaimo, where we are sitting. I ask Takao if there is anything we have missed or left out.

"Yes, we left out most of the interesting details—the fun stories."

"But that would be a book," I say.

"Exactly, that's it: you need a book! You're up to page 227 by now."

"Actually, only page twenty, and I'll have to pare it down."

Takao just laughs, and this time I detect no sense of irony. His face crinkles softly, and caught up in the moment, I can only laugh along with him.

Dr. Leonel Perra:
Quality of Education

D r. Leo Perra has retired from his work as a college administrator, but he's still so busy with consulting work that it took some time to fit me into his schedule. We agree to meet in the dining room of a hotel near the Vancouver International Airport, where he has another meeting with the Board of Indigenous Government. While I wait for him to arrive, I anxiously watch wet snowflakes drifting by outside the window, making the streets slippery and treacherous. Leo spots me when he enters the room and strides over with his hand stretched out, an easy, warm smile on his face, and lively eyes behind dark-rimmed glasses. I judge that here was a man who could instantly put people at ease—in my case, so much so that I stop worrying about the snow and the road conditions minutes after he begins to tell the story of his life.

He says that he had always been a practical person who was good with his hands and liked fixing things. When he left high school, there was no doubt in his mind that he would spend the rest of his life doing exactly that—but as a young man he had imagined fixing machines and engines, not educational institutions.

Leo Perra was born on November 13, 1939, in Spirit River, Alberta, a small farming community situated north of Grand Prairie and east of Dawson Creek, B.C., with a population of about eight hundred. Leo recalls that the winters were bitterly cold with the temperatures often dropping to 40 or 60 degrees Fahrenheit below zero.

Leo's father, Alex, had come from Saskatchewan and could turn his hand to any sort of business and be successful. At one time or another he

Dr. Leonel Perra, 2001

managed a restaurant, a rooming house, a farm, and a sawmill. In the 1930s he became a farm implement dealer and managed the dealership for many years. Leo's mother, Blandine, raised four children and ran a rooming house. In the 1940s the grain elevators in Spirit River burned down and when the carpenters and other workers flooded into the town to rebuild the elevators, Blandine packed them in. The Perra house was noisy and crowded, but it was filled with children's laughter and voices raised to make themselves heard above the inevitable din of people talking or joking with each other.

Alex and Blandine were hard workers, and so were their children. As the oldest, Leo was the one who helped his father at the dealership. It was either that or housework, and anything was better than dusting, washing dishes, or scrubbing floors. He was only six when he learned how to help assemble farm machinery, and when he got older he drove all over the surrounding countryside, delivering propane tanks.

Leo had an easy time at school, where he excelled in mathematics. The only subject that eluded him was English literature, in which he received rather poor marks. He also didn't particularly care because he wasn't planning to continue his education after high school. All he wanted to do was learn a trade and earn a living.

Alex had far more ambitious plans for his son. He had completed his schooling only as far as Grade Four, but despite his lack of formal education he was the chairman of the Catholic School Board, and he was determined that his children should at the very least graduate from high school. Alex wanted Leo to become a teacher. He had lived through the Depression and knew that even in those tough times, teachers had continued to work. Leo laughs at the memory. "He didn't tell me they weren't getting paid, just that they did have a job."

In those days there was a big shortage of teachers in the country. A person could graduate from high school, take a six-week summer course at the university, and start teaching in the fall. But no matter how his father tried to convince him that teaching would be an excellent career, Leo resisted the notion. While working with his father, he had become adept with machinery and wanted to be an electrician, perhaps even owning his own electronics business one day.

Leo studied electricity at the Southern Alberta Institute of Technology in Calgary for a year and the following summer got a job on a farm. One morning he made his lunch as he usually did, using some leftover pork roast from the night before. He was running the tractor that day. When rain suddenly came pouring down, he climbed off the machine, ran indoors, put his sandwich down on a heat register, and forgot about it. The next day he remembered about the sandwich and found it still sitting where he had left it. "Great," he thought. "There's my lunch." And he ate the warm pork sandwich. "How I managed to eat it, I don't know," he says. "I guess I must have been really hungry."

A couple of hours later his stomach started to heave, and he broke into a cold sweat. He got off the tractor and drove home. The next day he was so ill he was pretty sure he was going to die, and he was too sick to even care. On wobbly legs, Leo dragged himself to his doctor, who diagnosed a severe case of food poisoning and sent him to the hospital.

The doctors at the hospital ran a series of tests and took a number of X-rays. One of them showed a slight cloudiness in both of his lungs. His doctor told him that the cloudiness was cause for some concern and recommended that he stay in a clean air environment away from fumes and chemicals.

The doctor's orders meant that Leo had to make a different career choice. It wasn't easy. He'd been so sure of electronics that he had never even considered another option. As he pondered his future, he could think of only one career that seemed to fit the "clean air" requirement: teaching. So, on the Friday before Labour Day weekend, Leo decided that he would take his father's advice after all and become a teacher. Alex was delighted. Although it was only days before the school term began, Alex made sure that his son got into teacher's college: He called the superintendent for the local public school division, who phoned the dean of the faculty of education at the University of Alberta, and on the Tuesday morning after Labour Day, Leo started classes.

"I showed up on Tuesday morning—a country boy with no idea of what I was getting into," he recalls. "In those days school districts were so desperate for teachers they were willing to put up $600—half of which was a grant and the other a loan that was forgivable if you taught for two years."

Leo took the two-year teacher certification course, and then he taught high school for two years in Wanham, Alberta, a community with a population of about one hundred, only 35 kilometres from Spirit River. The small school taught Grades One to Twelve and had a total student enrolment of about two hundred.

Leo taught mathematics and French. He discovered that he was a good teacher. "I got turned on by students who learned while I was teaching," he says. "Every now and then you'd see a glimmer of light because you had done a good job. That excited me."

After two years, he went back to university for summer school and night courses to get his Bachelor of Education degree. While he studied, he taught in the Edmonton school district. After graduating, Leo was anxious to move back to a small town. "Being from a community of 800 people, I found life in Edmonton quite challenging," he says. "Particularly the business of driving for half an hour to get anywhere. We used to drive our car just to go a block, but we'd be there within a minute. And the streets were rough and dusty in Edmonton, and I'm kind of finicky about my cars. I don't like pounding them over the pavement."

He pauses in his narrative and laughs, recalling his priorities back then—moving to a smaller town because of his car. But he also wanted to live in a more rural community for other reasons too, one of them being that he liked the pace of life and the friendliness of smaller towns. He sent resumes to half a dozen communities in B.C., and the assistant superintendent of schools in Kamloops, B.C. was the first person to call.

After a ten-minute conversation, he asked Leo, "How's your discipline?"

"I haven't had any complaints," Leo said.

"Well, you're hired if you want the job."

Leo laughs. "Imagine, after a ten-minute interview, you're hired. These things just don't happen any more!"

At the same time as he had began his job hunt, he had married Carol, a girl from Victoria, whom he had met in Spirit River, where she had worked as a nurse at the local hospital. Leo recalls their meeting as a classic case of love at first sight. They hadn't married right away: Carol had taken time to travel and had then moved back to Victoria while Leo continued to study and work in Edmonton. In 1965, shortly after their wedding, Leo and Carol moved to Kamloops, where Leo taught French and mathematics in the local high school. The town was experiencing a construction boom at the time, and as a result, housing was in short supply; so Carol and Leo put their furniture and most of their belongings in storage and stayed in a motel while they looked for a permanent home. Unfortunately, the storage facility burned down, and they lost everything, with no insurance coverage either.

Faced with the expense of starting over, Leo looked for extra work. He got a job teaching summer school, where he met Jack Harrison, the director of adult education. Jack suggested that Leo might be interested in teaching French at night school. Leo said yes, he'd love to teach at night, but then Jack decided to teach the French course himself and made Leo the night school principal instead.

The job was chiefly administrative. Leo collected money, registered students, and helped with the programming four nights a week. During the day, he taught his regular classes, and because he was handy with equipment, he was also head of the high school audio/visual department.

The following summer he became the summer school principal, and when the next school year started, he went back to his night school/day school routine. While other teachers enjoyed long summer vacations, Leo got only two weeks off, but he didn't think of his long hours as a hardship. The way he saw it, he still had ten days off at Easter and ten days at Christmas, and that was a better deal than most working people had.

Meanwhile Jack Harrison was working with the Regional College Committee—a group of people interested in establishing a college in Kamloops. Leo helped Jack calculate budgets. He also helped him develop a statistical database to prove that a college was needed in the Cariboo. The chair of the Regional College Committee was also the chair of the Williams Lake school district, which was looking for a director of adult education. When Jack heard about the job opening he asked Leo, "Would you be interested in it?"

Leo was interested enough to investigate. He and Carol drove up to Williams Lake to take a look at the community. It happened to be the week before the Williams Lake Stampede and most of the population had already begun to celebrate. Men where drunk on the streets, weaving in and out of traffic, brawling, and being altogether disagreeable. The adult education centre was an old maintenance building and looked its age. Leo and Carol turned around and drove home, thinking, "No thanks."

Four days later, the Regional College Committee met in Cache Creek, about an hour's drive from Kamloops. Jack phoned Leo from the meeting. "Leo, do you think you could be interested in this job? They still need someone."

The job was tempting, but did he really want to settle in a town like Williams Lake and work in a building that looked like a glorified garage? "Should I go and talk to them?" he asked Carol.

Carol said he might as well, so Leo drove to Cache Creek and had a beer with the chair of the board at the local bar. When the chair offered Leo a 50 percent increase in salary, Williams Lake and the school building suddenly looked a lot more appealing; Leo took the job. The money was a definite factor in his decision; however, he had also discovered that he liked administrative work and was good at it. In many ways operating the Centre for Adult Education was like operating a company. Leo had grown up with an appreciation for the work in running a business, so he was prepared for a management position.

The federal government had just introduced the Canada Manpower system and the Occupational Training Act, so the funding was in place for creative solutions to unemployment, administered through the adult education centre. Since Williams Lake had a large Aboriginal population spread throughout the Cariboo–Chilcotin, the departments of Indian Affairs and Canada Employment were also providing funding for programs.

Leo's department set up programs from Williams Lake to Bella Coola. It was a vast territory, but Leo not only managed the programs on a balanced budget, he made a surplus and used it creatively. Some of his most innovative programming was in the Aboriginal communities. One day, an instructor suggested that the centre offer cooking classes to the Aboriginal people because there were no home economics facilities or classes offered anywhere in the region. Leo didn't think cooking classes sounded very exciting, so he filed the request away and had almost forgotten about it until one day when he was out on one of the Reserves talking to an instructor who was running an auto mechanics shop. Leo had taken his four-year-old son Michael with him, and when he was ready to leave, he couldn't find the boy. He located Michael at the family dinner table. He had been playing with the instructor's children, and when their mother called them in for supper, he had gone too. Leo walked in as the family and his son were filling their plates with potatoes, rice, macaroni, and bread. There were no vegetables or meat—just lots of filling, starchy foods. "When I saw that I thought, 'This is serious in terms of needing a cooking course.'"

Leo jumped into action. He found an empty trailer that the school district was no longer using, and with his small surplus, converted it into a cooking shack containing two sinks, two stoves, two ovens, a refrigerator, and kitchen cupboards. The cooking instructor travelled with the trailer to all the remote communities in the area, parking it in one place for about three weeks at a time. The women welcomed the lessons with more eagerness than Leo could have anticipated. Graduations for the cooking classes were often memorable with the food being provided by the graduates. At one graduation, the guests dined on an elaborate Chinese meal.

When Leo discovered there was a need for sewing classes, he bought a dozen portable sewing machines and made an arrangement with a fabric store to provide materials at a discount. He and the teacher would load fabric and pattern books into the back of the company station wagon and take it to the Reserve, where the women would choose their patterns and material. The following week the teacher drove up with plywood sheets—to serve as tables—and sewing machines and started the class.

Although Leo worked long days, especially from September to April, he was feeling fulfilled. Even when he encountered problems, he was satisfied with being able to find his own solutions. He was also never afraid to try something new. There were days when he thought he was learning more than his students. In the late 1960s the National Film Board offered a "challenge" series of films that were meant to make viewers think. When the brochure for the film program arrived on his desk, Leo read it and thought it a frivolous waste of the taxpayer's money, but he signed up for the program anyway. Later he went out to Dog Creek to discuss the success of the film course with the ranch woman he had hired to run it. She told him that one night as they watched a film that included a car race, when a front view of a car showed it coming directly towards them, one of the kids jumped underneath the table. "That child had never seen something like this before," Leo says. "That being the case, I thought this was something worthwhile to do just for the value of the general exposure to things that are going on in the rest of the world. People really lived an isolated life on some of the Reserves back then."

Leo set up the first Status of Women workshop in Canada because it seemed like the right thing to do. Almost two hundred and fifty people agreed with him because they plowed their way through two feet of snow to listen to speakers Judy LaMarsh and Judge Nancy Morrison.

In the year 1969 the plebiscite for a college in the Cariboo was held. Williams Lake was part of the region, so Leo put his energy and influence into campaigning for the college and getting people out to vote. Although Williams Lake was the community furthest from the college in Kamloops, it had one of the largest voter turnouts at 85 percent. Why did Williams Lake respond so favourably? Leo's influence was becoming widespread. He was well known as a man who cared about education and who listened to what people wanted. His innovative courses and approaches were proof of the value of education. There were others in Williams Lake who had also influenced the voter turnout, including the members of the school board and Anne Stevenson, a local resident who had been active in the community for years and was a strong advocate for education.

The plebiscite passed, and in 1971 the Centre for Adult Education became a department of Cariboo College, and Leo became the dean of continuing education. In that vote, Leo's region expanded to include the Lillooet school district and the northern half of the Cariboo school district.

In 1974 Leo became vice-principal of Cariboo College and moved back to Kamloops. He hoped that his new position would mean fewer hours on the job. Since 1968 he had been starting his days at 8:00 a.m. and finishing at 10:00 or 11:00 p.m. He liked the work; however, he didn't mind trading in the adult education hours for the more reasonable hours of a vice-principal's position. But his hopes of shorter hours were quickly shattered. The college was still in the early stages of development; it was a volatile period in its history. "Those were the days when everybody was learning," Leo says. "The faculty started sitting on selection committees. No one had experienced that kind of stuff before. Superintendents and principals might hire teachers in those early days. I was learning on the job."

The new faculty members had graduated from universities with what seemed like radical ideas. There were issues of conflict of interest and votes of non-confidence in the administration. The life span for a college principal in those days was about eighteen months. There were no precedents to follow because the board members had never dealt with a community college. Locals wanted the college to serve the needs of the community, and the faculty wanted to serve the needs of academia. New issues surfaced daily. To add to the general confusion, unionization in the college system had just begun, and the unfamiliar bargaining process was being developed.

Jack Harrison, who was the principal when Leo was hired, saw Leo as a much needed ally. Although Jack had strong community ties, he didn't have the academic credentials he needed to earn the respect of faculty leaders; so in 1978, the board of directors suggested it was time for him to move on. Leo calls it a tumultuous turnover. "It had the flavour of a palace coup."

With Jack gone, Leo stepped in as acting principal until the board could hire a new person to fill the position. By the time the college hired a new principal thirteen months later, Leo had brought order back to the institution. He wasn't afraid to be strong and to do what he thought was fair. When he was faced with a strike by the support staff, he locked them out, and when unions gave him ultimatums, he stood up for what he felt was right. During his principalship, a department head suffered a heart attack, and when she was ready to come back to work, the other department members told Leo, "If this person returns to her position, we're all going to resign."

He considered their threat for several days, then at the next meeting he said, "I very much appreciate your candidness, but I have spoken with the individual. She is prepared to return to her position, and I am prepared to support her. I will accept your resignations when you want to hand them in." He left the room and informed the board of what he had done. The board said, "It's nice to see administration making some decisions." What they didn't say, but implied, were the additional words of "for a change." None of the instructors tendered their resignations.

While Leo was involved in the madness of running the college, he was also studying for his Master's in Education degree through Simon Fraser University. He dubbed the study room, his "sanity room."

When the new principal took over, Leo realized he had enjoyed the job and felt reluctant to step down, so when Selkirk College in Castlegar (near Nelson, B.C.) advertised for a president, he applied. Selkirk College was established in 1965 and had gone through the same struggles as Cariboo College. In fifteen years, the college had had fifteen full and acting presidents. It was perceived to be so bad that when Leo told the chair of the board at Cariboo College that he had accepted the job of president at Selkirk College, the chair said, "Leo, you don't want to go to Selkirk College—you deserve better."

Leo now laughs at the memory. He ignored the well-intended advice and went to Selkirk College in 1980 with the idea of staying for about five years—bringing some stability to the institution and then moving on. He stayed for twenty years until his retirement.

He found his new job fun, exciting, and demanding. The hours were long, and grew longer with the years as Leo became involved with education at the provincial level; but the foundation at Selkirk College—which the founding president had put in place—was built by a strong ethos that valued quality of education, and Leo could fully embrace that philosophy. He had always believed that quality of education was the raison d'être of a learning institution. Quality could mean outfitting a trailer with stoves and ovens and hauling it up to an isolated First Nations reserve, or it could mean delivering top-notch academic courses: the purpose of the college was to teach students whatever subject they had come there to learn and to do it well. Leo found that the instructors felt similarly. Despite the conflicts between faculty and administration, they continued to be professional, delivering quality education.

Selkirk College had a history of difficult labour relations. In the late 1970s there had been a long strike by the support staff for the college and the school districts of West Kootenay. After almost four months, the government had legislated an end to the strike and brought in an arbitrator to work out a settlement. But even in 1980 when Leo arrived, there was still a good deal of resentment over the back-to-work legislation. The bad feelings resurfaced when Leo had to negotiate his first contract mere months after taking over as president.

To a large extent, Leo leaned on his experience at Cariboo College and the professional development courses in negotiation he had taken. He quickly gained a reputation as a tough but fair negotiator; some of his staunchest enemies from those days have now become his strongest supporters and friends. He had the capacity to look at all sides of an issue. His goal in negotiating was to reach a settlement that was fair to both the employee and to the taxpayers, who ultimately paid for it. "I had no set formula for bargaining," he says. "I think my approach came from my background and the values I have and from treating all employees equally rather than trying to favour one group over another." However, he was not above using every trick he thought would help him. If he showed an occasional flash of anger, it was to bring home the message that he meant business. Leo was also blessed with an excellent memory, and he did his homework. More than once he would listen to a negotiator, go through his briefcase, and pull out the relevant piece of paper. "This is a memo you sent me six months ago that's quite different than what you just said to the board." He was also blessed with a sixth sense and had an uncanny feeling for knowing when he had pushed hard enough and when it was time to back down.

Favouritism, or elitism, had thrived at the college when he arrived. The staff room was officially the faculty room; support staff and non-academic administration personnel were not welcome. Leo ordered the faculty lounge to become the staff lounge. He also believed strongly in gender equity not just for teachers but for all staff at the college. Female tradespeople, he argued, should be treated the same as men. He knew how tough some of the "menial" jobs on campus were. When there had been strikes at Cariboo College, he, along with the rest of the administration, had kept the campus running by washing dishes, cleaning up, and doing whatever the support staff had done. "I was certainly interested in treating everyone equitably," he says. "And so we reached settlements by treating everyone on an equitable basis."

As an administrator, he constantly looked for opportunities to bring more money into the college. In 1986 the B.C. government encouraged colleges and universities to recruit international students because of the economic benefit of bringing foreign dollars into the province. But the government also had a secondary motivation. Several private English as a Second Language (ESL) schools that had been established to teach English to foreign students had collapsed and left students with no classes. The government asked the colleges to provide ESL training to save them the embarrassment of having foreign students, who had paid their fees, finding a bankrupt sign on the school's door. Leo was one of the first college administrators to actively recruit Asian students.

As early as 1981 Leo saw the need to provide classes in computer studies. That year, Selkirk College had $200,000 in surplus funds. Much to the consternation of the main campus staff, Leo used the money to purchase computers for the continuing education division in Trail. "It was my sense of fair play," he says. "Here was this centre in Trail. It didn't have very much, but it was a good-sized community, so I thought, 'Let's put a computing lab in Trail.'"

The college bought about twenty computers, which were expensive in those days. They were primitive machines by today's standards—running strictly on floppy discs—but the adult education department used them for training, for summer camps, and for dozens of other successful programs.

Leo was so pleased with the results of the computer lab program that he decided to buy computers for the main campus with the next surplus. Since computers were still prohibitively expensive he shopped around for a bargain. The DEC Corporation was offering a desktop computer called The Rainbow, with a special educational price tag of about $2,600 each. Leo thought that was a great deal, but just as he was about to purchase them, the academic staff argued that the college should put its money into IBM equipment because business was heading in that direction. Leo followed the advice, and he has never regretted doing so. "I think one thing I have always tried to do is get technology into the hands of people in the institution," he says. "I've tended to support instruction at the expense of administration because instruction is what delivers the dollars to the institution. The institution will never be known for the quality of its administration, but it will be known for the quality of its instruction."

Selkirk College probably never had what Leo calls "the biggest or the nicest technological toys," but he made sure it stayed up-to-date. He encouraged the faculty to develop a curriculum that took advantage of modern technology. He also began to work with the local school districts to develop an interface between the high schools and the college. For years college students had been able to use some of their college courses as credits towards university courses. "We started working with the school district to try to start developing transitional pathways—for want of a better term—between students in the high school and students in the college, and we managed to get the college staff to recognize the work the students were doing in the high schools to give them advance credits," Leo says, with a bland smile on his face.

I smile. "That's a nice incentive to get kids into college."

He laughs. "You've seen right through me."

Although it was a clever ploy, the advance credits also helped students to shorten their studies, so it was a gain for everyone. "That was not an easy thing to achieve," he says. "Colleges always enjoyed the support of the universities in terms of transferring into them, but we never used to extend the courtesy to the K to twelve system. By the time I left Selkirk, I think there was good acceptance of that."

Leo did some things that had people marvelling at where he could possibly have come up with the ideas he had. In the early 1980s, Selkirk College had operated the David Thompson University Centre College in Nelson in partnership with the University of Victoria. In 1984 the government shut down the funding for the university college, and soon after that, the City of Nelson convinced a Japanese school to move into the empty building. The school was successful, but the administration wanted some Canadian students in the facility as well as Japanese. At that same time, Leo had been thinking about restarting the college's music program that had shut down years before for lack of funding. There were piles of unused musical instruments stored away in an old classroom, and it seemed an awful waste.

While he had pondered how to reintegrate a music program, his son Chris was developing an interest in an innovative music program at a school called MIT in Los Angeles. One day while Leo was in Los Angeles doing research for his doctorate studies, he dropped into MIT to investigate their program. MIT was turning out graduates in contemporary music who wanted to play in small bands or who wanted to do composition or engineering for the recording industry. "Very interesting," he thought.

He was beginning to put the two pieces together—the Japanese school and the music school—but he hadn't solved the funding problem. The province was spending a lot of education money, but not on innovative music programs. There was a movement in various communities to create university colleges; however, Selkirk was not one of the colleges selected to become a university college. This situation was the leverage Leo decided to use: He and the board presented their argument to the government that since they would receive no funds to become a university college, they should at least have some extra money coming their way for a music program, and that since music is an international language the perfect place to put the music program was in the Japanese School. If the Japanese students chose to enter the program, so much the better. It was logic the government couldn't argue with; the college started a contemporary music program that has been very successful from the start. "It was the right kind of thing for that community," Leo says. "It's an artistic community. I would stop for gas up in the Slocan Valley and have people tell me how much they appreciated the fact that this school was now in Nelson."

In 1989 Selkirk College received a $300,000 grant for music equipment. Following Leo's lead, the staff looked for bargains that would help them get maximum value for the grant. They managed to get Bryan Adams' old eight-track recorder and Oscar Peterson's old mixing console for a fraction of their original costs. They bargained for every piece of equipment they needed and ended up with a first-rate music studio at a fifth of the retail cost.

In 1994 Leo helped create the Post Secondary Employers' Association and became its first president. He was also a member of several other system committees at the provincial level. Shortly before retiring in 2000, he was asked to join the board of the Institute of Indigenous Government, a small educational institution set up by the province to help First Nations leaders learn the fundamentals of leadership and running a band. The provincial government came to Leo because he had earned a reputation for straightening out problems and bringing stability to educational organizations, and he also had a reputation for being smart, shrewd, fair, and honest. In addition, during his last years at Selkirk College, he had developed some expertise on policy governance, which is a model of how boards should organize themselves to be effective; so he was known as a man who knew how to work well with boards.

He became president of the Institute of Indigenous Government and is now past president. Late one night shortly after he had been appointed as interim president, he was watching Able Auctions on television, listening to the announcer talking about the failure of the dot-com companies. He saw that equipment could be purchased for amazingly low cost. The institute had just received a grant of $200,000 from the Ministry of Advanced Education to re-equip the school because its computers were obsolete and the furniture was literally falling apart. "We should look at this stuff," Leo thought. "These machines look like they're almost new."

Leo and some of the institute staff went to the auction and have been going to auction sales ever since. They have completely refurbished the school with new desks, modern computers, chairs, and accessories, and they still have money left over. In some cases they were buying brand new, still-in-the-box computers for $500.

Leo was asked to come on the board of the Institute of Indigenous Government to bring stability to the organization—just as he had brought stability to the Centre for Adult Education in Williams Lake, to Cariboo College in Kamloops, and to Selkirk College in Castlegar. I met with him sixteen months after he took on the job. "I believe they're well on their way now," he said.

In 2001, one year after Dr. Leonel Perra retired from Selkirk College, he was awarded the Order of British Columbia. Leo remembers receiving a phone call from the secretary at Government House in Victoria. The secretary said, "I'm calling from the Lieutenant Governor's office with respect to the Order of B.C."

Leo had recommended Audrey Moore, a former mayor of Castlegar, for the Order of B.C., and he was pleased that he was getting a phone call to tell him she was about to receive the award.

"Do you know why I'm calling?" the man said.

"Yes, you're calling to let me know that Audrey Moore is the recipient of the Order of B.C. That's just great!"

"Oh no," the secretary said. "It's you."

"What?" He was totally surprised. He says now, "Sure, I've done lots of things. And I did some of them well. But I was paid to do those things. I always saw that as part of my job."

He didn't stop feeling just a bit sad about Audrey Moore until the committee in Ottawa accepted his nomination of her for the Order of Canada.

Leo did many things in his 35 years in education. He worked with people from all levels of society throughout the province, but what he remembers most fondly are the cooking classes, the sewing machines, and the adult education classes at the Canim Lake Reserve, south of 100 Mile House. He remembers how eager those students were to learn. One woman had a baby on a Friday afternoon, and on Monday morning she was back in the classroom. Leo remembers creating a welding trailer to drag welders around, and he remembers flying in and out of Bella Coola in a Beaver aircraft to deliver education. "Those are the things you can't create—they're just there. And they are the things I will never forget," he says.

His proudest achievement at Selkirk College is that after twenty years, he was still accepted by the board, administration, staff, and faculty. In 1999 at the staff Christmas dinner, Leo discovered that his staff had nominated him for a leadership award from the Chair Academy—an international association of educational institutions— and the nomination had been accepted. Early the next year, he received the award. "It just blew me away," he says. "And I was crying." Leo's staff also nominated him for the Distinguished Service Recognition Award from the College Presidents' Network of the Association of Canadian Community Colleges. He received that award in May 2000.

His most cherished memory of his twenty years at Selkirk College is the party the staff and board gave him in recognition of his ten-year anniversary. Since he knew nothing about the party, he had made plans to go to Kamloops that Saturday for the twentieth anniversary celebration of Cariboo College. A few days before the event, Walter, a friend from Victoria, called and said he wanted to come up to talk to him about a particular foundation in Toronto. Leo agreed to have dinner with Walter and delay his departure for Kamloops until later in the evening.

When he arrived, Walter said, "Let's go up to the golf club and have dinner there."

They pulled into the full parking lot, and Leo said, "Walter, we're never going to get in here. The place is packed."

"They're probably all out on the golf course," Walter said.

They walked into the building. "The place is packed," Leo said. "Walter—it's full. There's a banquet going on."

The fact that there were familiar faces around him didn't register until Walter pointed up to a big banner strung across the wall. "Congratulations, Leo, on your 10th Anniversary."

Leo attracted that kind of loyalty and recognition because he is dedicated and fair-minded. In Williams Lake, he didn't have to create a cooking class; he didn't have to create a welding trailer; and he could have ignored the film series. But he believed it was his job to provide the education people wanted and needed, even if it meant putting in extra time and energy. By his definition, that commitment counted as quality education, which is all he ever hoped to achieve.

Ric Careless:
An Arbitrary Optimist

I don't think I have ever met anyone who is so eager to talk about wilderness preservation—his vocation—or someone who does it more eloquently than Ric Careless. A half-hour after I ask my first question, Ric asks me, "And what was your second question?"

Ric was born in Toronto on February 22, 1951. His father J.M.S. (Maurice) Careless was the head of the University of Toronto's history department and was known as Canada's premier historian. He received the Order of Canada for his work and educated many of the historians across the country. Ric was the middle of five children. He calls himself the black sheep—the troublemaker—but he was bright and clever and enjoyed participating in the spirited intellectual conversations that invariably took place at the Careless dinner table. The underlying theme of those conversations was responsibility and a sense of duty, especially to country. Ric's mother, Elizabeth, was a seventh generation Canadian. She and Maurice were proud of their country and did their best to instil that sense of pride in their children.

Ric was a downtown kid who got up to all the usual "city kid" pranks, but he also lived close to the Don Valley. Although the river was polluted, it was also an oasis of wilderness. In the spring when the snow started to melt, Ric and his friends would build dams in the river and then release enormous amounts of water to spill over into the city streets.

His teachers recognized his quick, intelligent mind, and they enrolled Ric in an enrichment course for bright children. Every Saturday,

Ric Careless, 1994

about 30 youngsters from across Toronto would gather to discuss a wide range of topics from geography and law to questions of ethics. When he was in Grade Six, Ric attended a one-week outdoor school on the islands that lie in Toronto's harbour. During that week, he banded birds, mucked around in the marsh, and began to understand how the natural world works as an ecosystem. "I know that that was the place that first turned me on to the natural world."

When he was twelve years old, Ric had his first experience of summer camp in the Haliburton country, north of Toronto. He learned how to paddle a canoe and went for overnight trips into Algonquin Park. "That really twigged me on to the wild country."

But the solitude of Algonquin wasn't enough to satisfy his secret desire. From the time he was a very young child, he had wanted to see mountains. He read books about Norway because he loved the landscape of the mountains coming down to meet the sea, and he drew pictures of the Norwegian hills and fjords. It wasn't until he was in his 40s, after he had moved to Gibsons on the edge of Howe Sound, that he realized it wasn't Norway he had been drawing—it was Howe Sound and the Coast Mountain Range. "I always felt that I was born in the wrong place," Ric says. "I was meant to live in the mountains, so British Columbia has always been my home."

When Ric was fourteen, his father took a summer posting as a visiting professor at the University of Victoria. The family rode the train across Canada. When it was due to come into Jasper, Ric got up at 5:00 a.m. and climbed up to the dome car, where he knew he would have the best view. He watched the dawn light wash over the distant purple-grey foothills. As the train rolled on, the mountains loomed larger and larger, and for the first time, Ric understood the scale of the mountains he had loved long before he had ever seen them. "They were actually real. They were three-dimensional! "That was just a tremendous thrill. The train went by Mount Robson, and it was clear and glorious, and it was just so exciting."

That summer in Victoria, Ric raked leaves, mowed lawns, and did errands to raise enough money to take the overnight train to Kamloops and then ride back down the Fraser Canyon. A few weeks later, he travelled up to Lillooet and rode the train back down, surrounded by mountains. "Either mountains are in your soul or they aren't," he says.

"Now when I go back to Toronto I'll find that I'll be looking at the clouds and thinking that they're mountains. They're definitely the anchor for me."

Although Ric's earliest wilderness campaigning involved the coastal rainforest, the places he has always held most dear are B.C.'s mountain wilderness areas. "My work is intensely spiritual," he says. "I work on a lot of levels. I work strategically and intellectually. I can run the numbers out and crunch them; I can do the artistic with the images and the pictures; but I really believe that underneath it all is the spiritual. I think this is what this stuff is about. This is what my life is about."

That fall, Ric's family returned to Toronto. The summer Ric graduated from Grade Twelve, his father was invited back to the University of Victoria (UVic) for a year, so Ric enrolled at UVic as a science student. But he soon found the subject limiting and restrictive. He believed in a world that was more than rational and logical—a world where the intuitive and inspirational lived side by side with science. He transferred to the honours geography program, which he enjoyed immensely, and when his family went back to Toronto, he stayed behind.

In his second year, Ric met Brett Wallach, a professor who had taught at the University of California at Berkeley and had been doing leading work in geography and conservation. Wallach introduced Ric to the writings of men such as Henry David Thoreau, John Muir, and other great wilderness conservationists. Wallach had his class study the transcripts of the U.S. Congress on conservation issues, which fascinated Ric. "I got this desire to one day testify before the United States Congress," he recalls. "He was a tremendously inspiring man and really did connect me with my life's work."

Ric joined the UVic Outdoors Club, becoming its first conservation director. He started travelling out to the west coast of Vancouver Island, to Long Beach, and Clayoquot Sound to explore the natural beauty of the island. In Ric's third year at UVic, Ken Farquharson, the founder of the Vancouver branch of the Sierra Club and one of the first and leading conservationists in the province, visited Victoria. "We've got to have a Sierra Club on Vancouver Island," he told the members of the UVic Outdoors Club, and Ric agreed.

He was already a member of the U.S. Sierra Club, so he simply took their letterhead, clipped off the logo, pasted it on a blank piece of paper, and taped the words "Vancouver Island" under it. Voila!—a new Sierra Club logo had been created! As far as Ric was concerned, it was enough to make their club official. Eventually the mother organization heard about the unauthorized club on Vancouver Island and sorted it out, but not without a good deal of consternation and surprise, and not before Ric had run his first campaign for the preservation of the Nitinat Triangle under the auspices of the Sierra Club.

The Nitinat Triangle was an old-growth forested valley on the west side of Vancouver Island adjoining the West Coast Trail, which encompassed a cluster of three pristine wilderness lakes and became the site where Canadian citizens first campaigned to protect an old-growth rain forest.

The forest company B.C. Forest Products wanted to log the lowland valley, where 1,000-year-old cedars and Douglas firs grew. Ric, his girlfriend Karen, and Gord Price, another member of the outdoors club, set off to save the valley. "We were university kids who didn't know better—that you're not supposed to do these things," Ric says. "We were really starting from square one. There were no templates or examples of how to do it."

Ric, Karen, and Gord went to Nitinat to map the area. There were no trails and no roads; the river was their path. They waded upstream, often up to their necks in water, dragging their canoe past rapids and through immense old-growth forests and giant ferns while spawning salmon shot past them and swam through their legs.

For Ric, Nitinat was exciting, but it was also cold, wet, uncomfortable, depressing, intimidating, and scary. The dark clouds hovered low in the sky, and the chill and gloom were unremitting. After what seemed like an endless trek, they caught their first glimpse of Hobiton Lake. At that moment, the dark rain clouds parted and a shaft of light sliced through, touching the water. The high, forested ridge behind Hobiton Lake towered over the scene. "There was just a sense of spirit," Ric recalls. "It was a very magical place. It was almost as if the land was speaking to me, and I just had a desire to keep this place special forever."

Ric, Karen, and Gord explored the lakes in their canoe for several days. During the next year the Sierra Club cleared the first trails into the Nitinat Triangle. That year, Ric met John Willow, a man who had been a resistance fighter with the Polish underground during the Second World War and a faller for forest giant, MacMillan Bloedel. He had decided that clear-cutting was something he simply could no longer do. At age 50, John Willow was one of the older campaigners for Nitinat, but as such he brought guidance, knowledge, and solid experience in laying strategic plans. John also helped cut the first portage trails connecting the lakes.

Whether younger or older, the Sierra Club activists knew they had to give people the opportunity to see the area before they could understand what was at risk. While the club cut trails, B.C. Forest Products built a road into the area as quickly as it could. As the sounds of blasting came closer, the group felt an increased sense of urgency to save Nitinat.

The club organized meetings to raise public awareness. As the trails were completed, they took members of the media out to Nitinat to show them the wilderness. They contacted a man with an airplane, who took them up to photograph the area, and Ric found an award-winning filmmaker in Seattle, who spent two weeks documenting the Nitinat. Ric directed, wrote the script, and mixed the sound at the local radio station. "We didn't know how to do any of this. I did it completely backwards, but it ended up playing on national television."

Club members enlisted the help of politicians, and Ric started lobbying the cabinet ministers of the W.A.C. Bennett government. "Here I was—a kid about twenty years old—lobbying these sliver-haired politicians. It was very intimidating, very scary, yet it was so clear to me this is what I had to do."

The minister of forests, Ray Williston, initially told Ric there was no way he was going to put forests aside for parks. In further meetings with him, Ric realized that the best way to relate to Williston was to assume the role of a son to his father. Using this approach over the next year, Williston's attitude changed. One morning when Ric visited him, Williston said, "You know, I just went in and flew over the Nitinat the other day. I can see what you're talking about. I think we're going to have to do something about it."

"It was pretty amazing," Ric says. "But even at that age I realized that it's not there until it's there."

As the campaign continued, the government called a provincial election. Ric and his group knew they would have to bring the issue to a close before election day or begin again with a new government. They talked to the media across the province and held public speaking events in Vancouver and all across Vancouver Island. To culminate the campaign, Ric invited Jean Chrétien, the federal minister for national parks, to speak at a rally in downtown Victoria. Ric and his friends promoted the event for six weeks, appearing on radio shows and plastering the city with posters. On the night of the rally, the auditorium was jammed. Several provincial politicians were in the audience, and one of them remarked that the energy in the room was reminiscent of a religious revival. When Chrétien got up to the podium to speak, he pulled out his prepared speech, read a few lines, pushed it aside, and leaned forward on the podium, and said, "I just want you to know that tonight I am committing myself and my government that we are going to protect the Nitinat Triangle."

Twenty-five years later, when Jean Chrétien was campaigning across Canada in a federal election, he talked about a meeting he had had with W.A.C. Bennett before the rally for Nitinat. "I'm going to make you a deal," he had told Bennett. "We're going to protect a place called the Nitinat Triangle." Ric had not known at the time about the private meeting between Chrétien and the premier, where the deal was struck, but he was gratified that Chrétien had remembered it.

Just before the provincial election in 1972, the B.C. government committed not to log the Nitinat Triangle, but despite that commitment, Nitinat did not achieve national park protected status until 1985. Ric says, "One thing I learned over the years is that it's not done until it's done. That was the one where I got my start. That was the one where I learned about lobbying. And then I began to wonder, 'What other opportunities are there on Vancouver Island?'"

In 1972, the summer he graduated from the University of Victoria, Ric secured a student employment grant to research wilderness areas that were still intact on Vancouver Island. He and other members of the Sierra Club looked at thousands of air photos and plotted every logging road and every clear-cut to determine what was left that was worth saving. Such a project had never been attempted before anywhere in Canada. By then, the misunderstanding with the U.S. Sierra Club had been cleared up, and the organization gave Ric a pilot to take him and some others over Vancouver Island on a reconnoitering flight. When they flew over the Schoen Valley, northwest of Campbell River, they knew they had found a wilderness area deserving of provincial protection. It contained dramatic mountains and a spectacular landscape, but what made it especially interesting was the complex of meadows on the eastern side of the mountains, which provided a natural habitat for the then highly endangered Roosevelt elk.

Bob Williams, the resources minister with the new NDP government, had taken a liking to Ric; so Ric took advantage of that fact to lobby him to protect the Schoen Valley. Williams very quickly committed his government to protecting it, and Ric began to wonder what other areas in B.C. needed protection.

Meanwhile, at the beginning of that summer, the Parks Canada department in Ottawa had offered Ric a job as a parks planner. Ric had accepted, but after working on the Schoen Valley campaign, he called National Parks' director John Nichols, and said, "I hate to tell you, but I'm not going to take the job because I just can't imagine moving back to Ontario."

"I'm sorry to hear that," Nichols said. "But would you be interested in doing a contract for us instead?"

The department hired Ric to identify potential parks in the Interior of B.C.—something no one had ever thought of doing. Ric drove up and down and across the province, living and sleeping in the back of a little Datsun truck. Everywhere he went he asked people, "If you could protect any area what should the priorities be?"

During the Nitinat Triangle campaign, when Ric spoke to B.C.'s minister of parks, he had learned that only 3 percent of B.C.'s land base was protected parkland. "And that's just about right," the minister had said. Ric didn't agree; however, he knew if he was to see the B.C. parks system grow, there was a lot of work to be done.

During his employment for Parks Canada, he was the only person in Canada actually being paid to protect the wilderness. In his travels, Ric met Art Twomey, a bearded mountain man and U.S. draft dodger living high in the Purcell Mountains in the Kootenay region of B.C. He told Ric about his vision for a protected Purcell Wilderness area.

When Ric came back from his trip, he created the first map to identify a system of parks to protect endangered wilderness areas. The Sierra Club of B.C. gave some money to the project, but the majority of the funding that allowed Ric to work as the Western Canadian conservation representative came from some wealthy Albertans who were interested in preserving wilderness in both Alberta and B.C. Catherine Whyte from Banff, who had been married to the well-known photographer of Banff, Peer Whyte, was a particularly strong believer in wilderness; she became Ric's main benefactor.

As the Western Canadian conservation representative, the first issue Ric chose to work on was the Purcell Wilderness. Art Twomey had already started a public campaign using tactics that Ric and the Sierra Club had used at Nitinat and in the Schoen Valley. He was also a gifted cinematographer, so he shot a film of the Purcells, which he showed in every community in the Kootenays.

At that time, the government had just established a new agency: The Environment and Land Use Secretariat, which reported to cabinet ministers and whose responsibility included everything to do with the environment and land use. Shortly after the agency was created, Bob Williams, the minister of resources, asked Ric to join the staff. "For the first couple of times he asked me, I thought he was just trying to block me," Ric says. "My job was to stay true and lobby for wilderness, but eventually he convinced me to join. I vowed I was going to try to use the opportunity to advance the cause of wilderness."

As one of his first acts in his new job, Ric proposed that the government protect the Purcell Wilderness area. With Bob Williams' support he convinced the cabinet that the Purcell Wilderness would benefit the province, so they created a 300,000-acre wilderness area, which at that time was the largest protected wilderness in southern B.C. "That was very exciting," Ric recalls. "It was very, very exciting."

The forest companies were angry and lobbied for years to dismantle the park. They viewed the land as a means to create jobs and earn money. "For many people in the forestry business, a tree is a just a bunch of fibre standing up on end that's supposed to go through a sawmill," Ric says. "Many people do not see the point in leaving a forest intact for its ecological, recreational, and spiritual values."

The citizens of the Kootenays kept fighting back and in the 1990s when the government brought in the commission on land and resources to complete the protected areas in B.C., they insisted that the Purcell Wilderness needed not just to be retained, but enlarged. They were successful in having it expanded from 300,000 to 500,000 acres.

After his success with the Purcell Wilderness, Ric turned his attention northward to Spatsizi, a 1.75 million-acre expanse of wilderness located halfway between Smithers and the Yukon, which is often referred to as "Canada's Serengeti."

Spatsizi had been proposed for protection for many years but without success. In this campaign Ric joined with Bristol Foster, who was then head of the B.C. Ecological Reserve Branch, to finally put Spatsizi under official protection. Once again Ric spoke to Bob Williams who fully agreed with the plan, but just when Ric thought he'd won the campaign for Spatsizi, the government called a snap election. Ric and Bristol Foster worked with a sense of urgency reminiscent of the Nitinat campaign, and days before the election, they were successful in having the government declare Spatsizi a protected area.

When the new Social Credit government headed by Bill Bennett stepped into power, Ric worried that they might dismantle the park on the pretext that it had only been created as a political act. But just at that time, the media published a story about a wilderness guide in Spatsizi, who had violated the Wildlife Act on numerous counts, illegally shooting undersized and protected species. The public was outraged that this had been allowed to happen, especially in an area of such exceptional wildlife value. The public's support of the newly created Spatsizi park grew so strong that the new government not only convened a review of the Wildlife Act, but it also confirmed its solid support of it.

In 1976 Ric left his government agency job to accept a commonwealth scholarship to the Joint Centre for Environmental Studies in New Zealand. But within a few weeks of beginning studies towards his master's degree, Ric proposed to quit. After years of front line campaigning to protect parks, advising cabinet, and writing wilderness legislation, graduate work didn't excite him. The scholarship committee then offered him a fellowship to study for his PhD, but six weeks into his studies, Ric left. "I knew the academic world. I realized that if I got a PhD all I would end up doing was become an academic or a senior bureaucrat and neither interested me."

Instead, he travelled and visited the wild places and protected areas in New Zealand, Australia, the islands of the South Pacific, and other parts of the world. When he got back to Vancouver with no job and no money, he found work in Smithers, running the youth employment program for the northern two-thirds of the province. "I just used the opportunity to continue to work on conservation projects." He worked on a variety of environmental assessment projects and took a six-month tour of the national parks in B.C., the western U.S., and Central America.

In 1980 Ric moved to Nelson and then Cranbrook, where he managed an Energy Conservation Demonstration Centre sponsored by the federal, provincial, and local governments. The project proved it was possible to economically build full-scale houses that would heat on the energy output equivalent to two pop-up toasters in a minus-40-degree winter. When the price of oil went down, the government and the public lost interest, and the centre closed down.

For some years, Ric managed nature interpretation contracts for provincial parks in southern B.C., and then in 1985 he went to work on the issue of South Moresby—one of the Queen Charlotte Islands. The public had been trying to save and protect South Moresby for ten years. "The government had been running people through processes. It was a 'talk and log' situation," Ric says.

The public became more and more outspoken in its anger over South Moresby, and although the government might have gone on ignoring this, it could not as easily disregard some of its biggest supporters.

Bryan Williams, who went on to become the president of the Canadian Bar Association and Chief Justice of the Supreme Court of B.C., had long loved the wilderness and had been a member of the group that had worked with Ken Farquharson in the 1970s to save the Skagit Valley, near Hope, from being dammed. In 1985 he took a group of top industrialists and financiers to South Moresby Island in a sailboat. They came back united in the decision that the place had to be saved, and then sent a letter to Premier Bill Bennett, urging him to do so.

At the next cabinet meeting, the subject of South Moresby was debated again. When the same old chorus of "Oh, these are just a bunch of radical environmentalists" began, Bill Bennett said, "Well, I think you might like to see this letter from some of our most steadfast supporters and business leaders." When he read the letter to his cabinet, the members knew they would have to take the issue seriously. They established the Wilderness Advisory Committee to review South Moresby. They also later set up a committee to look at the future of sixteen different wilderness areas in B.C., including the Stein Valley, Khutzeymateen, and Tatshenshini.

Some cabinet members regarded the Wilderness Advisory Committee as an opportunity to discredit the environmentalists, so they appointed industrialists to the committee. However, the premier had named Bryan Williams as committee head—an appointment Williams had refused to accept unless he had at least one leading conservationist on the committee—he selected Ken Farquharson. Over the next six months, the committee held a series of meetings across the province. Hundreds of people came to them, and one by one the committee members realized this was a serious matter, and they began to change their minds.

At the Cranbrook meeting of the Wilderness Advisory Committee, the issue of the Purcell Wilderness resurfaced. After Ric made a passionate presentation to the government, urging them to not just retain the Purcell Wilderness but to expand it from 300,000 to 500,000 acres, he was approached by a group of local guide outfitters who had heard him speak. "There's a wilderness area adjoining Banff National Park on the B.C. side of the Great Divide in the East Kootenay, which is about to be logged. Would you be interested in working on this?"

"Please take this on," they said. "It's called Height of the Rockies. It's very spectacular with 26 peaks over 10,000 feet, old-growth forests, and extraordinary wildlife." To demonstrate his commitment each outfitter reached into his pocket and pulled out a cheque for $1,000 or $2,000.

They told Ric that ten years previously, the Ministry of Forests had promised not to log the area, but by 1987 the industry had logged out the lower valley. "And they'd run out of wood, so guess what they were going to do?" Ric asks me. "They were going to renege on their deal. The guy who had been the head of that process for government had gone on to become chief forester, and he knew he'd reneged."

By now Ric had learned about power politics. "You either preserve Height of the Rockies as was originally promised, or there is going to be a tremendous public uproar," he told the chief forester. "If you want another South Moresby erupting, you're going to get it in Height of the Rockies, and you will be seen as reneging on your promise. If you want to convince the citizens that the ministry of forests lives by its word and really does care about the wilderness, you'd better protect Height of the Rockies. Otherwise your failure to honour a deal will generate a backlash clear across the province at a time when the public's appetite for wilderness is growing fast."

Ric proposed that B.C. should follow the lead of the U.S. "Let's amend the Forest Act to set up Forest Service wilderness areas so that the Forest Service can also protect the wilderness." The government liked the idea because it gave the government a way to hold onto its land base while meeting the public's demand for wilderness, so the Forest Act was amended.

In 1988 a number of adventure tourism operators, who had seen the success of the Height of the Rockies campaign, banded together to form the Wilderness Tourism Council (WTC) to represent their interests in protecting land and water resources upon which their businesses depended. Ric accepted the WTC's proposal that he be its director.

Shortly after the establishment of the WTC, a Smithers-based group of steelhead fishing guides asked Ric and the WTC to help them preserve the Babine River, one of the premier steelhead rivers in the world. Forest companies were planning to log the Babine right down to the water's edge. Ric used a different strategy to protect this wilderness, which involved analyzing the dollar values associated with the river's steelhead industry and its tourism value as compared to the money that could be derived from logging. When he had gathered enough evidence to prove that preservation dollar values exceeded those that could be gained from logging, he met—on the behalf of the newly formed WTC—with the senior level members of the ministry of forests. "What these folks are asking is reasonable," Ric told the forestry officials. "The value of the resource for tourism on the Babine is extremely high. By contrast, the forest resources are limited. We can make a case. And, by the way, you're not going to be dealing with just a couple of local operators; you're going to be dealing with the tourism industry as a whole."

Within 30 days, the Ministry of Forests made the decision to protect the Babine River. Shortly afterward, Johnny Mikes, a river rafting guide and one of the founders of the WTC, asked Ric to come and look at a river called the Tatshenshini. On many occasions he had made the same request, and Ric had repeatedly told him that he couldn't spare the time; the Tatshenshini was too far away—right on the Alaska– Yukon border. But Johnny persisted, and in 1989 Ric went down the Tatshenshini on a raft with a small group of guides. He encountered a new immensity of wilderness. "It was on a scale like I had never experienced before."

The Tatshenshini is the heartland of a 10,000-square-kilometre area. The river is more than a kilometre wide and cuts through the St. Elias Mountains, the highest range in Canada. It took them twelve days to traverse the 257 kilometres down to Glacier Bay National Park in Alaska, and as the group drifted farther down the river, they travelled back into the ice age. On the lower reaches they passed glaciers, some sixteen kilometres wide, and heard the air reverberate with thunder as 46-metre high towers of ice broke into the river. "It was of the calibre of the Grand Canyon," Ric recalls. "It was the most spectacular area that I had ever seen."

The Tatshenshini was the only unprotected area surrounded by national parks in the Yukon and Alaska: it was the missing piece. It was the home of the biodiversity of the region, and it was being threatened by a proposal for an immense open-pit copper mine. A major exploration camp had already been built, and the right of way for a 120-kilometre road was being slashed in. The ore in the proposed copper mine was 40 percent sulfide, and when the ore is stripped open and exposed to the air and moisture, it forms vast amounts of sulfuric acid that has the potential to leach out toxic metals, resulting in those toxic metals poisoning the river and its fish, effectively killing it for over 10,000 years. Ric believes this copper mine was the most dangerous mine ever proposed in Canada. "I remember thinking: this is an area no one has ever heard about. How are we ever going to be able to deal with this issue in the time available?"

Initially Ric and the others, who organized to protect the Tatshenshini, sat down with the mining company to see if they could arrive at a compromise solution. That proved impossible, so Ric looked for a different tactic and found the flaw in the proposal: the mining company had to ship their ore from Alaska. Ric doubted that B.C. would forgo the economic values in the mine regardless of the environmental costs, but the U.S.—which was downstream from the mine's proposed acid drainage—had everything to lose. It would kill American salmon and devastate Glacier Bay National Park.

Ric and his wife Dona developed a coalition that linked 50 of the largest environmental organizations in North America, representing about ten million people. Together, these groups lobbied senior levels of government in B.C., Alaska, Ottawa, and Washington, D.C. Ric's project caught the attention of a senator from Tennessee, Al Gore, who gave it his support. When Ric testified in front of the U.S. Congress, he fulfilled the vision he had had so many years earlier as a young university student.

All those involved in the Tatshenshini campaign were pleased with the responsiveness of the U.S. Congress. In order for the mining proposal to go through, it needed 31 permits from the U.S., so without American support, the mine could not go ahead.

The mining company fought back. Premier Harcourt commissioned a blue-ribbon panel to review the issue, but it found 86 serious unsolvable problems and twelve potentially catastrophic-scale risks associated with the project.

As a result, in the summer of 1993, Tatshenshini was declared a protected area. The following year it was named a United Nations World Heritage Site. Preserving the Tatshenshini region and linking it to the adjoining national parks in Alaska and the Yukon created the largest international protected area in the world.

Ric felt exhilarated by the victory, but the backlash from the mining industry was intense. For two years, the industry did everything it could to reverse the decision while Ric and the others involved in the Tatshenshini campaign fought to preserve what they had won.

In 1994 Ric was awarded the Order of British Columbia for his lifetime achievements, but especially for his efforts with the preservation of the Tatshenshini wilderness. "I really loved the process of being nominated for that award because it really is a citizen's process," Ric says, adding, "I've always done this wilderness conservation work because I've felt it's important. I also feel it is a privilege to pass wilderness onward. My dream is that some kid three generations from now will come down to the edge of the Tatshenshini, and while he'll never know anything about me, he'll have the chance to see a grizzly bear. That's what this is about. When I received the Order of B.C., all of a sudden I saw that what I'm doing does mean something to society." Ric has received a number of national and international awards since, but it is the Order of B.C., he says, that means the most to him.

Ric has continued to work with many other British Columbians in establishing protected areas in places such as the Stikine Valley, the Okanangan, the Babine Mountains, the Chilcotin, and others in the province, but he says that his job was changing. "Other people are now handling the puck. My job is to be a little more like a coach or to be an enabler. I'm interested now in helping to mentor the next generation of leadership on environment. I had the chance to be a star on the ice for a while. Now my job is to enable star conservationists who can do it even better."

By 2001, about 13 percent of the land base in B.C. had been protected. Ric says the job of the environmentalists now is to make sure those areas stay protected, and he believes they will be successful. He calls himself an "arbitrary optimist" because he believes the worst he can be is wrong. There is already too much pessimism in the world, he says, "So I choose to seek the impossible and achieve it. I believe what has hobbled us so many times in the conservation movement is that we have a tough story to tell. People often cast us as people yelling, 'The sky is falling!' But in fact, we're the canaries in the coal mine. We are saying that human survival is at stake. It's not just the endangered life forms that are at risk. The endangered species potentially is us." Society's dilemma, he says, is that it is too often inclined to kill the canary rather than listen to what the canary has to say. Conservation is a tough life. You don't get rich. Sometimes you barely survive. But the rewards are great: the Tatshenshini, South Moresby, Babine, Height of the Rockies, the Purcell Wilderness—these are the rewards.

Ric says, "I really believe that it is our wild lands that make us Canadians. We may be divided by heritage, by language, and by history, but the one thing that unites us as Canadians is our wilderness. When others think about Canada, they imagine our wild country. The wilderness and Canada's wildlife are symbols on Canada's currency. At the same time, Canadians clear-cut the precious wilderness without considering the implications. To me, when we log some of these places, it's like the moneychangers in the temple. We're doing something that is approaching sacrilege."

Ric also believes that when it is done right, logging and wilderness can coexist. He believes that when we log indiscriminately, however, we are depriving future generations of biodiversity, recreational opportunities, and more importantly, wonder and beauty. Ric likens clear-cutting in places like Nitinat or Clayoquot Sound to chopping up the *Mona Lisa* for kindling. He believes that the challenge is to figure out how to use the forests to create jobs and at the same time recognize that there are areas that are too precious to log.

As we go over our allotted two hours, I feel certain that Ric could go on talking about his passion for wilderness for the rest of the day and never run out of words. I'm sure he has been successful in his campaigns not just because he cares passionately about wilderness, but because he is smart, does research, and knows how to talk to the people in power. The last words I say to him as we end our meeting are, "I'm so glad there are people like you doing this job."

Joan Acosta, 1994

Joan Acosta:
The Power of Language

I find I am at ease with Joan Acosta the minute I meet her in her tiny office, where she publishes *Westcoast Reader* at Capilano College in North Vancouver. I'm not sure why, perhaps because I was expecting someone cool and intellectual, and Joan isn't anything like that. She has an impressive mop of curly brown hair, a clear, direct way of looking at people, and a great, infectious laugh that I hear often during the two hours I spend with her. I like how "ordinary" she seems; although I also wonder, "How ordinary can this woman be?" when I see some of the framed awards on her office walls. I notice the Woman of Distinction Award, the Order of British Columbia, and a letter of appreciation from Jean Chretien. When I comment that it is quite an impressive array, Joan says, "I was just doing my job."

Joan Acosta's job is to produce a monthly newspaper called *Westcoast Reader*. The publication reaches adult literacy students, English as a Second Language (ESL) students, high school students, people in rehabilitation centres, deaf adults and children, people in First Nations' programs, and many more. It uses simple language, reflects no political agenda, and often includes puzzles, projects, or recipes to involve the reader.

With a circulation of 85,000, *Westcoast Reader* is one of the most widely read newspapers in Canada; but where other major publications employ a staff of editors, reporters, and dozens of support people to get their product to the public, Joan Acosta relies on only one part-time assistant and, of course, herself. Joan certainly gets paid for the work she does, but she's also dedicated because she believes in the power of language and literacy.

Joan says that her favourite stories are about the triumph of the human spirit over adversity, and I suspect that is simply because she has found plenty of evidence in her life of the inherent goodness in humans and how the human spirit can conquer many hardships.

Joan's belief in the goodness of people partly stems from her childhood. She grew up in Guatemala, a land of warmth, sunshine, and friendly people. Her father, Wilson, was Welsh and her mother, Kathryn, American. Wilson was working for a steamship line that stopped in Guatemala, and he stayed because he fell in love with the country. Kathryn had gone to Guatemala to visit her brother, who was working there. She met Wilson, fell in love, and married him. In 1937 they had twins, Diane and David, and Joan was born seven years later.

The family lived in Guatemala City, which Joan remembers as a small and charming town. Now when she goes back to visit, she says it's unrecognizable as the place in which she grew up. She remembers the people of Guatemala as extraordinarily warm and kind. Her fondest childhood memories are of long days spent with family friends at Lake Atitlan high up in the mountains, where they swam in the warm water and visited the markets in the surrounding towns. Each town had a different market day, and each market was bright, noisy, and as colourful as a carnival with vendors laughing and bargaining over their goods.

Joan attended the American school in Guatemala City, where the children were taught in English for half the day and Spanish the other half, becoming completely bilingual. Joan had as many Spanish friends as Americans.

I ask her if she was aware of any racism while she was growing up.

"I'm sure it existed," she says. "But I wasn't very touched by it."

When she was sixteen, Joan went to boarding school in Wellesley, Massachusetts. "I really wanted to go," she recalls. "My brother and sister had gone to school in the States, and I thought that would be a cool thing to do. Once I got there, it was a little harder."

Massachusetts, with its New England winters and brick buildings, was a big contrast to the warmth, lush vegetation, and sunshine of Guatemala. "It was hard to be away from such a beautiful and idyllic homeland," Joan says. "And I had never experienced winter, which was hard. Exciting the first time, but as the months went on and I had to bundle up, it was kind of hard."

I am curious to know what she means by "hard?" "Did you get lonely?" I ask.

"Not really lonely," she says.

"Did you cry?"

Joan pauses and says, "I probably did. I don't remember that very clearly, but I remember feeling homesick. I had lots to do; it was just a feeling of missing home."

She eventually adapted and made friends. She worked harder than she ever had at school in Guatemala. For the first time, she had to do research and write essays, and she had acquired none of those skills in her previous school.

When she graduated, her brother David convinced her to go to the University of California at Berkeley. "He thought Berkeley was a wonderful place—great profs and all that," Joan says. "And I was ready to go somewhere very different from New England, and California was very appealing."

She had no career plans. She took all the core subjects such as anthropology, English, and science and assumed that in two years she'd have a clearer idea of the direction she wanted to take. The only real problem Joan ran into at Berkeley was housing. Diane was working in New York at the time, so she came to California to help her sister find accommodation and familiarize herself with the university. There were absolutely no vacancies and the more they looked, the more depressed they got. They finally found Joan a boarding house in a seedy part of town. Joan's fellow boarders were a female roommate and six Iranian men. Joan remembers that Diane was literally shaking. "Is my sister going to be safe here?" she asked Mrs. Boyle, the landlady.

"Oh yes," she said. "I have one rule. The women always have to have one foot on the ground."

With that scant reassurance, Diane flew back to New York.

"I was scared," Joan says. "I was really scared. I was very uncomfortable in that situation."

Joan quickly realized she had nothing to fear. The men treated the women with great deference, and Mrs. Boyle was a warm woman and an excellent cook who served up big communal meals in the evenings and put out a smorgasbord of food for breakfast. But after her first semester, Joan and her roommate found an apartment and moved.

Berkeley in the 1960s was one of America's hubs of liberal thinking. Students cared about social issues and were anxious to be involved and to help make a difference. They cared about segregation, racism, and poverty. The streets around the campus were lined with cafés, shops, and alternative food restaurants. Students wore beads, frayed jeans, dashikis, flowing peasant skirts, and sandals. Berkeley suited Joan, as David had predicted.

In her third year, she went to the University of Madrid on an exchange program, where she lived with a family that she remembers as kind and open and who treated her like their own daughter. It was the end of the Franco era and Spain had just opened its borders for the first time in years. The students were hungry for American and British literature and bombarded Joan with questions about the U.S. Joan's classes were taught in Spanish, and she began a lifelong love of Spanish literature.

Back in California, she completed her studies at Berkeley with a degree in Spanish Literature, but even after four years of studies, she still didn't know what she wanted to do. "I had a degree in Spanish Literature that I didn't think was going to get me anywhere. So I thought I'd have to go to graduate school—or do something." That "something" turned out to be joining the Peace Corps. The only reason she can think of for doing so was because it was Berkeley, and it was 1965. "Berkeley was very political, and people were doing that kind of thing," she says. "They were going to the south to register voters. People were going into the Peace Corps. There was that real push for youth to help in some capacity."

Joan wanted to go back to Latin America to do community work, but instead the Peace Corps sent her to Liberia on the west coast of Africa, where her assignment was to teach children to speak, read, and write English. She could have turned down the job, but she believed teaching English was important and it was something she could do.

Before embarking for Africa, she had three months training in San Francisco, part of which involved learning one of the 27 dialects spoken in Liberia. The new recruits also learned about Liberian culture and how to teach English as a second language. From San Francisco, the group flew to Key West, Florida, for practicums in ESL classrooms with Cuban children. "They were so cute," she recalls. "That was such a good experience, and I learned a little bit about how to manage a classroom."

When Joan stepped off the plane in Liberia it felt like she was walking into a sauna. She had grown up in a warm country, but nothing had prepared her for the intense heat and humidity of the swampy coast of Africa. She was also one of very few white people in Liberia. "It was probably one of the first times in my life when I felt that I stood out so much."

She had seen poverty in Guatemala and Mexico, but not to the same degree as the poverty in Liberia, where beggars wore rags and lepers walked on the streets with fingers missing and faces disfigured. "That was hard," Joan says. "I didn't know anything about leprosy because I had never seen it in Guatemala."

The Peace Corps assigned her to teach in the elementary school of Ganta, a small town with a population of about one thousand. Her Grade One class consisted of 100 students, whom she was expected to teach in a classroom that she describes as "the size of an office."

"I can't do this," Joan said to the principal. "I can't fit them in."

"You must," he said. "They paid their fees."

She managed to cram 50 children into the classroom. The other 50 clung to the chicken-wire fence outside, listening in. The principal would periodically come around with a switch and beat the children off, but as soon as he had disappeared, they came back and hung on, shouting out answers to questions along with the children in the classroom. "You couldn't keep them away," Joan says. "They really wanted to go to school. The kids were just dying to go to school."

The children had never had a teacher like Joan, who interacted with them, told them stories, and even asked them questions. She had no textbooks, but she pulled stories out of old magazines, and as she settled in to the job, she began to take the children's own stories and write them down on the blackboard or on big pieces of paper. "I can't believe this, but in my two years there I think I taught every kid to read," she says. "I don't know if you could do that here—if you could take 100 first graders who didn't even know their ABCs and teach them all to read in a year. It wasn't me so much; it was their absolute desire to learn. They came to school early. They were so enthusiastic."

Joan conveys to me the excitement of that time, gesturing with her hands and her voice full of expression. I get the impression she would love to even show me photos of those children. "It just made me feel incredible," she says. "They were great little kids."

It wasn't easy for the children to go to school. Many of the first graders were older because they had had to work in the fields, and their families had struggled to buy a uniform and to pay the $6 fee. Some of the older girls were pregnant, but they didn't care—they just wanted to go to school. "They all managed to learn," Joan says. "I think it was mostly their enthusiasm and desire to get ahead. Education seemed to be really, really important to them."

Joan's school encompassed Grades One through Six, and although the children were eager to stay in school, the attrition rate was high because they had to help their parents work on the farms. By Grade Six the classes had dwindled in size to about 25 students.

Near the end of her teaching job in Liberia, Joan contracted amoebic dysentery, and after almost four months of battling the illness and losing weight, she was admitted to a mission hospital. A week later, weighing just 90 pounds, Joan flew to Brazil to be with Diane, who lived in Rio de Janeiro at the time. When Joan got off the plane, her sister thought she looked like a ghost. A doctor in Brazil treated her with medication, but she still felt ill. When she flew home to Guatemala, she saw her old family doctor, who prescribed a different medicine. Treating amoebic dysentery was not an exact science, so Joan's recovery was slow.

In 1970 Joan went back to Berkeley to teach in the Educational Opportunity Program, which had been created to help minority students fill gaps in their studies. Most of Joan's students were Chicanos and African Americas, and the majority of the work she did with them was improving their language skills. Joan agreed with the university that without a good understanding of English, these students were not going to do well in other subjects.

In 1972 she went to Mexico City, where she taught in a bilingual school. Two years later, she went to Montreal for a year, and then to Toronto, where she taught ESL at Greenwood School in the city's east end. Greenwood was a "reception centre," which meant it enrolled newly arrived immigrants, many of them so new they were still in culture shock and couldn't speak a word of English

By the time she arrived in Toronto, Joan had had plenty of experience teaching English to people from other cultures, but in the Greenwood classroom she was confronted with students, many of them refugees, who came from China, Greece, Chile, Yugoslavia, Cyprus, and other countries. Her classroom was a stewpot of languages. "The students were great," she says. "The job was just fabulous."

"But how do you teach kids who don't speak a word of English?" I ask.

"I don't know. You just do it. You start with the basics: 'What's your name? Where are you from?'"

She taught them to understand the questions they would be asked in their new country. Those who were suffering from severe culture shock would just sit and listen. "I think when you learn a new language, you take in so much before you actually produce anything," she says. "A lot of the students were absorbing it all and putting it all together and kind of suddenly one day they were able to say a few things, and we'd all get so excited."

Joan may have been the students' biggest supporter, but the class knew the struggles each person was enduring because they were all in the same situation, so they cheered each other on with boundless enthusiasm. "There's a lot of controversy over whether students should be put right into a regular classroom or whether they should be selected out the way these students were," Joan says. "I really think that that sort of reception idea worked really well for them. They were incredibly scared and intimidated when they came. I know some students would do okay in a regular classroom. It might take them a little longer, but for many students who came from very impoverished backgrounds— from rural areas where they had maybe not even been to school very much in their own language—I think this transition was good."

Joan taught at Greenwood School for four years. During that time, she met and married David Porter, who taught at the same school. When David found work in the North Vancouver school district they moved to the West Coast. Joan became one of the first instructors hired by Capilano College to teach ESL. The college established the ESL program in Highlands Church in North Vancouver with funding from Canada Manpower.

In 1979 a lot of Vietnamese refugees were arriving in Vancouver. They were dubbed "boat people" because they were crowded into old, unseaworthy tubs that drifted slowly across the Pacific Ocean for weeks. They lived in deplorable conditions before arriving on the West Coast. The great majority of Joan's students were Vietnamese, ranging in age from seventeen to men and women in their 50s. Often an entire family would come to class. They generally arrived at the school in a state of shock. They had been in refugee camps and had endured the most appalling conditions on the boats, and now they were in a country that was so far removed from their reality, it may as well have been another planet. They were thin and sometimes unwell, but as eager to learn as the Grade One Liberian children had been years before.

Joan became very fond of many of her students, and they returned her affection. They invited her to their homes, gave her tea, fed her, and when she became pregnant, they knitted baby sweaters with blue being the colour of choice. Joan laughs. "They told me I was going to have a boy. 'Oh teacher, it will be a boy. You will have a boy, teacher.' It was supposed to be a compliment." But when she had a baby girl her students said, "Oh she's so nice. She's so beautiful. The next one will be a boy."

"When she was little I used to bring her to visit them," Joan recalls. "And they just love children, as so many cultures do. I think we really miss that in our society. They would just pick her up and carry her around."

Years later, Joan still sees some of the students who became her friends. "They all have children, and the kids have children, and they've all assimilated into the community … and it's amazing because they had such a hard time coming here. I don't think people recognize that: how very difficult that was for them."

"I get the impression you really cared about these people," I say.

"Oh yes, I think probably more than any students I had. I really related to them. Perhaps it was that I was more mature and could understand some of what they had gone through, and they were such good people—so hard-working and so anxious and so happy to be there. They were so appreciative of having arrived in Canada and having people look after them and help them."

In 1982 the ESL program moved to campus. That was also the year Joan became the editor of *Westcoast Reader* newspaper. The idea for the newspaper had come out of a meeting of about twelve ESL teachers in 1981, who said the one thing they desperately needed was a publication that would be easy for ESL students to read and that dealt with adult material, in other words, a newspaper for newcomers. At that time, there was a similar newspaper called *Newcomer News* that was being published by the Ontario government. The teachers liked the paper, but not the political influence.

At that meeting, the teachers formed the board of the newspaper, and one of them took on the project for a year, publishing the first three editions of *Westcoast Reader*. The funding to produce the paper was initially almost nonexistent, but during those twelve months, the board developed more sources of income and offered the job to Joan. She had produced about four issues of a small newsletter for her students called *Canada and You*, and the board felt that was enough experience to qualify her for the position. The pay wasn't much, but Joan believed in the project. "I thought it was fabulous—and it was scary too," she says. "I had never done anything before that had a distribution like this. But it sounded like a neat idea, and I thought it was going to help people. I could tell from my own ESL students that they needed that kind of thing. That was a real incentive." Joan continued to teach ESL classes while publishing five or six issues of *Westcoast Reader* each year, which was all that the budget allowed.

Westcoast Reader was full of information about Canada and B.C. because Joan had learned that ESL students wanted to learn about their new country and province. Along with the newspaper, Joan wrote teacher's notes to take the place of the material ESL teachers had previously been creating on their own.

She taught herself to do layouts, and because she wanted the newspaper to be easy to read and understand, she spent a great deal of time simplifying material. She got permission from *The Vancouver Sun*, the *The Province*, and the *North Shore News* newspapers to use their articles, and each day she scoured the papers for stories about immigrants and about people overcoming great odds. When those kinds of articles were scarce, Joan would dream about a staff reporter or about going out to get those stories, but the funding was inadequate to do so. She also wrote articles on health and safety, and she included recipes because cooking, she says, is a universal language. In some issues, she created special inserts that focussed on such topics as AIDS, wife abuse, family literacy, and family law. With each special edition, the board had to find additional funding, and sometimes Joan helped track down the money. *Westcoast Reader* still has no guaranteed funding, and each year Joan and the board worry that the provincial funds will not be made available.

Although the provincial government holds the balance of financial control over the newspaper because of its funding, it once wanted total control. In the early 1980s, when it was recognized that *Westcoast Reader's* audience was perhaps the most easily influenced in the country, a ministry agency in the Social Credit government tried to take over the publication. ESL teachers in the province protested vigorously. They knew they could depend on Joan Acosta to put out an unbiased product, and they did not trust the government to do the same.

The news media heard about the issue, and editorials in *The Vancouver Sun* and the *The Province* denounced the government for trying to take control of the paper. Influential people such as the director of Legal Services in Vancouver wrote letters in support of *Westcoast Reader*. "No," they said. "You can't do this. *Westcoast Reader* is like a textbook. You can't fill it with government propaganda."

The government received thousands of letters, and then Paul Gallagher, who was the president of Capilano College at the time, negotiated with the government to keep *Westcoast Reader* as an independent newspaper. "It isn't just a little paper," Joan says. "It's a paper that people thought they had saved. The people felt they had won."

In 1990, the International Year of Literacy, Joan formed a partnership with a colleague from Vancouver Community College and *The Province* to insert a page in the newspaper once a week called "Newsreader." Like *Westcoast Reader* , the "Newsreader" ran stories that were simple to read.

When *Westcoast Reader* began publishing ten issues a year in 1992, its production became Joan's full-time job. In 1982 the paper's circulation was 8,000; now it is 85,000. Joan divides her time between working out of her Capilano College office and her home, which she calls both a blessing and a curse. She finds it all too easy to walk into her home office on a Sunday afternoon and start to work when she should be taking time off.

During her twenty years of publishing *Westcoast Reader*, Joan Acosta has also produced three books. Her first, *Coast to Coast Reader*, was inspired by the newspaper and is filled with upbeat, easy-to-read stories from across Canada. She wrote her next book, *Canada Coast to Coast*, at the request of teachers who wanted a textbook of exercises to accompany *Coast to Coast Reader*. She worked as project coordinator on a third book, *Newcomer's Guide to British Columbia*, which has become the province's most popular government publication. The easy-to-read book is for newcomers to the country and covers topics such as telephones, banking, housing, and the medical system.

Joan recalls that when the government asked her to write the *Newcomer's Guide*, it was looking for a quick fix. They had hired a consulting company to create the book. The company hadn't taken sufficient time to research the book's proposed audience, and as a result, it was too difficult for the newcomers to read, and it also contained unsuitable information such as: "How to get a boat licence."

"How many newcomers are going to own a boat and need to get a boat licence?" Joan wondered.

"Please plain-language it," the representative from the Ministry of Multiculturalism said to Joan.

She laughs. "I thought that was a great verb I had never heard before."

She said to the representative, "No, I can't do that. I have to start from scratch, and I have to start from the reader's point of view, and we'll have to field test it."

"This is going to be very costly," protested the representative.

"Yes, maybe, but if you want it done right, that's how you have to do it. You have to do it in simple language and you have to take it from when the person gets here from the airport—maybe he has to use the bathroom or the telephone or mail a letter."

The government representative thought Joan's suggestions were very clever. Joan thought they were just plain logical. "That was seen as a very innovative publication," she says. "But really it wasn't anything special. All that happened was they had a person do it who knew the audience, and that doesn't often happen."

Joan has also worked with two other instructors on two small books for Co-Development Canada, a B.C.-based non-governmental agency.

Those books are about community projects that have had an impact in Canada and around the world. They feature community gardens and small businesses, and once again, the stories are largely about people succeeding against great odds.

Westcoast Reader continues to be Joan's most important project. Perhaps one of the biggest rewards she gets for her long hours of work on the newspaper is the letters from students and teachers.

John Collins of the West End Seniors Network in Vancouver wrote these words:

> Thank you for producing *Westcoast Reader* and circulating it free to groups learning English as a second language … My students, who are elderly, get great enjoyment from the articles and quizzes that you run. You have the gift of providing materials that are relevant and interesting. Keep up the good work. It is greatly appreciated by ESL students and teachers. Certainly this teacher and his students are grateful.

A group of students in Mission, B.C. wrote to her:

> We are a group of fifteen ESL students at Mission Adult Learning Centre. Every month we receive *Westcoast Reader*, which we enjoy very much because we take our copy home and share it with our family. We want to thank you for sending it to us. The *Westcoast Reader* is an important contribution to our knowledge and skills. The worksheets are very useful. We enjoy very much completing them at home.

A Grade Five student in Burnaby, B.C. also sent a letter:

> I really enjoy your newspaper because it has such good information about Canada and what is happening in the world. I also enjoy the little comic strip at the bottom of the first page that always makes me laugh and I really thank you for that because my parents stopped ordering the *Vancouver Sun* so I have nothing but *The Westcoast Reader*. You have a very good newspaper. Keep them coming.

The newspaper has collected hundreds of such letters over the years.

Joan was awarded the Order of British Columbia in 1994. She recalls her feelings when she received the telephone call, informing her she had been selected to receive the award. "I was shocked. Me? Little old me?" She asked why she had been chosen. The official told her that the award was for her work in literacy, and Joan thought, "But that's my job. I'm just doing my job." And though she still feels like an ordinary person, Joan says, "I think the idea of *Westcoast Reader* is very powerful."

She recalls her investiture, when she took her place on the podium with people like Haida artist Bill Reid and Dr. Michael Smith, who had won a Nobel Prize, as one of the most special moments in her life.

In 1996 Joan's life suddenly became more difficult when her sister Diane fought and lost an intensive bout with cancer. "That was the low point of my life," she says. "That was really, really hard. I was very close to her … She was single, and I was her main person, so that was hard. She went through a lot of surgeries and treatments. That was very, very hard. I saw a lot of her at that time and it was tough, really tough, to go through that."

A brighter element in her life is her daughter Erin, who Joan calls "a good product." "She's also a good writer," Joan says, "which pleases me no end. We're a close family. We've travelled a lot with her, and that has been fun."

In 2001 Capilano College created the Joan Acosta *Westcoast Reader* Award. The annual award of $700 goes to an ESL student with financial need who has displayed excellence in class and set an inspirational example in the ESL program.

As I read the description, I can't help thinking that it seems somehow fitting that the word "inspirational" should be associated with an award that has Joan Acosta's name on it.

Corporal Ross Purse, 1993

Ross Purse:
For the Love of People

When I meet Ross Purse and his wife, Vivian, at their retirement home in Parksville, a resort community on Vancouver Island, I notice a FOR SALE sign on the front lawn. Shortly after shaking hands and introducing myself, I ask, "Why are you selling? This is such a beautiful home."

Ross explains that he and Vivian had moved to the adult community because its beauty had captured them, but that he misses his friends, chatting with his cronies in the local coffee shop. He also misses the company of young people. "I love being around people," he explains to me. "I love to communicate."

As a former managing director and secretary-general of the Canadian National Institute for the Blind (CNIB), it might be expected that Ross is legally blind. He describes his limited vision for me: he can make out where I am sitting and he can detect shapes and movements, but he needs special magnifying equipment to use his computer, which he uses a great deal to keep up with his reams of correspondence. He writes to people like Boris Zimin, who heads the All-Russia Association of the Blind, and to Zimin's secretary, Lucy Tsesarakaia, whom he has never met but with whom he exchanges family photos and stories like old friends.

Ross says that connecting with people is important to him, and I later learn firsthand what he means. Several days after our interview, he telephones me to say he's sending me a videotape of an interview he had had with the Canadian military about his experience as a prisoner of war in Japan. He also invites me to lunch. When his house finally sells, and he moves back to the neighbourhood in Nanaimo where his friends live, he calls to give me his new telephone number. I feel honoured by this connection with him because Ross Purse is an exceptional man with a loving and gentle heart.

He and his twin sister were born on September 10, 1918, in Roland, Manitoba, a tiny town with a population of 500. His father, Charles Chester Purse, worked as a grain buyer, and his mother, Ethel, stayed home to look after the four children. Charles Chester died in 1928, leaving the family with a $5,000 savings account. The grain company had owned the house, and Charles had had no life insurance.

Ethel Purse used the $5,000 to make a down payment on a house, but she had no means of paying the mortgage. Ross worked on weekends, delivering groceries, but it wasn't enough. Four years later the bank repossessed the property, and Ethel and her daughters moved in with a married sister, and Ross and his brother went to live with another sister.

I ask Ross how he felt about his father's death. He says that he was too young for it to seem real to him.

"How did you feel about your family splitting up?" I ask.

"I'm not quite sure. It was sort of the way of life at that time. Things were tough for everybody. It was just after the 1929 collapse, and everybody was just doing the best they could."

When Ross finished high school, he got a full-time job at the grocery store until he and his older brother, Clair, enlisted in the Winnipeg Grenadiers on his 21st birthday—September 10, 1939. He joined the army because it was the thing to do at that time. "I think everyone pretty much thought that was going to be a real experience."

He received his basic training in Winnipeg and shipped out with his unit to Jamaica to supervise a prison camp. Jamaica was officially pro-British, but many locals—including the prime minister—had tried to assist the German navy ships that sailed the waters of the Caribbean; they were incarcerated in the camp.

Eighteen months later, Ross's unit was recalled to Canada to exchange their tropical uniforms for standard military issue. They shipped out of Vancouver on the TSS *Awatea*, a New Zealand ship. "We had no idea where we were going," Ross recalls. "About twelve hours or less at sea we were told that we were going to Hong Kong, and that was kind of exciting—the idea of seeing another country that was going to be so totally different." When the 2,000 Canadian men arrived in Hong Kong, they joined the British in their garrison at Sham Shu Po to help protect the island.

Ross begins to take long pauses in his narrative. Later, when I watch the videotape he gives me that had been filmed a few years earlier, I hear the off-camera interviewer asking Ross some of the same questions about his experiences that I have. His answers were almost identical. He tells his story with precision and detail, as though he was a detached observer of the events that took place, rather than a participant. Maybe it's the only way he can tell the story and get through it.

On December 7, 1941, several hours after the attack on Pearl Harbour, the Japanese bombed Hong Kong. The ship that had been carrying the unit's heavy artillery was sunk. As a result, the men were badly armed, and the garrison almost helpless. "We were overwhelmed," Ross recalls. "We had no chance at all."

On Christmas Day, Hong Kong surrendered to the Japanese, who dropped thousands of leaflets over the city, ordering the soldiers to turn in their arms and give themselves up by evening. If not, they would be shot.

Corporal Ross Purse and three other Canadian soldiers went to meet the enemy at Happy Valley, Hong Kong's racecourse. "It was a terrible experience," he recalls. "We were allowed to carry no arms, of course. We just had to keep moving towards the enemy lines until we were captured. It was very frightening. They had all been drinking, and they were pretty uncontrollable."

The next day, the Japanese marched their prisoners up to the Peak, the mountain that towers over the city, where they sorted them into their units. A day later they forced the men to march down the peak to North Point, which served as the internment camp. Many of the soldiers were wounded. They were given no rest, no aid, and no special consideration. They had to keep up or die.

I ask Ross if he remembers how he felt.

"No," he says. "You know, it's an interesting thing, but when you're in the army it's a day-to-day thing. At that time we really didn't register what was happening. We were trained to simply carry on as best we could."

The men were imprisoned at North Point for just over a year. Their rations were about 700 calories a day, which is less than it takes to keep a body's vital organs functioning properly. "The conditions started to appear—pellagra and beriberi, the swelling of the legs. And so the deterioration became obvious. And dysentery—we lost a lot of people through that."

Each day Ross watched as Chinese citizens tried to bring packages of food to the prisoners, who were their sons, husbands, and fathers. "When they'd get about 50 or 60 feet away, the Japanese would open fire on them. They would just take cover, leave their dead lying on the street, and when the firing stopped, they'd come right back out, pick up the parcels they had left, pick up their dead, and come right up to the gate. They were just amazing people. I believe the Japanese soldiers took pleasure in killing or injuring the Chinese. If they caught a pregnant woman, they beat her on the stomach until her baby was aborted."

Many prisoners sat huddled on their bunks most of the day. Ross worked with the camp doctor, Captain H. Beadnell, in what passed for a hospital but was little more than a shack. After the war, Beadnell wrote a letter of commendation for Ross.

> During the fifteen months I have known Corporal Purse, he has worked as a medical orderly under myself in this prisoner of war camp, and I have formed a very high opinion of his character and ability. Although not a trained medical man, he has stood out among such trained orderlies in this camp for his energy, hard work, and reliability, His manner has always been pleasant, both towards the medical officers and towards the patients; he has never lost his temper in the most trying circumstances, and has done considerably more than his share of the medical work during the entire period. Although several trained medical men were available, Corporal Purse has always been the main prop of the sick quarters in the camp.
>
> In circumstances in which most men have shown themselves selfish, unwilling to make any effort to help their own fellows in misfortune, and worried only about themselves, Corporal Purse has been prominent

as one of the few men with the character and sense of duty to enable them to remain superior to the majority. The fact that he has been himself sick for the greater part of this time he has not allowed to interfere with his efforts.

After about sixteen months, the prisoners were moved to their former garrison at Sham Shu Po. Six months later, every man still capable of doing even the most minimal amount of work was shipped to Japan. Ross and the others were crammed into the hold of a reconditioned coal carrier and were at sea for nineteen days. "You had room to squat, but you couldn't lie down and you couldn't stand," Ross recalls. "They lowered the food in buckets, and it was really some kind of garbage—fish, bones and all—and then for the toilet they lowered the same bucket, I guess. I don't think they changed them. It was just awful. It was really like a slave ship. You know, I often say, when I hear about all the problems in the Third World with people starving, I can appreciate what's happening."

The ship finally docked in Osaka, Japan. From there the men travelled in freight cars east to the labour camp of Oeayama, located across the sea from Vladivostock in Russia. The prisoners were put to work in nickel mines that ran across the surface of the ground. Each day the men were transported to the mines in cattle cars while children stood on the embankments, throwing rocks at them through the slats. They worked ten hours each day on 350 calories of rice.

Ross hands over an old photocopied newspaper photograph of the camp that shows two men sitting on a bench in what could be underwear or loincloths, their arms like twigs, their ribs sticking through transparent skin like the skeleton of a ship's frame. Not surprisingly, every man in camp was a medical emergency. Their abdomens were swollen, and bodily fluids filled their joints.

Seeing this disturbing image and listening to Ross's calm, almost monotone voice, I want to weep. "How did you feel? Did you shut your emotions down?"

"Yes," he says. "I think that's what you do. The conditions were so bad that you never thought about it being over. You just lived within yourself. Beriberi and other conditions were so advanced at that point that you couldn't even go to the washroom because your hands were so swollen. As a matter of fact, it was so awful that I find it difficult to believe that it truly happened."

Ross worked in the mines until he was too weak to pick up his tools. But again he didn't lie on a bench and shut his eyes; he went to work in the hut that was the makeshift hospital. The only medicine they had was a disinfectant to clean wounds. Men were dying of diphtheria. Many of them had gangrene, and one of Ross's jobs was to amputate rotted fingers and toes that had lost all sensation. "I amputated them and applied disinfectant. You could do it without any anesthetic. It was just one of those things that took place, and you did what you could."

The nightmare continued for two more years. When the U.S. dropped the second atomic bomb, the Japanese guards fled. Of the approximately 2,000 prisoners who had entered the camp, about 1,500 were still alive. They commandeered a train and told the conductor to take them to Tokyo. When they arrived on September 10, 1945—Ross's 27th birthday—and stepped onto the platform in their prison uniforms, the first man Ross spoke to was a U.S. general with an entourage of about thirty soldiers. The general nodded at Ross and asked, "Do you know a fellow by the name of McNaughton?"

"Of course I do," Ross replied. "He was with us."

"No, I'm talking about General McNaughton."

"Oh, did you serve under him?"

"Not really. We were sort of buddies."

"Well, what's your name then?" Ross asked.

"General McArthur," the man replied.

Ross laughs. "Geez, he was such an easy person to meet."

"Do you think you'll remember this day?" McArthur asked.

"I hope so," Ross replied. "It's my birthday." Ross Purse was 27 years old and his sight was failing; he had cardiac beriberi, and his pulse raced dangerously when he walked more than twenty feet. In Tokyo, he was taken to an interrogation centre, stripped of his prison clothes, bathed, deloused, and disinfected. With a towel wrapped around his distended stomach and his ribs sticking through his skin, two nurses examined him—one with a stethoscope to his chest and one with her finger on his pulse. The nurse with the stethoscope listened to the rapid-fire beating of his heart. "Did you get his pulse?" she asked the other nurse in disbelief.

The second nurse looked at Ross. "Has your pulse always been this rapid?"

"Well you're the first girl I've laid eyes on in four years," Ross joked.

The men were shipped from Tokyo to Guam, where they were hospitalized for two weeks to regain their strength and be treated for their various diseases. From Guam they travelled to Hawaii for another ten-day hospital stay and then were flown to San Francisco. The Canadians were sent on to Esquimalt on Vancouver Island and shipped home from there.

When Ross (who is five feet, ten and a half inches tall) arrived in Winnipeg on October 20, 1945, he weighed 108 pounds. His girl, Vivian, had waited for him to return home. They were married on January 5, 1946, despite the fact that he was still very ill, that he was legally blind, and that he could not bear to be in a crowd.

For eight months Ross visited the hospital each day. When he was discharged, he decided he had to get away. He had continued to correspond with acquaintances from the army, who lived in the West Indies, and through them he obtained a job managing a dairy and citrus farm. "But I continued to have health problems. I had visual problems and emotional problems, and so I took shock treatments, which settled me right down. I was bad tempered, I was really miserable, but after three treatments I was fine."

When his doctor advised him that staying in the tropics was bad for his continuing malnourished state, Ross and Vivian returned to Winnipeg, where he continued to receive extensive medical treatment for nerve damage, eating disorders, and bowel problems. "There were just so many things that were associated with malnutrition."

When he felt capable of returning to work, Ross took a job in the forest entomology department at the University of Manitoba. For nine months, he and a pilot flew over the northern part of the province, mapping the countryside. The pilot's job was to fly the plane; Ross was supposed to make observations and draw the maps, but each day when they landed, the pilot would ask him, "What did you see?"

"Nothing," Ross said. "But let's do something with the maps anyway."

He now laughs, "We just made it up."

The next year, the head of the department, impressed with his previous performance, asked Ross to fly the plane and take his own crew out. Ross confessed, "I can't even drive a car."

"I decided I'd better go and have a talk with the CNIB," Ross says.

He enrolled in a six-month catering program with the CNIB in Toronto and worked in their Manitoba catering department for a short while before realizing it was a job he didn't want to do. He wanted a career.

The CNIB sent him back to Toronto, where he took an administration program, and when he returned to Winnipeg he began working as a field secretary, doing casework with the visually impaired. "I enjoyed that," he says. "I think I enjoyed it because I saw these people who had lost their sight, and I think I could understand." Two of the people with whom Ross worked went on to become heads of the CNIB years later.

After three years in Manitoba, Ross was transferred to Regina, where he took on the role of district executive director of southern Saskatchewan. Eighteen months later he became the superintendent of the Saskatchewan division of the CNIB.

"I seems that you were rising up the corporate ladder rather quickly," I say.

"Well, I had a good wife," Ross says. "And I liked what I was doing. I like people. I got along with people in government."

While he was in Saskatchewan, he enrolled in a two-year diploma program. "I wanted to get a better understanding of what the administration is all about. I thought that if I had a better understanding of management and a better knowledge of what was right and wrong in administration, I would know if what we were doing was right."

In 1964 Ross became the director of the BC/Yukon division of the CNIB, and in 1969 he was transferred to Ontario to lead the largest division of the organization. Within months, he was promoted to assistant managing director of the national division, the second highest position with the CNIB.

During that same time, from 1969 to 1973, Ross became the Canadian representative to the American Association of Workers for the Blind (AAWB), which was formed to promote the development of services for blind people in the Americas. He held the position of secretary for two terms. During his years with the AAWB, he won the prestigious Ambrose M. Shotwell Award, which recognizes outstanding contributions in work for the blind and prevention of blindness. He was only the third non-American citizen to be awarded.

"Why did you get the award?" I ask. "What did you do that was special?"

"I guess I brought in a couple of things they liked," Ross says. "I introduced ideas on rehabilitation to modernize the service of agencies."

He spearheaded the updating of audio libraries for the blind to make them fully available to all of the association's clients. He also made sure that Canada was given special status as a sovereign nation in the AAWB, and as a result forged closer ties between the AAWB and the CNIB.

In 1973 Ross was promoted to managing director and secretary-general of the CNIB, the top position in the agency, which he retained until he retired in 1980 at the age of 61. As a member of the World Council for Welfare of the Blind he travelled around the world, advocating for improved services for the visually impaired. He became regional director of the North American/Oceania region and was elected to the International Agency for the Prevention of Blindness, where he served as regional director for the U.S. and Canada. Ross also established the first Canadian arm of that group.

I try to estimate the hours Ross would have had to work to fulfil all his duties. "Did you work seven days a week?"

"Every week. And I worked every night. But I enjoyed my work so much it didn't matter."

"Why did you enjoy it so much?"

"It was all about people. I just enjoyed people. I was deeply interested in seeing what could be done."

Ross says he was so concerned about the welfare of blind people that before his retirement, he took the risk of alienating many of his colleagues and friends. He said to the council of the CNIB, "I think it's about time we asked blind people what they think about the CNIB. Let them tell us instead of us telling them what we think we should be doing for them."

"I knew that by doing that, I was opening up the proverbial can of worms," Ross says. "But I wanted blind people to tell the CNIB what improvements could be made. I was convinced that we had become too many things to too many people. I wanted to enlist the help of government and non-governmental agencies to provide services for blind people, and I wanted to see blind students moved from basic training into the academic environment. I found out that lots of blind people were docile. They weren't saying a lot of things that were on their minds because they didn't feel free to do it, and I wanted to give them an opportunity to come out and say precisely what they felt was lacking."

The council agreed to his proposal on the condition that he enlisted the support and participation of the government. The government agreed to share the cost of the survey with the CNIB provided that Professor Cyril Greenland, noted for his accomplishments in social work and psychiatry, was appointed the coordinator of the project. Every person on the twenty-member committee that Greenland appointed was visually impaired, and only one was employed by the CNIB. Thousands of blind people across the country were surveyed. "It really identified the changes that should be made to modernize services for the blind," Ross says. "We learned that services that were established way back in 1918 should be thoroughly examined and changes be made."

The completed document stated that blind students should be fully integrated into the public school system; blind people should be offered the opportunity of receiving a higher education; and blind people should be moved into integrated housing. "I always felt it was stupid that blind people should be shut up in housing because then they had no guidance and no one to assist them visually," Ross says.

The report also indicated that visually impaired people wanted the government of Canada to create more programs and be more involved in their welfare. "It just brought into focus the number of services the CNIB was trying to do on its own. That had to be changed," Ross says. "We had to involve other groups that had an association with blindness. I felt for the first time that blind people felt free to openly express their views. Although they felt proud of the CNIB, they felt changes had to be made to meet the needs of the future."

Change occurred quickly. Residences for the blind began to be integrated. Today, blind children attend public schools, and blind youths are getting a college or a university education.

Ross says the survey is his proudest achievement. "I took a real chance. I knew that I would offend a lot of people. I knew that my predecessors would be hurt, and they were hurt. But I said to them, 'I hope you understand that I'm not doing this to damage anyone's reputation. I'm doing this to try to bring the CNIB into the 21st century.' But I know that some people—including a good friend of mine—felt it was very extreme. But you take those chances."

Soon after completing the survey in 1980, Ross retired and moved with Vivian to Vancouver. He was exhausted from years of working long hours and imagined that nothing would be finer than doing absolutely nothing. For a few months idleness was pure bliss, but when he started moving the rose bushes from the front yard to the back yard, he got his real estate license and went back to work. The fact that he couldn't drive his clients around to look at properties didn't hamper him. He used to tell them, "Now look, you don't have to worry about me. You can go out with another agent, and I can be walking down the street and you can drive by and I won't know who the hell you are." He did well in real estate, and when Vivian joined him, they became a team. Within two years Ross was managing two successful real estate companies.

In 1987 the Canadian Opthamological Society presented Ross with a special award of merit. At about the same time, the CNIB created the Ross C. Purse Doctoral Fellowship, a $12,000 scholarship, awarded annually to encourage and support theoretical and practical research and studies at the graduate or doctoral levels in fields of blindness and visual impairment. Part of the sponsor's message reads: "This fellowship has been established in the name of Ross C. Purse … in recognition, on his retirement, of the significant contribution he has made to the advancement of work for the blind and prevention of blindness at home and abroad."

In 1993 Ross was awarded the Order of British Columbia in recognition of his military service, the work he has done as the regional director for the CNIB in B.C, and for the work he has done for the blind all across the country. "I was surprised," he says. "I don't know why I was surprised—I just was. But I was so pleased to receive it from the Honorable Dr. David Lam. It was a great honour."

At the end of our interview, while Ross hunts for photographs to give me, I walk around his office. On the walls are hung the Ambrose

Shotwell Award, the Order of British Columbia, his military medals, and other citations. But what really matters to him is people. He has friends all over the world. He shows me letters from Dr. David Lam and from his friends in Russia and other countries. "My life has always been about people," he says.

"One would think that after your experiences in the war, with all the inhumanity you witnessed, that you wouldn't care, that you would have isolated yourself," I say.

Ross's voice grows softer. "Coming out of that prison camp, I think I'm the only one that went on to a senior position. I know one person that became a doctor and another one who became a very good writer, but most of them fell victim to other problems."

"How did you rise above those problems?" I ask.

"I don't know. I like working. I like challenges. And Vivian— we've been married 56 years—and the encouragement I've had from my family has made the difference."

I believe it is what Ross has accomplished with that encouragement that has really "made the difference."

Robert Bateman:
A Passion for Sharing

I sit with Robert Bateman in his studio on Saltspring Island while fat flakes of wet snow drift down on the towering cedars outside and collect in great blobs in the rims of the skylights overhead. While he talks, Bob sits on a stool with his feet resting on the bottom rung of his easel. He's delicately layering depths of colour on *Asian Jungle Fowl*, one of several paintings that will appear in a new book. He never stops working as we talk, only pausing now and then to look at me briefly or to think of a name or a date. Knowing his schedule and his deadlines I don't mind not having his full attention. Afterwards I realize that for the two hours I was there I felt he was intensely focussed on the interview. I wonder, too, how many people have asked him the same questions I have; yet he makes it seem that every answer he's giving is fresh and newly considered.

The Batemans' home is wonderful. It is situated near the end of a narrow road that winds along the shore. Even with the snow clinging to the shrubs, his Japanese-style garden has an air of serenity and makes one want to pause. Although the upstairs section of the big sprawling house is a wonderfully cluttered studio, the lower floor where the family gathers emits the same sense of repose as the garden outside.

Bob was born in Toronto on May 24, 1930, as the oldest of three children. He grew up in exclusive Forest Hill village but on what he calls "the wrong side of the tracks." People like the Eaton family lived on the "right" side. The family house on Chaplin Crescent backed on to the old Beltline Ravine, which was a wild place with a creek running through on its way to the Don River. Bob spent hours exploring the banks of the willow-shaded creek, where he observed minnows and

Robert Bateman, 2000

tadpoles swimming in the shallow water. One day he even found a painted turtle. "It was a wonderful place to grow up and explore," he says. "To just climb down the embankment at the bottom of our garden, and there I was in another world."

Migrating birds passed through the ravine in the spring and fall, and Bob became as fascinated with them as he was with the animal life on the ground and in the water.

"What was it about birds that interested you?" I ask.

"I don't know," he replies. "That's one of those questions like, 'Why did Gretzky skate, or, why did Glenn Gould play the piano?' Maybe I was just born that way."

Neither of his parents was artistically inclined nor were they naturalists. His father, Wilbur, was an electrical engineer; his mother, Annie, who came from a shipbuilding family in Nova Scotia, stayed home to raise her three sons.

Bob's friend, Al Gordon, was also fascinated with creatures and birds. They used to borrow Al's father's old First World War field glasses to get enthralling close-up views of the local birds. At age twelve, Bob, Al, and Don Smith, another school friend, joined the Junior Field Naturalists at the Royal Ontario Museum, where their monthly meetings were led by members of the staff. "We became ornithology department groupies," Bob recalls. "The staff worked on Saturday mornings back in those days, and two or three of us guys would go into the back rooms."

Bob greatly admired Terry Shortt, a scientist, naturalist, and excellent illustrator of birds, who was in charge of exhibits for the natural history department of the museum. "He became kind of a mentor, and I would bring my stuff down and show him what I was working on."

At school, Bob had a reputation as an artist and a naturalist, but he didn't talk about his habit of watching birds. "In the 1940s you couldn't be a boy bird watcher and expect to be accepted by your peers," he laughs.

As the class artist, he had a group of admirers whom he entertained with cartoon drawings of teachers and friends. They would follow him home after school and lean over his shoulder while he painted air battles between Spitfires and Messerschmidts, and drew cartoons of Hitler. But clever as he was and as much as he loved drawing, he never planned to become an artist. "Art as a career was not an option," he says. "There were no nature artists in those days that I was aware of—not nature art that you would hang on walls." Bob believed he would be painting seriously for the rest of his life, but it was not important that he exhibit or sell his work.

One day Hiles Carter, Bob's Grade Eight science teacher, asked if he could buy one of Bob's bird paintings.

"I can give you one," Bob said. "You don't need to pay me for it."

"No, I want to buy it," he said.

"Why would you want to buy it when I want to give it to you?"

"Because," Hiles Carter said, "I want to be able to say that I am the one who bought the first Bob Bateman painting."

When Bob discovered that he could indulge his love of nature with books as well as outdoors, he became a keen reader. "I had to walk many, many, many blocks to borrow the books at St. Clemens Library, which was the closest public library," he says. "I went through virtually every nature book every year, especially things by Ernest Thompson Seton and Sir Charles G.D. Roberts."

At age sixteen, Bob graduated from the Junior Field Naturalists and became a voluntary leader and instructor. "I was a teacher long before I was a teacher, and I absolutely loved it." In 1947, at the age of seventeen, Bob took a summer job as a "joe boy" at the Wildlife Research Camp of Algonquin Park in north-central Ontario. He dried the dishes, dug garbage pits, filled in potholes, and performed any other duty assigned to him. He was one of two employed in that position, but because he could identify birds, he was also given the job of running the breeding bird census. Every week, Bob walked up and down quadrants of the park, counting the scarlet tanagers, the black-throated green warblers, the least flycatchers, and the other breeding birds. "It was a turning point in my philosophy," he says. "It was an absolutely pivotal time. A lot of the people who were at the Wildlife Research Camp were well-known naturalists that I either knew to see, or had been on hikes with through the museum connection, or had heard about. And so here were older mentors in the field of natural history and nature study, but they were wildlife biologists."

On Friday afternoons, Bob joined the biologists as they sat under the tall spruce trees and listened to their scientific discussions, progress reports, and critiques. "This was a new kind of species that I had not encountered in North Toronto. These were rugged, outdoor guys who knew how to properly paddle a canoe with a 'J' stroke, and they knew how to sharpen an axe properly, but they were also intellectuals. One would be reading Emmanuel Kant or they would be reading literature or poetry. There would be literature readings at lunch hour and folk singing in the evenings, and this was in the '40s when folk singing was a fairly rarified thing. I was used to the North Toronto bourgeois, where you were respectable and you went into business or engineering or something like this, and on weekends you'd get dressed up and go to church and go visiting. These guys got dressed down on weekends and went for hikes. I knew right away that they were my kind of species. They were kindred spirits."

He spent three summers at the Wildlife Research Camp. At the end of the first summer when he went back to Toronto, he discovered he missed being a member of the Field Naturalist's Club. The museum had a junior and a senior club—which Bob and his friends unjustifiably regarded as a "bunch of old fogies"—but nothing for people their age. So Bob and his friends formed an intermediate field naturalist's club, which quickly attracted a strong and influential group of naturalists. Many people in the club later became heads of university departments or filmmakers with the National Film Board of Canada. Bristol Foster, who became Bob's lifelong friend, was one of two members who later became directors of the Royal British Columbia Museum in Victoria.

When he graduated from high school, Bob enrolled at the University of Toronto, still unsure about his future career. "I'd heard horror stories about calculus, so I knew I was not going to be a biologist," he chuckles. "I have no genes for math and no genes for clerical stuff or anything along that line."

In his second year Bob decided to take an honours course, and when he analyzed his options, he remembered a speech he'd heard in his high school auditorium: "You can be whatever you want to be in life. There's one secret; all you need to do is associate with those people."

Of the subjects Bob had been studying, he ruled out psychology, archeology, and art because he didn't want to associate with psychologists and archeologists, and he never considered art as a career. He enjoyed the company of biologists, but he couldn't do mathematics. He decided geography was the ideal choice because it involved rugged outdoor activity and fieldwork. It was also a clean, clear, scientific subject that didn't require mathematics. And because Bob had chosen geology as an option in his curriculum, he could do field work in the summer, which meant travelling to wild and remote parts of the country. In his spare time he could paint.

"I was a Group of Seven groupie by then," he says. "I wasn't painting birds any more. My Algonquin years moved me into The Group of Seven—the Tom Thomson mythology—working directly in the field. I didn't even have a studio."

Like The Group of Seven artists, Bob owned a twelve- by sixteen-inch box that contained his oils, brushes, and palette, with slots on the outside for canvases. Like them, he became a "purist" and finished a painting on location. "It was a point of honour not to go back to it in the studio. You'd lose the essence," he says. "And I have stacks and stacks of these things, most of them with embalmed blackfly corpses that committed suicide in the gooey oils."

We both laugh. "But were they good?" I ask

Bob pauses for a couple of seconds and smiles. "They were not as good as Tom Thomson."

He obtained his first summer job as a university student at the fisheries research laboratory at Opeongo Lake in Algonquin Park, and once again he found himself working with men with whom he felt a genuine kinship. Even today, in his 70s, Bob is a youthful, handsome, blonde-haired, blue-eyed man. That summer, when he was in his twenties, he was strong and fit, his hair bleached by the sun, and his muscles solid and firm. He recalls that he had never felt better or more alive.

During the next summer, when Bob joined a geological survey team in Newfoundland, he spent much of his spare time on his hobby of collecting small mammals. He had developed an interest in them at the Royal Ontario Museum, where York Edwards, who later became the director of the Royal British Columbia Museum, had shown him how to catch and prepare the specimens. His summer field trips provided a rich venue for trapping and collecting in areas where no one had trapped before. To Bob's delight, museums around the world were eager to take his specimens. He jokes, "If I go down in posterity it may be through my mice. I have specimens not only in the Royal Ontario

Museum and the National Museum of Canada, but the Smithsonian, the British museum, the Chicago Field Museum, and quite a few of the major museums in the world. They all have, somewhere in their drawers, a little row of things with 'Robert Bateman, 1950-something' written on the label."

Bob still believes that the summer he worked in Ungava in Arctic Quebec was the most exciting of his life. The Inuits on the team told him and the three other Caucasians that no man had set foot on this land before, not even their people. "It was such fabulous pristine country," Bob recalls. "You'd catch a beautiful, big Arctic char with every third cast. Now wealthy sportsmen are flying in to fishing camps, and it's being fished all the time."

Bob painted the lakes and rivers and caught more specimens of a very rare breed of mice than existed in all the museums in the world. "The scientific name of the mouse is Phenacomys Ungava," he explains. "And the common name is Ungava Phenacomys." I stare at him and he starts to laugh. "In case you don't like scientific names."

"You were just waiting to tell that one, weren't you?" I laugh.

Bob finished his degree in geography and chose to become a teacher—not just because of the long summer vacations, he says; although the holidays were definitely a factor because they would allow him time to paint. "But I really loved teaching. I used to say that I taught for fun and I painted for real."

Bob liked ideas and philosophy, and he shared his thoughts with his students. He never wrote assignments on the blackboard or told the youths to be quiet and get to work. He talked, presented ideas, shared insights, and invited questions and discussions. His first year as a teacher oddly resembled his student days. He left his parents' home each day to go to school, and each day he came home and went to his room to paint. The only differences were the direction he was facing in the classroom and the subject of his paintings.

Bob read the Canadian art magazines and changed or evolved to conform to the current style. When he tried post-impressionism, Van Gogh and Cézanne were strong influences. His guiding philosophy became, "Art begins were nature ends."

"I still believe that's true," he says. "That's what you do with nature—play with it to turn it into art."

In his late twenties and into his 30s, Bob started painting in the abstract expressionist style, but always—no matter how abstract the art—he took his easel, canvases, brushes, and oils to a field or a rocky shore and painted in the presence of nature. "I'd sit in front of a willow tree in the winter with a three- by four-foot board laid out, and I would look at the willow tree and I would think 'willowness,' and I would get in a willowy mood and I would attack the canvas and just try to get the feel of what 'willowness' was like."

One day in 1956 Bristol Foster telephoned to say he had just completed his master's degree and wanted a break before going on to get his PhD. "I want to go around the world in a Land Rover," he said.

Bob thought he was joking.

"Come with me," Bristol said.

"I tried to give him all the reasons why I couldn't do that," Bob says. "I was in first-year teaching, I had a job, and what would happen to my job, and etcetera, etcetera. But I didn't have a permanent girlfriend. I wasn't married. And being a high school teacher, there were tons of jobs. Back when I started there were about a hundred jobs for every teacher."

Bristol said, "I'll phone you back next week, and if you can think of five good reasons not to go, I'll accept them. Otherwise, we're going."

When Bristol telephoned seven days later, Bob said, "I can't think of any good reasons. Let's go."

So on a Sunday afternoon, Bristol and Bob plotted their trip, using a school atlas, and worked out a budget of $2,000 each for fourteen months, which included the price of the Land Rover, the sea voyages, and all their provisions. They picked up their Land Rover in England, sailed on a freighter to Ghana, and drove across equatorial Africa. "This was just at the end of the colonial era when the going was good," Bob recalls. "Kenya was still a colony, and Uganda was a protectorate, so it was quite safe."

From Africa, Bob and Bristol travelled third-class on a passenger ship to Bombay, and then drove north to Nepal and Darjeeling. They got special permission to go into Sikkim, where they visited the Crown Prince. They took a Japanese ship to Rangoon, Burma, where they received authorization from the British ambassador to drive out of Burma even though wars were raging along the country's borders.

"Virtually no one had driven out, and you still can't do it," Bob says. "It was very dangerous. You were likely to get shot by the army because they'd think you were insurgents. We were allowed to drive only during daylight hours, and it was just wonderful. The people were wonderful and the landscape was picturesque."

When they crossed the border into Thailand, they were placed under house arrest. "It was one of the most sensitive areas in the world," Bob says. "So they held us for four days, and we had a delightful time exploring caves and getting involved in a Buddhist festival."

They continued to Malaya and were waiting for the post office to open one morning when a British captain walked by. Bristol looked at him through the window of the Land Rover and said, "Peter Fairclough, what are you doing here?"

"Bristol Foster, what are you doing here?" the captain replied.

The two men had been high school classmates, and in the course of the ensuing conversation Fairclough said, "If you guys are around in a week, I think I can arrange for a trip by helicopter into the interior of Malaya."

"So that's what we did," Bob recalls. "We dressed up as British 22 SAS paratroopers, and they helicoptered us into a piece of forest that had been dynamited out. We landed there and it was like Ungava: We were in an area that is now totally changed. There was a beautiful race of people that was almost pygmy-like that hunted with blowguns and had had virtually no contact with the outside. We saw pristine waterfalls and tropical rainforests. We were so lucky to have been alive at this period of history to see a bit of the world the way it was." From Malaya they continued to Singapore, Australia and across the outback, and then by ship back to Vancouver, and home to Toronto.

Bob returned to teaching geography and art. When Nelson High School reorganized departments and gave him the choice of becoming either head of the geography or art department, Bob chose art. "I picked art for several reasons," he says. "One, there's less marking; two, you could be more independent—you didn't have to coordinate with other teachers; and three, you could create your own little world in which you could get close to the kids who were really keen on art. The relationship with the students became a very important part of my life—and of our lives after Birgit came along."

One day in 1962 an old friend from the Ontario College of Art, Gus Wiseman, said to Bob, "Have you been down to see the Wyeth show at the Albright Knox Gallery in Buffalo?"

"No, I haven't."

"Well, you should go."

"Why?"

"He's a damn fine painter."

Interesting, Bob thought. "I was an abstract painter, Gus was an abstract painter, and here he was raving about this realist. So I thought, 'Okay, I'll go and take a look at it.' It was my road to Damascus."

Bob recalls walking into the gallery and seeing the art of Andrew Wyeth for the first time. "My heart was beating faster. It was, quite literally, transforming. I would go to every single art show at the Art Gallery of Ontario, and I enjoyed them. And I'd keep up with what Harold Town was doing, and what Jack Bush was up to, and the rest of them, but I wasn't thrilled. I was asking myself a very penetrating question: If my paintings were hanging in this show, would I walk across the room and spend ten seconds looking at one? And the answer was, 'Well, maybe.'"

When he saw Wyeth's paintings Bob knew he would cross an entire city to stand in front of one of them and just stare and stare. "I couldn't pull myself away. I kept going up closer and looking at them, and the guard was telling me to stand back. And what it turned out to be—and this is pivotal in my whole philosophy—was here's an artist who cared about the actual planet earth, the actual textures and particularity of the world we live in. He cared that this was the bark of an old maple tree, or that this was an old stone wall, or the flank of a young bull."

Bob had become well known as a naturalist. He was an executive of the Ontario Federation of Naturalists, and he was a member of as many as five boards at a time. He was teaching educators how to present nature to children, and he was in demand as a public speaker on the subject of the natural world. "So, here I was, saying how important it is to know the particularity of the planet—to know the names of your neighbours or other species, and yet when I was painting nature it was just great gobs of paint splashed all over the place. So here was a guy who cared about that, and I hadn't been, and it was a real eye-opener. But it took me about two years to get out of my abstract art snobbery."

At about the time that he discovered Wyeth, Bob met Suzanne, who became his first wife. "Suzanne was the only girl I'd ever met who was both an artist and a naturalist," he says. "And I was ready for marriage."

Suzanne was ten years Bob's junior and had never travelled, so he decided to take her to Africa, the continent he had found so attractive in his travels, before building a home on the ten acres of land he had purchased on the escarpment in Burlington. "One of the reasons I'd moved to Burlington was because of the Niagara escarpment," Bob says. "It was beautiful rough country not far from Toronto, so you can get to the art galleries and theatre. So I'd bought ten acres with a stream and a view for $4,500 in 1959."

He applied to the external aid department to teach in Africa, and in 1962, he and Suzanne travelled to Nigeria. Bob taught there for the next two years. Their first son, Alan, was born there. Bob also continued to paint and trap mice, which he skinned, stuffed, and used as subjects for scientific drawings.

During one holiday Bob and Suzanne flew to Nairobi to join Bristol Foster and his wife Anna on a trip through East Africa to visit wildlife biologists. One day Bob noticed a sign in the window of the East African Esso headquarters, advertising a calendar competition. Bob took one of the flyers and entered a painting of a *Thompson's Gazelle* and another of a *Superb Starling*. He did not win the competition, but he took the top two spots in the public popularity poll. A local art dealer, an American woman who owned the Fonville Gallery, located Bob by making inquiries through Bristol Foster and said, "I could sell paintings like this." She convinced him to paint more wildlife, which she took to shows; they sold instantly.

"Was that exciting?" I ask Bob.

"I felt amused," he says. "I didn't need the money, and I didn't think it was a great career or anything like that. I thought it was nice that people liked it, and I did it the best I could. So I had a wafer thin but extremely wide reputation as an international wildlife artist before anyone knew me in Burlington except as the local art teacher."

When Bob and Suzanne came back to Burlington, he designed his dream home, drew the blueprints, and created every detail right down to where the wall plugs should be positioned. In his new home studio, Bob was now painting wildlife. "I thought I was painting nature as no other artist had ever painted it," he says. "It was almost true. There are one or two people I have discovered since who were doing similar things."

Bob's paintings were different because he placed each bird or animal in its natural habitat, and he created the surrounding landscape with as much painstaking care as he did the animal. "I was taking into account all kinds of things. And all my influences, including cubism and post-impressionism, were still there but kind of hidden underneath the particularity."

Canada's centennial year, 1967, caused excitement and patriotism across the country. Thousands of individuals and communities involved themselves in centennial projects. As his contribution, Bob decided to paint his neighbourhood, Halton County, as it was in 1867. He talked to the owner of the Alice Peck Gallery in Hamilton about exhibiting his work.

"We don't just take people who walk in off the street," Alice said. "We have very high standards here."

"I know that," Bob said.

"We have a very good stable."

"I know," Bob said. "That's why I came to you."

"What did you say your name was?"

"Robert Bateman."

"Doesn't mean anything to me. Who are you?"

"I'm the art teacher at Nelson High School."

"Oh," she said. "I think I've heard of you. Well, okay, I'll take a chance."

Bob brought his paintings to the gallery and the show sold out on opening night.

"I didn't expect to sell any," he says. "I was surprised. I kept saying, 'I'm not painting living room art. I don't think this is going to sell but that's okay. I don't care. I'm just painting stuff to please myself.' And it started a feeding frenzy, which has lasted more or less throughout my career. I've always had more demand than I've had paintings to supply it."

Despite his sudden fame, his attitude towards his art has never changed. "I paint easel paintings to please myself, " he says. "If someone wants to buy them, then they buy them."

From then on, Bob was affiliated with the Beckett Gallery, and Tom Beckett was his main dealer. When the gallery announced a new

Robert Bateman exhibition, lineups formed hours before the gallery's opening time, and when the doors finally opened, people rushed in to fight over paintings. Husbands and wives plotted to split up with one of the pair racing to take possession of one painting while the other grabbed another one. Bob didn't attend the openings. He heard about them from Tom afterwards, and the reports Tom gave him didn't excite him. "My interest was in the painting," Bob says.

He kept his prices affordable. Speculators bought them and then resold them for many times the original price. *Winter Cardinal*, for example, originally sold for $1,800. The buyer resold it for $35,000 two years later, and when it last traded hands it sold for nearly triple that amount.

By 1971, Bob was married to another art teacher, Birgit, and his life was soon to change in another way. The Nairobi gallery, which still represented him, was bought by the largest and most prestigious wildlife gallery in the world: Tryon Gallery in London, England. Under the terms of the sale, Bob was sold with the gallery, much like a hockey player is sold to a new club. In 1975 Bob had a one-man show at the Tryon Gallery. Before the show opened, he said to Birgit, "This will be an omen. If I succeed at the international level, I will leave teaching."

"By that time I was paying more income tax on the proceeds of my art than on the proceeds of teaching, in spite of me trying to keep the prices down," he says. "They kept going up. I knew I could sell everything I did at the local level, but I said, 'If I succeed at the international level and have a good show, then I will leave teaching.'"

His show sold out, and Bob left teaching the next year. In the years that followed, Bob and Birgit made frequent trips to Vancouver with their boys, Christopher and Rob. In the fall of 1979, Bristol Foster, who was then the director of ecological reserves for the province, arranged a boating trip for them up the coast. "Here we were with this beautiful heavenly weather off the northwest coast of Vancouver Island, with the sea otters and the bald eagles, and our eating fresh seafood, and I got this severe case of B.C.-ophilism," Bob says, "And I said to the scientists, 'I'd like to put a down payment on some waterfront property. Where would you suggest I start looking?'"

"Saltspring Island," they said.

Before they left to drive back home through the Rockies in their Volkswagen camper, Bob and Birgit purchased a post-and-beam view home on a southwest-facing slope on Saltspring. They added to it with the help of architect Hank Schubart and made it their permanent home in 1985.

Today Bob and Birgit live and work in their home, which is large enough to accommodate the office staff he employs to handle the multiple demands on his time. "I had no idea that I would become famous," he says. "It was never my goal. In fact, when my first book came out in 1981, that's when people started saying, 'I'm so happy for your success. How are you handling it?' And you see, there's something wrong with that. What they meant was, 'How are you handling all this fame?' Well, if one's goal in life is to be famous, then I was achieving a little bit of success. But my goal in life was never to be famous. My goal is to have a balanced life—nature, my family, art … and I loved teaching. I still love teaching—talking, explaining, and ranting—it's one of my joys in life. This fame stuff, such as it is, has given me a soapbox, and I will use the soapbox to do some good if I can." One of the ways in which he shares his ideas is on his website "batemanideas.com," where he expounds on a variety of topics, ranging from ecology to education and art.

In 1999 Bob discovered that he had been named to receive the Order of British Columbia in 2000. He had met a friend at the Vancouver International Airport, who had read about the award in the *Vancouver Sun* newspaper. "Congratulations," his friend said.

"For what?" Bob asked.

"You've been awarded the Order of B.C."

"Oh," Bob said. "That's very nice. That's an honour."

Awards mean little to him. As well as the Order of B.C. he has received nine honorary doctorates and the Order of Canada. His citation for the Order of B.C. reads in part: "Since the 1960s, he has been an active member of many naturalist and conservation organizations, and has used his wildlife paintings and prints to raise millions of dollars for these causes."

The list of those causes in Canada and the U.S. is enormous. Each year, Bob Bateman donates between 200 and 300 prints as well as original paintings, which are auctioned to raise money. When an organization advocates the causes of nature, Bob tries to support it, but the demand has become so overwhelming that he is forced to be increasingly selective.

On his website, Bob addresses his critics, who have said that his art is not avant garde because it does not deal with important issues.

> An artist is an artist, be he/she high, low, or decorative. Artists are artists because they can't help it—they just are and they do art for the love of it or because they can't stop themselves. Their prime motives are not the market or what will the critics think or whether they are "High" or "Decorative" or "Tough" or "Easy." This is their piece and they do not need to defend it. The buck stops with them. Take it or leave it.

If it were up to Bob Bateman, he would change the structure of the education system and take children out of the classroom and into nature and let them learn and become respectful and reverent about the world around them. "I've been told that young people can recognize hundreds, if not up to a thousand, corporate logos, and they'd be hard pressed to name the names of ten local species near their house. It's a tragedy of the first order."

If it were up to Bob, we would care more about the world and the beauty of it, and we would help our children discover it. "I love sharing," he says. "That's one of the main things—that's the teacher in me and partly why I paint and why I do these books."

Bob's philosophy about painting has not changed since the day he encountered the art of Andrew Wyeth. He paints the world to reveal the texture of its surface and what is underneath it. "A lot of my art is totally intuitive and emotional and spiritual," he says. "I have no idea why a given thing will turn my crank. It just comes out of left field somewhere. A phrase I sometimes use is 'metaphorically slamming on your brakes' and stopping and saying, 'Aha! That's worth a look, and that combination of things is worth a look.' I give quite a few artists' workshops, and you can't teach that. There's no answer. That is what is so joyful and wonderful about humanity."

Bob sometimes muses that the salvation of the world might be something very simple indeed—something as simple as all the closet birdwatchers, especially perhaps the little boys, coming out of the closet. "The world would be a better place if everyone was a bird watcher."

Index

Biography of Author

Goody Niosi was born in Karlsruhe, Germany, in 1946. At age five she immigrated to Canada and grew up in Ontario. She recalls learning to read intuitively and falling in love with books, promising herself at age ten that she would be a writer when she grew up.

Goody didn't become a writer until she was 49. Her first career was as a film editor in Toronto and Vancouver.

"What you do in your life gives you a partial picture of a person," Goody says. "To really know someone, ask them what their passions are. I am passionate about ideas and ideals … about walking with my dog through dark and snowy woods, while Robert Frost's words circle through my head … about truth and justice … about seeing people smile with their eyes and hearts. If I can do one thing in my writing, I hope to be able to make a difference."

Magnificently Unrepentant, the story of Merve Wilkinson and Wildwood, was Goody's first book. In *Ordinary People, Extraordinary Lives*, she has once again chosen to tell stories of people who have made a difference in the world.

Goody writes for the *Nanaimo Daily News, Harbour City Star*, and other publications. She lives above a stable in the country with her dog, Lizzie the Labrabrat. When she is not outdoors or involved in various community activities, she can probably be found plunked down in front of her computer.